D1452426

The Future of Catholic Higher Education

The Future of Catholic Higher Education

The Open Circle

JAMES L. HEFT, S.M.

OXFORD

UNIVERSITY PRESS

OXFORD
UNIVERSITY PRESS

Oxford University Press is a department of the University of Oxford. It furthers
the University's objective of excellence in research, scholarship, and education
by publishing worldwide. Oxford is a registered trade mark of Oxford University
Press in the UK and certain other countries.

Published in the United States of America by Oxford University Press
198 Madison Avenue, New York, NY 10016, United States of America.

Library of Congress Cataloging-in-Publication Data
Names: Heft, James, author.
Title: The future of Catholic higher education : the open circle / by James L. Heft, S.M.
Description: New York : Oxford University Press, [2021] |
Includes bibliographical references and index.
Identifiers: LCCN 2020058612 (print) | LCCN 2020058613 (ebook) |
ISBN 9780197568880 (hardback) | ISBN 9780197568903 (epub)
Subjects: LCSH: Catholic universities and colleges—Philosophy.
Classification: LCC LC487.H44 2021 (print) | LCC LC487 (ebook) |
DDC 378/.0712—dc23
LC record available at https://lccn.loc.gov/2020058612
LC ebook record available at https://lccn.loc.gov/2020058613

DOI: 10.1093/oso/9780197568880.001.0001

5 7 9 8 6 4

Printed by Integrated Books International, United States of America

Contents

PART IV: COCURRICULAR AND CURRICULAR DIMENSIONS

Acknowledgments

Over the years, I have found that one of the best ways for me to think is to write. Many have helped me with my writing, beginning with the Marianists at the high school I attended in Cleveland Ohio. They asked me to write a monthly column for the school newspaper. Fr. Philip K. Eichner, S.M., was one of my best teachers and has remained a lifelong mentor. Several professors in college had a profound effect on me, one in particular, a historian of philosophy, Fr. Bernard Newbauer, S.M. Two professors in particular helped me in graduate studies: Harry McSorley and Fr. Leonard E. Boyle, O.P., both of whom seamlessly directed my dissertation. Many people during my time at the University of Dayton helped me in many ways. Bro. Ray Fitz, S.M., president for many years at the university, invited me to give talks to the faculty; Una Cadegan, one of my best students at the University of Dayton, and now a professor of American Studies, has taught me a great deal about both writing and thinking. The comments, feedback, and generous critiques of other faculty, including Steve Dandaneau, Paul Benson, Richard Sapphire, Fred Pestello, Chris Duncan, John Geiger, Jan Stets, Sean Wilkerson, Kevin Hallinan, and many others, have helped me think more carefully about these issues. Mary Jude Brown, my assistant while I served as provost and now author of an important book published by the Catholic University of America on the "heresy trial" at the University of Dayton in the mid-1960s, was a source of constant support and sanity.

Sr. Alice Gallin, O.S.U.; David O'Brien many years at Holy Cross College; Mark Roche at the University of Notre Dame; and Charles Taylor have also been great colleagues and sources of inspiration for me. I could also name many colleagues at the University of Southern California who have also been sources of wisdom, criticism, and encouragement. To all of them named and unnamed, I am grateful. I wish to thank Cynthia Read, my editor at Oxford, and the two reviewers of this manuscript—their comments helped me to sharpen my argument and make some key points clearer than they were. Any mistakes in this book are due to a failure on my part to say something fair, important, or well.

I dedicate the book to my parents, Berl and Hazel Heft, both raised on farms in central Ohio, and who raised me and my four siblings in an ecumenical household.

Introduction

The Ongoing Conversation

The Invitation

In 1980, three years after finishing graduate studies and joining the faculty at the University of Dayton, I received a phone call (email didn't exist then) from the president, Brother Raymond L. Fitz, S.M., asking me if I would accept an appointment to a university-wide task force to discuss the mission of the university. I accepted the invitation. Then he asked me if I would be willing to chair the task force. Being young and more subject to flattery then, I agreed. A good number of the veterans of the university, as well as two deans, had already been appointed to the task force. It didn't occur to me at the time that I was way too young to chair this distinguished group; it should have.

I remember vividly our first meeting. After introductions, I quite confidently underscored the importance of the task force and then suggested a few of the key themes that I thought we needed to discuss. Before I had finished, the veteran chair of the Physics Department audibly sighed and asked, "Haven't we had this discussion before?" I don't recall exactly how I replied, but emboldened by my recently acquired PhD in historical theology, I probably spoke with more confidence than I should have that it was an important conversation and that we needed to have it since, as the times change, so might our understanding of the university's mission. Well, I wasn't wrong in saying that, but I did underestimate the challenges that lay ahead. I also didn't realize that leading, participating in, and learning from such conversations would become a central concern for me for the rest of my life.

In subsequent years, that physics professor and I became good friends—he even tried to explain quantum mechanics to me, more than once. But ever since then, I have heard faculty raise the same question when asked to discuss the mission of the university: "Do we need to talk about this again?" Perhaps they thought that having heard, if they did, about the university's mission when they were hired, they didn't need to hear about it again. In truth, it should be admitted that many mission conversations have hardly been riveting. Nevertheless, I and others have found that they are critically important and that they should continue, always.

The Future of Catholic Higher Education. James L. Heft, S.M., Oxford University Press. © Oxford University Press 2021.
DOI: 10.1093/oso/9780197568880.003.0001

Catholic Tradition and the Open Circle

I did my doctoral studies in medieval history and theology. I have continued to study history as an indispensable resource for understanding events both past and present. Beginning in the nineteenth century, we learned a new way to understand history, tradition, and even Christian teachings. We discovered it to be a dynamic process, as something that "develops" (thanks to St. John Henry Newman), marked by periods of continuity, discontinuity, and adaptation. A central theme of this book is to preserve the continuity of the Catholic intellectual tradition, but also recognize how it might need to be adapted, how it has been adapted and even changed, and to do all this through dialogue and research carried on not just within the Catholic community, but with scholars of many disciplines and of other religions.

In 1964, an English translation of Gabriel Marcel's important 1940 book (*Du Refus á Invocation*) was published with the title *Creative Fidelity*. The subtitle for this book, *The Open Circle*, suggests a similar combination of continuity, discontinuity, and development. I have tried to capture both continuity (the circle, a community of believers) and development within and beyond it (its openness). Later in this book, especially in chapter 8 on academic freedom, I contrast the model of a university as an "open circle" to that of a closed circle, on the one hand, and to the "marketplace of ideas" on the other. These models are ideal types, the kind that philosophers often create. Few institutions embody perfectly a single model. Even though the model of the open circle is, I believe, the most difficult to sustain, it is the most promising to ensure that Catholic higher education has a future.

The image of the circle was used by Cardinal Nicholas of Cusa (1401–1464), a brilliant mathematician, theologian, and scientist, to illustrate how our knowledge of God in this life can never be complete. We might say today that all knowledge is asymptotic, that is, at best, an approximation. Cusa explores this idea in the first book of his classic, *De Docta ignorantia* (*On Learned Ignorance*).[1] But an emphasis on the limitations on what we can know has for centuries been explored in forms of thinking called apophatic, or in the Christian tradition, the *via negativa*. We find it in Pseudo-Dionysius the Areopagite (late fifth and early sixth century), who influenced many theologians, including Thomas Aquinas, whose carefully developed doctrine of analogy reminds us that there is always more about God that we don't know than we know.[2]

By the image of an "open circle," I wish to convey two things: first, a faculty committed to an intellectual tradition distinctive enough to sustain a community with a common discourse, and second, a faculty eager to learn from other traditions. Grammatically, the metaphor "open circle" is both a noun and an adjective. To be a circle, a Catholic university needs to foster and engage critically a particular tradition, the Catholic intellectual tradition in all its rich complexity and surprising diversity. In other words, the circle ensures that there will be a community that shares enough in common to make it possible for vigorous and informed debate and development. Without that circle, almost every discussion will be in search of first principles and often not arrive at compatible ones. The smaller the circle is, the more closed the community, and the larger it is, the more diverse it can be.

A Catholic university in the modern world should want to be both distinctive and open—distinctive, of course, because without it, there is no "competitive edge," to use market speech. But why be open? Because the very nature of a university communicates hope. The theologian Nicholas Lash wrote, "Optimism and despair already know the outcome—they prematurely complete the story."[3] Optimism and pessimism are implicitly totalitarian, he explains, where hope is open and confident about the future. There is always more to learn, even if full comprehension remains forever beyond us, especially in thinking about God. A closed circle has given up on the rest of humanity, and the marketplace of ideas lacks a center for discourse. Both of these alternative models of a university, along with that of the open circle, are developed at greater length in the chapter on academic freedom.

Scholarly Contributions

In our own time, gifted scholars have described how over time the church has continued to learn as it encountered other traditions and faced new challenges. I am thinking, for example, of the ways scholars have described the way Christian doctrine has developed over the last two thousand years (Jaroslav Pelikan), the creative Patristic period (Newman himself), the dynamic medieval period (Marcia Colish), the shape of modern and contemporary Catholicism (John O'Malley, S.J.), the history of Christian spirituality (Bernard McGinn), and the interaction of history and doctrine (Yves Congar, O.P.), to name only a few. These historians do not paper over the dark moments of church history, but their careful even-handed assessment of the triumphs and failures of the church gives grounds for hope.

Focused more sharply on the history of Catholic higher education, several Catholic writers and scholars have made their own contributions to the mission discussion. I would have been a lot more prepared in 1980 to chair that task force had I read their writings. But Philip Gleason's magisterial study, *Contending with Modernity: Catholic Higher Education in the Twentieth Century* (1995), had not yet been written. But I had no excuse in 1980 for not knowing about George N. Schuster's 1930 complaint about the lack of intellectual distinction among

Catholics, their "markedly puritanical spirit" and lack of intellectual creativity. Later in that same decade the young leader of the University of Chicago, Robert M. Hutchins, speaking to some members of the National Catholic Educational Association, criticized Catholic universities for putting more emphasis on sports and vocational training than on research and the humanities. Then there was John T. Ellis's 1955 article, "American Catholics and the Intellectual Life," which documented the lack of intellectual achievement in nearly all of Catholic higher education. His article ignited a huge debate, more intense than similar critiques going all the way back to middle of the nineteenth century, when Orestes Brownson complained about the absence of any intellectual activity among Catholics, and then in the late nineteenth century, when both Archbishop John Ireland and John Lancaster Spaulding called for a national Catholic university of distinction. But by 1955, America had emerged as the world power. The country was filled with rising expectations. The GI Bill, the Servicemen's Readjustment Act of 1944 that provided benefits for World War II veterans, made access to higher education possible for millions of veterans who otherwise would never have gone to college. It is not hard to understand why, in the mid-1950s, Ellis's essay created such a firestorm. In Gleason's words, it popped "the cork on long-suppressed discontents."[4]

The Post–Vatican II Debate Starts

The Second Vatican Council generated its own optimistic expectations and opened even wider the gates for change in the church. Shortly after the council ended, Paul Van Thomson published an article in *Columbia College Today*, with the provocative title "Should Catholic Colleges Be Abolished?"[5] Though he thought they had a future, he believed that to remain relevant, they had to change. He argued that they needed a more dynamic mission than transforming "the proletariat into the bourgeoisie," to quote Evelyn Waugh's remark made just after visiting the United States in the 1950s. Thomson wanted more emphasis on the liberal arts and praised those few Catholic colleges that had developed "new habits of experimentation, a sense of creativity, and a new broadness of intellect." The key, Thompson believed, was for old and staid Catholic colleges to break out, to cease being "a mere transmitter of orthodox religious ideas from a fortress-like Church to an unruly world."[6] For Catholic colleges and universities to thrive, they had to overcome their timidity, isolation, and rigidity and be academically relevant and socially concerned. He singled out two Catholic colleges for praise, Immaculate Heart College in Los Angeles and Webster College in Missouri. Neither exists today as a Catholic college.

Not everyone was that confident about the future. It was one thing to lament the rigidity and mediocrity of Catholic higher education; it was quite another to suggest that Catholic colleges and universities weren't worth the time, money, and effort needed to keep them afloat. In a *Commonweal* essay published in June of 1967, John Cogley wrote that the Catholic university had no future:

> The idea of the Church's conducting something identifiable as a "Catholic university," in the sense that Marquette, St. Louis, Fordham, Notre Dame and Georgetown and the Loyolas are today considered Catholic universities, will one day seem as anachronistic as the papal states, the error-has-no-rights "Catholic State," the Catholic penitentiary, or the Catholic bank.[7]

Cogley believed that the passing of "classical culture" and the arrival of modernity meant that the Catholic university "no longer has anything to give the world but memories."[8] That same year, he took issue with Fr. Hesburgh, C.S.C., then president of Notre Dame and leading spokesperson for Catholic higher education in the United States, who was quoted in an article published earlier in *Harper's Magazine*.[9] Hesburgh stated that a Catholic university, though not to be equated with the church, was nevertheless *of* the church. Cogley thought this was nonsense:

> [Hesburgh] suggest[s] that the Church is the bearer not only of revealed truth but the arbiter of all truth—that the Church can authoritatively determine the truth not only about what has been revealed but what is known from science, philosophy and the social disciplines. I think this is nonsense both historically and logically.[10]

Putting to one side the question of whether Cogley properly interpreted what the author of the article quoted Hesburgh as saying, Cogley asserted that no authentic university derived its authority from any institution outside itself. Were a Catholic university to do so, it would never be an authentic university. It would lack, Cogley argued, the necessary independence that all great universities possessed. Interestingly, however, Cogley still believed that every university should teach theology as a recognized discipline. In other words, if a "secular" university" did not teach theology, it would be as anomalous a term as George Bernard Shaw's "'Catholic' university." To be clear, Cogley thought that a secular university should teach not just Catholic but all Christian theologies. Otherwise, a Catholic university would end up "favoring" a particular theology and not give equal time to others.[11] If a university teaches only one tradition of Christian theology, then it is not really catholic, and therefore, Cogley concluded, it fails to be a true university. Not long after the appearance of this article, Cogley left the Catholic Church and joined the Episcopal Church. He also sent his son to Harvard.

Seven weeks after *Commonweal* published Cogley's essay, Fr. Hesburgh convened a group of leaders of Catholic higher education at Notre Dame's retreat center in Land O' Lakes, Wisconsin. They issued what became known as the "Land O' Lakes" statement. They boldly claimed that "a Catholic university must have a true autonomy and academic freedom in the face of authority of whatever kind, lay or clerical." At the same time, they stated that a Catholic university must be a community of learners and scholars "in which Catholicism is perceptibly present and effectively operative."[12] Hesburgh did not oppose the study of other theologies or even other religions but insisted that Catholic theology and philosophy remained the core of a Catholic university's intellectual mission. Their statement reflects the optimism and confidence of the immediate post–Vatican II period.

It didn't take long—just two short years after the closing of the Second Vatican Council—for scholars and academic leaders to stake out strong, and even opposing, positions on the nature, mission, and future of Catholic higher education in the United States. By the early 1980s, the Vatican decided that it needed to weigh in on the matter. In 1990, after extensive consultation with leaders of Catholic colleges and universities from around the world, the Vatican issued an apostolic exhortation, *Ex corde ecclesiae*, translated as "from the heart of the Church." In choosing that title, the Vatican wanted to remind the leaders of Catholic higher education that just as in the twelfth century, so also today a close relationship between the church and Catholic universities remains important and needs to be sustained. Although *Ex corde* affirmed the institutional autonomy and academic freedom of Catholic universities, when implemented in the United States in 1999 it added, without consultation, the requirement that Catholic theologians should ask for a *mandatum* from their local bishops. It also stated then that at least 50% of the faculty should be practicing Catholics, including the president of the university. Since 1990, this landmark Vatican document has set many of the terms of subsequent debates. Overall, its presentation of the mission of a Catholic university has been positively received in the United States. Some debates erupted initially about its implementation, but since then things have been mostly quiet—at least with reference to *Ex corde*. Discussions, even debates, about the nature and mission of a Catholic university, however, continue.

I have described this conversation about the mission of a Catholic university as necessarily ongoing. One example of how the debate continues may be found in a recently published article in *America* magazine (February 1, 2016), coauthored by Michael Naughton, the late Donald Briel, and Kenneth Goodpaster. Taking a very different tack than Cogley, who saw no future for Catholic universities, these authors wanted to make sure that they have a future. They worried about mission drift, or *teleopathy*, an occupational hazard with a distinct, three-stage pattern. Institutional leaders 1) fixate on limited goals and make them ultimate aims, 2) rationalize these goals as the principal purpose of the Institution and 3) eventually detach their institutions from their fundamental purpose and "reason for being."[13]

Citing *Ex corde*, the authors defend two principles on which they believe the mission of Catholic universities stands: (1) the unity of knowledge and (2) the dialogue between faith and reason. They believe that commitments to "social justice," "educating for responsibility," "sustaining the environment," and "celebrating diversity" become hollow when they are detached from the "theological and integral core" of the Catholic tradition. Without "distinctively Catholic criteria in hiring, curriculum, research and promotion," the faculty, they believed, becomes more attached to their own disciplines, while the Catholic character of the university gradually atrophies. Since faith and reason are integral to that core, they advocate for a strong program in Catholic theology.

Their worry about mission was not shared by Catholic historian David O'Brien. In a letter to *America*'s editor, he bluntly stated that the authors were "simply wrong": "American Catholic higher education is alive and well despite decades of criticism by popes, bishops, a handful of faculty and lay Catholics convinced that Catholic colleges and universities have sold their souls for academic respectability."[14] O'Brien puts little faith in "confessional" colleges or "set-apart Catholic Studies programs" and recommends instead "a sense of shared responsibility for the common life" of the country. For O'Brien, the authors should not have assumed a countercultural stance that ignored many good things that could have been discovered and shared had they advocated instead solidarity with the rest of the citizens of the United States.

Preliminary Diagnosis

Should the leaders of Catholic universities, assuming as I do that Catholic higher education should have a future, be more worried about "mission drift" or a failure to see as their primary mission addressing challenges faced by the country? One way to think about these different positions is to diagnose the current state of Catholic higher education in the United States. In a 2015 letter, historian Dr. Una Cadegan and I invited scholars to participate in a conference on the current state of Catholic intellectual life in the United States. We included in the invitation a diagnosis of the current strengths and weaknesses of Catholic higher education. That diagnosis included some of the key points of this ongoing debate over the state and future of Catholic higher education. I have grouped them under four topic areas: changes in the culture, in the US Catholic Church, in Catholic colleges and universities, and in leadership and finances.

First, there have been some *profound cultural changes* in the United States. We now have a "culture of choice" brought about by increased mobility, the growth of a market mentality, and the decline of intergenerational formation. As a consequence, membership in religious organizations becomes increasingly voluntary, sorting religious communities into enclaves of the like-minded. We also witness a deepening polarization of culture in society and in religious communities as a result of the rise of pluralized and fragmental communications media in the form of cable and satellite television, the Internet, and social media. Finally, our culture's polarized ways of thinking about sex, stretching from hypersexualization to Puritanism, exacerbated by the sexual abuse crisis in the Catholic Church, have diminished the church's teaching authority, especially in matters of sexuality and gender.

Second, besides changes in the culture, *within the Catholic community* we find serious divisions in which official teachings are selectively put at the service of political partisanship rather than at the service of the truth, the unborn, and the poor. Except for immigrants, we in the United States now have a largely affluent Catholic population, successful beyond their grandparents' greatest hopes, with large percentages of the younger generation acquiring university educations, and segments of Catholic higher education, despite significant setbacks and challenges, still flourishing in many ways unforeseen by previous generations. At the same time, however, the church is experiencing a significant and growing number of younger Catholics, some of whom graduate from Catholic universities, who no longer identify with any religious tradition.

Third, we described the *state of Catholic higher education*. We now have a larger, more broadly educated cohort of scholars, many of whom have received excellent educations in secular universities and offer an opportunity for bridging the divide between religion and the academy in new ways. On the other hand, we have few Catholic intellectuals to engage in that conversation. We now have several generations of theologians, most of them laypeople, educated outside the seminary, using different methodologies and bringing their perspectives to the study of theology and the academy. Unfortunately, the highly developed, too-little-known or -used body of social thought available to be brought to bear on the great public questions of the age remains largely unused, is sometimes ignored, and is susceptible to politicization when disconnected from other key aspects of Catholic theology and social life. And finally, persistent doubts are expressed about whether Catholics in the United States and faculty at some Catholic colleges and universities are cultivating the kind of rich intellectual life and culture that previous generations imagine as the goal and challenge of the freedom Catholics have in the United States.

Fourth and finally, there are *leadership and financial issues*. Given the rapidly increasing cost of Catholic colleges and universities, many families, including not just poor but also middle-class families, are unable to afford a Catholic education. Many institutions have small endowments and depend, sometimes precariously and almost exclusively, on tuition. The membership of the religious orders that have founded and built 90% of the Catholic colleges and universities has been in a freefall for the past fifty years. Some lay leadership hired to solve financial problems does not sufficiently appreciate Catholicism as an intellectual tradition.[15]

This diagnosis is sobering. The picture it gives of Catholic higher education is, in my view, mixed, the challenges multiple, and many of the resources available to respond thoughtfully to these challenges underutilized, in scarce supply, or even unknown. Some Catholic universities are doing a decent job embodying their mission, some are drifting, some are in financial crisis, and some are mediocre. The collection of essays coedited by Dr. Una Cadegan and me addresses this diagnosis, *In the Lógos of Love: Promise and Predicament of Catholic Intellectual Life*. The choice of the word "predicament" was inspired by Catholic novelist Walker Percy, who thought we lived today between a world that has ended and one yet to be born:

> One sign that the world has ended, the world we knew, the world by which we understood ourselves, an age which began some three hundred years ago with the scientific revolution, is the dawn of the discovery that its world view no longer works as we find ourselves without the means of understanding ourselves.[16]

If we are at the end of one age and not quite sure of the shape of the next, do Catholic intellectuals, as Dr. Cadegan pointedly asked in her chapter, have anything enduring to say to our own unsettled and polarized times?[17] She and all of the scholars who contributed to the book believe that Catholic intellectuals indeed do have something enduring and worth saying to the modern world: Catholic higher education is important not only for the Church and our country but also for the world.

The mission conversation is important and will continue. In retrospect, I am grateful for my first innocent and unprepared plunge into this important conversation in 1980. I have remained a part of it ever since, giving lectures and publishing articles on various aspects of Catholic higher education. That physics professor was right: he already had participated in that conversation. In fact, it has been going on in the United States since the beginning of the nineteenth century. Moreover, in our own time, it needs to continue, attentive to both the Catholic intellectual and spiritual traditions, making careful nuances, and engaging in a thoughtful reading of the cultures of the United States, the church, and the academy.

I have grouped the chapters of this book under four headings, the nature of which I explain at the beginning of each new section. Group one, North Stars, are people whose lives and thoughts I think ought to play key roles in shaping the mission of a Catholic university. In the second group, I locate Catholic universities in the United States within the national culture, with its growing secularism, and then globally with the Catholic Church, giving particular attention to the 1990 Vatican document, *Ex corde ecclesiae*, and the way the American bishops struggled to implement it. The third group, the faculty, explores a variety of issues, ranging from what faculty do, teach and research, and how they and their Catholic university ought to think about academic freedom. And finally, in the fourth group, I have two chapters, both dealing with the intellectual and moral development of students. While all these chapters treat the same subject, the Catholic university in the United States, I have tried to reduce, if not eliminate, repetition.

The Institute for Advanced Catholic Studies

In this book, I add my own reflections to this continuing conversation. I have benefited immensely from the many scholars who have been contributing to this discussion, many of them theologians, historians, philosophers, members of the hierarchy, and others. At the University of Dayton, I was privileged to serve for six years as chair of a large and then somewhat contentious theology faculty, as a provost for eight, and finally as the university professor of faith and culture and chancellor for ten—positions that required me to think more about the overall mission of the university than I would have had I remained only in my own academic discipline and department.

For over fifteen years before leaving the University of Dayton in 2006, I led many interdisciplinary faculty seminars. I also helped design two-day off-campus seminars on "hiring for mission," which I describe in this book. These experiences underlined both the importance and complexity of faculty development. Cogley was right: we need to understand many theologies today; just as importantly, we need to find the connections that should exist between academic disciplines. For Catholic universities, Catholic theology and philosophy and the humanities should remain their primary, if not their exclusive, academic commitment. Professional education, in conversation with Catholic social teaching, bridges the Catholic university and the culture.

Since 2006, my religious community, the Society of Mary (Marianists), has allowed me to take up an academic position at the University of Southern

California (USC) in Los Angeles where, since 2012, a small Marianist community exists two blocks north of campus, right in the middle of the student neighborhood, a practice common at Marianist universities.

I have devoted the rest of my life to establishing the stand-alone Institute for Advanced Catholic Studies (ifacs.com), where scholars of many disciplines and many faiths will be able to spend nine months in research and conversation about their own disciplines and religions, with the Catholic intellectual tradition forming the hub of the conversation. In planning the institute, a committee of distinguished scholars, some of whom had been in residence at centers for advanced studies, recommended that the institute should be located in a major metropolitan area where scholars would like to have their sabbaticals, in a diocese where an independent Catholic research institute would be welcome, and at a major research university that was not Catholic. There are some fine universities located in small towns, like New Haven, Connecticut, and Princeton, New Jersey, hardly major metropolitan areas. Some bishops, especially in the Northeast, were suspicious of our initiative, among them Cardinal Law, who reported us to the Vatican, more specifically, to Cardinal Ratzinger, then head of the Congregation for the Doctrine of the Faith (CDF), the office responsible for orthodox teaching in the church. After some research of his own and consultation with my archbishop, Daniel Pilarcyzk, Cardinal Ratzinger gave us a clean bill of health. A longer and more involved story of this exchange needs to be written. It wasn't our only run-in with highly placed ecclesiastics.

The daunting character of trying to establish such a research institute was brought home to me in the late 1990s, when I had a conversation with Fr. Theodore Hesburgh, then recently retired president of Notre Dame. When I described my idea of the Institute for Advanced Catholic Studies, he was visibly enthused but said, "I always wanted to do that at Notre Dame, but wasn't able to raise the money for it—getting endowment money for faculty research is the hardest sell." I audibly gasped. Fr. Hesburgh couldn't raise the money? What in the world did I think I was going to be able to do?

Finally, it may seem at first sight counterintuitive that we did not want to be at a Catholic university. But there are several good reasons for that decision. First, Catholic colleges and universities in the United States compete against each other, often for students, donors, and even members of the same religious order. The institute exists to serve higher education in general and especially all Catholic colleges and universities; we do not compete with any university. Also, if we located at a Catholic university, we would not have the independence we do as a 501 (c)(3) organization with our own board of trustees. We wanted to be at a major research institution because that is what we do: research. There have been and are some wonderful opportunities for conversation and collaboration with some leading scholars here. But we are at, not of, USC, though its continuous support of our mission has been unfailing. USC has been immensely supportive by donating one of their development officers to the institute. It also allows gifts given to the institute to be counted as gifts to the university (the institute has no alums; it is a start-up).

Moreover, independence for an institute for advanced studies is critically important; without independence, it has no credibility. While every university has its propaganda, locating a Catholic research institute at a nonreligiously affiliated research university offers both the appearance and the reality of more independence than would be the case if we had located at a Catholic university. Being at a university that is not religiously affiliated allows for a more neutral environment for scholars of different religions than being at a Catholic university would. We believe that interdisciplinary and interreligious dialogue and research are critically important for universities that tend to fragment knowledge and a world that misunderstands the role that religions can play in contributing to the dignity of the human person and welcoming the "stranger."

Why was and is USC so supportive of a free-standing Catholic research organization? At that time the president, Steven B. Sample, wanted two things: First, he wanted a research center for Christianity (they already had one for Judaism and were in the process of establishing another for Islam). Though not a Catholic then, Sample wanted the Christian research institute to be focused on the Catholic intellectual tradition ("You guys have the long tradition," he once remarked to me). Second, he wanted USC to be among the top five universities in the country, a distinction that depends heavily on publication of original research—precisely what the institute does.

Fifty years from now, the conversation about the mission of a Catholic university will be different from the one we are having today, and certainly different from the one that I, terribly unequipped, was invited to lead forty years ago. The vast majority of the two hundred Catholic colleges and universities in the United States will be in the hands of lay leaders. Very few religious will be full-time faculty. The phenomenon of globalization and nationalism, with all their variations, tensions, and possibilities, will continue to intensify. And surely some veteran professor in a committee established to discuss the nature and mission of a Catholic university will once again audibly sigh and ask why the conversation had to be taken up again. I hope that all the chapters of this book, unified by the conviction that mission discussions should continue, will reflect a deep continuity with the Catholic tradition and an openness to truth from whomever and wherever it can be learned.

PART I

TRUE NORTHS

I have given the first three chapters of this book the title "True Norths." The North Star has long been famous in literature as an image for what counts most in life, what gives reliable direction, especially in the midst of darkness. For sailors, it has functioned as an anchor in the northern sky. The axis of the earth always points at it. It remains stationary while other stars circle around it. It offers not only guidance for sailors but also inspiration and purpose to those still navigating their earthly journey.

While there is only one North Star, there are many north stars, anchor points, for Catholic higher education. For any Christian, the first star has to be Jesus, the Son of God and source of the Holy Spirit. I believe that He and his Mother Mary, educator and Seat of Wisdom, offer both a foundation for a Catholic university and insight into its distinctiveness. Beginning a book on the future of Catholic higher education with chapters on Jesus and Mary might appear pious, even inappropriate, but I think otherwise.

How, it may be asked, is it possible to speak about Christian education and never mention Christ? Education at the university level, or any level for that matter, that ignores mothers, ignores also something live-giving, holistic, and nurturing. Admittedly, my life as a Christian and as a Marianist has influenced my thinking about these two north stars. An understanding of the humanity of Jesus and of Mary's role in his education is still relevant for all educators.

I am also including a third north star, St. John Henry Newman. His *The Idea of a University* has remained a classic, not just because it is a masterpiece of English prose, but also because it goes to the heart of what a university education should be: a formation of the mind and the heart that seeks to integrate all knowledge, and to do so through living in a moral community.

In each of these three chapters, the human context of learning—the reality of the quotidian and the importance of lived experience—grounds reflections about education that otherwise might remain merely abstract, a perpetual danger for those living in the modern academy.

1

Jesus and the University

Introduction

Not so long ago, thousands of young men and women wore brightly colored cloth wristbands with the initials "WWJD" followed by a question mark, which stands for "What would Jesus do?" Denounced by some as a cheesy marketing triumph that trivializes the complex process of discernment, the wristbands were promoted by others as visible reminders of the only question that serious Christians should be asking. I was reminded of these wristbands when I began thinking about what Jesus would do in a Catholic university.

To start with, would Jesus even want to be part of a university community? Some surely would say, "No, not at all!" They would insist that he, like Martin Luther King Jr., would be engaged in acts of civil disobedience, speaking truth to power, and serving time in jail. They would picture him as they would Mother Teresa, caring for the dying and the outcasts, ministering to people in great physical and spiritual need, touching their souls as they wash and heal their bodies. They would insist that Jesus would not waste his time thinking about justice; rather, he would fight for it. He would not devote his precious time to the education of social workers and physicians, but rather would actually be counseling the troubled and assisting the sick. In other words, what would Jesus do, really? Don't we in the academy have to ask whether at all costs he would avoid ministering to the well and the well-to-do or joining ranks with those who have the leisure to be scholars who teach middle- and upper-middle-class students—the children of privilege who today populate most of our Catholic universities?

For the sake of discussion, let us suppose for a moment that Jesus would want to be a part of a university community. We then can ask where in a Catholic university he would choose to be. Would he locate himself in campus ministry or instead in the theology department, or would he prefer that the two would not separate the pastoral and academic dimensions of life as they do? Or, would he join a faculty of law that emphasized social justice and the defense of the poor, rather than protect wealthy clients and big corporations? Or again, would he choose to be a part of one of the social sciences, seeing in them, on the one hand, a blend of scientific rigor—an obvious entrée into the modern mindset—and, on the other, a concern for people and communities? Would he choose to be in a school of business, where he could make clearer what belongs to Caesar

The Future of Catholic Higher Education. James L. Heft, S.M., Oxford University Press. © Oxford University Press 2021.
DOI: 10.1093/oso/9780197568880.003.0002

and what to God? Would he choose to be in the music department, where he could demonstrate that besides love one of the closest things to God is music? Would he choose to be in the visual arts department, where he could create imaginative works so needed in a flat world of efficiency, standardization, and commercialism? Being a great teacher, would he teach teachers? Would he join the biology department and make it clear once and for all that the theory of evolution and the doctrine of creation need not be in conflict? Or finally, would he choose to be in administration, where he could provide overall direction for the community, articulate its vision, and focus on the common good, but also worry about balancing the budget, deal with lawsuits, raise money endlessly, and go wherever the board of trustees tells him to go?

On the surface, my speculations may seem facetious. For me, and I know for others, they are not. I admit that asking where Jesus would locate himself in a Catholic university may not be the best way to formulate my concern. Later, I will pose the question in another way, one that I hope is more helpful. As confident as I am about the importance that Jesus has for a Catholic university, I am also aware that others may not see it this way. Many Christians, including Catholics, think that their relationship with Jesus is a personal matter, best kept private unless someone asks them about it. In our secular culture, they have difficulty imagining that Jesus and the Christian tradition are rich sources of what should be an integral part of the real business of a university, of its intellectual work carried on publicly. But the truth is that most Christian academics would be hard pressed to draw any explicit correlation between their belief in Jesus and their academic work. Christian philosophers would be puzzled, I think, if they were asked how the person of Jesus should influence their research.[1] Even though Catholic theologians might be clearer about the importance of Jesus in their academic work, they may still wonder whether Jesus ought to have anything to do with the rest of the academy.[2]

It seems to me, then, that it is not unfair to conclude that most Christian faculty have trouble imagining any intellectual relevance the person of Jesus should have to their academic work. They might fear that if they tried to overcome this divide they would lose status as academics. Would they be seen as fundamentalists? Would colleagues question the objectivity of their scholarship? Questions like these concern me. They make me ask whether what I am suggesting is really rather unreal, except for fundamentalist Christians, believers not known for their scholarship. So again, I ask myself, where indeed and in what ways should Jesus be a part of a Catholic university? Why this chasm between our intellectual training and personal religious beliefs? Is it possible to overcome this disconnect in appropriate ways that validate and even enrich our academic work and strengthen the distinctive academic mission of a Catholic university?

"What Does Jerusalem Have to Do with Athens?"

I am not the first person to pose the question. Throughout most of Christian history, Christians have been asking this question in different ways in different historical periods and in different cultural contexts. Already in the late second century, for example, Tertullian (c. 160–c. 225) asked the question this way: what does Jerusalem have to do with Athens? Or, as I am posing it, what does Jesus have to do with the academy? Tertullian thought they had nothing to do with each other:

> Our principles come from the Porch of Solomon, who himself taught that the Lord is to be sought in simplicity of heart. I have no use for a Stoic or a Platonic or a dialectic [i.e., Aristotelian] Christianity. After Jesus Christ we have no need of speculation, after the Gospel, no need of research. Once we come to believe, we have no desire to believe anything else; for the first article of our faith is there is nothing else we have to believe.[3]

I don't agree with Tertullian, who believed that he was simply restating St. Paul's words spoken in Athens where the Greek intellectuals spent their time "in nothing but telling or hearing something new" (Acts 17:21). These Athenians are the kind of people who are distracted by their "itchy ears" (2 Tim. 4:3), chase after gossip, and lose their focus on what is truly important. According to Tertullian, Paul already saw in Athens "the ensuing conflicts between philosophy and the truth." At first, Paul attempted to speak to these intellectuals and poets in their language, even quoting some of their own poets. Beginning with the reality of creating things, Paul reasoned his way to the existence of a God "in whom," he explained, "we live and move and have our being" (Acts 17:28). However, when he told them about the resurrection, some of them scoffed, while others invited him to come back again, but not anytime soon. Paul left Athens and went to Corinth, where in the strongest possible terms he denounced the pretensions of human wisdom and vain curiosity and preached instead Christ crucified, not in "lofty words or wisdom" (1 Cor. 2:1) but in the power of the Spirit. He wanted the faith of the Corinthians to rest "not on human wisdom but on the power of God" (1 Cor. 2:5).[4]

However, Tertullian's dim view of the academy did not win the day, nor did Paul's distrust of intellectuals prevent the early Christians from finding wisdom in pagan philosophers and poets. Try as Tertullian did to disparage human learning, philosophy, the arts, and the cultural achievements of the Greeks and the Romans, he was unable to win over to his view the major Christian thinkers of the early centuries. Tertullian's position represented something very un-Catholic: it imposed either/or choices—either Jerusalem or Athens—when both/and responses were necessary.

Christians realized that even though they had received a revelation, they still needed to ponder what it might mean in new contexts and different cultures. They realized that even though they believed that Jesus was the fullest revelation of God, their understanding of that revelation was always limited, and therefore needed to be rethought, questioned, refined, and even reformulated to state more adequately its meaning. They also realized that in some implicit way the spirit of Jesus had already been active in cultures before Jesus arrived in the flesh.

Clement of Alexandria (150–c. 215), perhaps the first Christian humanist, stressed the importance of the intellect—the baptized intellect. He set out to answer his contemporary, the sophisticated pagan philosopher Celsus, who had dismissed Christianity as a religion for the ignorant. In response, Clement carefully avoided on the one hand Gnosticism, which equates salvation with knowledge that only the elite possessed, and on the other an insecure faith that fears serious intellectual work. Clement chose both faith and reason. He was a both/and thinker.

At about the same time, following the lead of such thinkers as Origen, the Cappadocians Basil, Gregory of Nyssa, and Gregory Nazianzen, and then later Augustine, the Christian community found in the Greek and Roman classics a *preparatio evangelii*. These Christian thinkers gave birth to Christian humanism. If Jesus were truly human, then nothing human, nothing that embodied the creative work of humans, could be alien to those who believed in Him. For Christian humanists, Jerusalem could be enriched by Athens, even if Athens had yet to embrace Jerusalem.

But tensions between Jerusalem and Athens—between, if you will, faith and reason, or the heart and the head—have persisted over the centuries. In the twelfth century, just before the birth of the great medieval universities, the eloquent monastic leader Bernard of Clairvaux, mystic and master of the ways of the heart, sharply opposed the philosopher Abelard, whose restless and lively mind raised more questions than he answered. In the thirteenth century, the age of scholasticism, two great theologians, Aquinas and Bonaventure, both great believers and scholars, drew respectively upon Aristotle and Augustine, creating differences in emphasis if not contradictions that continue today. In the fourteenth and fifteenth centuries, writers like Thomas á Kempis accused the scholastics of arid rationalism, of being too at home in Athens. In his widely read and still in print *Imitation of Christ*, he stressed the need for simplicity of the heart, reminding his readers that it was more important to experience compunction than to define it. Though a scholar, Martin Luther called for a return to the scriptures and an end to arid scholastic philosophy.

By the eighteenth and especially the nineteenth century, the Enlightenment had taken over many of the major academic centers in northern Europe. It radically reduced the church's intellectual influence, defended freedom of conscience, and, especially in German universities of the nineteenth century, used the scientific method as the most valid and useful form of knowledge. For many Enlightenment thinkers, Athens banished Jerusalem from the academy. Even though at the beginning of the nineteenth century most academics were religious believers of some sort, they were most comfortable as deists—people who 𝗑 believed in an intelligent creator but mostly ignored Jesus as presented in the New Testament. In the midst of these developments, most Catholic thinkers understood the Enlightenment's demand for religious freedom as a desire to be free from religion. The Catholic Church vigorously rejected this "enlightened" thinking. Only at Vatican II did the Catholic Church officially embrace religious freedom, not as freedom from religion, but as the freedom from any coercion in matters of religion.

To conclude this brief history of Western thought, throughout the twentieth century, a century when Enlightenment ways of thinking continued to dominate, Catholics worked to find ways in which faith and reason could play their proper roles. At the beginning of the twenty-first century, Catholics need to defend reason, especially against forms of postmodernism that distrust all "metanarratives" like Christianity, and against postmodernism's influence on critical studies in the humanities and social sciences that focus their attention on power and gender. As a result, no institution has become quite as secular as the modern academy, where the question is no longer "What does Jerusalem have to do with Athens?" but rather "Is there anything other than Athens?" or "Is truth reducible to power and position?" Put simply, most of the Enlightenment opposed faith and most of postmodernism reason. As a consequence, as we shall see, it has become difficult to find a balance, an appropriate place in the academy for the person and teachings of Jesus, except at a number of small and conservative religiously related colleges and universities, where many secular intellectuals would hardly imagine even the possibility of a robust intellectual community thriving.

This reduction of knowledge to what can be empirically verified or imposed is especially unfortunate since Catholics are neither fundamentalists in their understanding of scripture nor empiricists when it comes to reliable sources of knowledge. Nor do Catholics despair of finding something of the truth of things, while still recognizing that race, power, and gender do influence perceptions of reality. Philosophically, the doctrine of analogy uses reason to uncover truths that are beyond the empirical and mathematical. Thomas Aquinas's doctrine of analogy locates real knowledge between the univocal (same with the same—identical) and the equivocal (opposites); it uses metaphor and analogy when

𝗑 Except in the US, where most academics were still christians speaking of God (some understanding but not full comprehension). There are admittedly personal and cultural factors that influence perception, but that need not lead to subjectivism.

Three Powerful Secularizing Forces

Three trends in modern culture help us to understand more clearly why religiously affiliated universities find it difficult, but not impossible, to sustain a fruitful conversation between Jerusalem and Athens. One pervades American culture, a second influences the academy's epistemology, and the third is economic in nature. The difficulties posed by these forces have been exacerbated within the church by some Catholic leaders who themselves have fallen into sterile false dichotomies, forms of either/or thinking that darken counsel, thinking that opposes grace and freedom, the individual and the community, and believing and questioning.

Consider, for example, the separation of church and state in the United States; on the positive side, this has made it possible for different religious communities to live together in relative peace. In this country, no religious group should be favored by the federal government. Each religious community enjoys the same rights and restrictions. Believers have the freedom to establish religiously affiliated colleges and universities. But as I explain in chapter 8, in the eyes of leading secular thinkers, religiously affiliated colleges and universities do not qualify as true academic institutions. Therefore, most religiously affiliated colleges and universities lack status, at least when compared to the Ivy League schools and the major research universities.

The second force, more directly affecting the academy, is the dominance exercised by those who, on the one hand, use the scientific method as the only reliable way to produce worthwhile knowledge, and those who, on the other hand, are committed to postmodern ways of thinking and distrust science's objective claims. Many people give the benefit of the doubt to knowledge arrived at scientifically (except when for the general public the topic is evolution and global warming), while postmodernists distrust universals, whether scientific or religious. I will describe in a moment some of the characteristics of postmodern thinking as it relates to the academy. For now, the achievements of science in medicine, genetics, and technology should be applauded, just as some feminists and critical studies scholars have unmasked power presented as truth.

Whether scientists or postmodernists, academics in the academy in the United States have become, as a group, very secular. Philosopher Charles Taylor recently noted that most academics conform to an unbelieving academic culture. As a rule, academics who are personally religious keep that to themselves.

Taylor finds it remarkable "that academic culture in the Western world breathes an atmosphere of unbelief." Why remarkable? Because, he goes on to explain, "perhaps we aren't surprised enough by this phenomenon, which is a feature of this important subculture in our civilization, rather than of the society in which it is set."[5]

Most academic disciplines, formed as they have been over the last century when the scientific method has stood almost alone as the measure of academic achievement, have reduced, if not completely left out, not just the religious but also the ethical issues that are actually already an integral part of most academic disciplines. By the middle of the twentieth century, the moral dimensions of life and learning had been transferred to the humanities, an area least valued by the dominant academic culture. The moral formation of students has been left to campus ministry, which on nearly all secular campuses draws no financial support from the university. By the late 1960s, universities relieved themselves of "parental" oversight, absolved themselves of acting *in loco parentis*, and claimed responsibility only for the intellectual development of their students, a responsibility actually made more difficult to meet in the absence of moral formation. Academics in nearly any discipline who wish to study ethical and moral issues, and especially if they explicitly relate these issues to religious traditions, find it difficult to get external funding. And if they undertake such research on their own, their academic peers sometimes penalize them for going beyond the approved limits of their discipline. Needless to say, very few of the most prestigious refereed journals would publish an article on neuroscience and the soul.[6]

An essential part of "secularism," from the Latin *saeculum*, meaning "the age," emphasizes the present. A secular society neither looks to the past nor embraces a normative tradition. Typically, it is suspicious of all normative traditions because norms create restrictions on personal freedom and needlessly create guilt. Intellectuals distrust normative institutions, especially religious ones, which draw their authority from past revelation and typically have little to do directly with the academy. Drawing on the work of intellectual historian James Turner, historian Sandra Mize described the American intellectual as the person who "stands alone—the descendent of no tradition and the toady of no external authority. The intellectual hero or heroine rejects traditional interpretative frameworks, suspends all beliefs except in his or her ability to forge new and truer insights into the way things really are. He or she is a sort of Gnostic with a streamlined cosmology who arrives at these new insights through empirical evidence discovered through observations and even better, experimentation. In other words, science as practiced in the laboratory provides a near universal model for all intellectual pursuits."[7]

Of course, not all intellectuals fit this description. But it is still hard to be taken seriously as a scholar if you think that your religious faith might be a source of useful academic knowledge. It is even difficult for Christians to imagine that fundamental and verifiable insights into the human condition could have been revealed by an individual who lived for a short period of time in a distant province of the Roman Empire and died, was crucified as a criminal, and, according to his disciples, rose from the dead.

But the empirical method is not the only epistemology influencing the academy. As already mentioned, in more recent decades postmodernism has also found a foothold. In its most lethal form for any religion, it proclaims the end of metaphysics, the end of all "totalizing" narratives, and the reduction of all knowledge claims to various forms of power. Obviously, such a position is deadly for Christianity. It attacks Christian teachings as ideologies of control and oppression—the efforts of a patriarchal system to impose nonexistent universals that stifle personal freedom.

It must be admitted that Christianity has at times, and sometimes for long periods of time (condemning slavery formally and officially only at Vatican II), both wittingly and unwittingly, oppressed minorities and reduced women to second-class citizens. At the same time, it ought to be recognized that subjectivity (not to be equated with subjectivism) plays a role in all thinking. Purely objective and totally accurate expressions of reality are impossible. Nor can the realities of power, gender, and coercion be ignored: all concepts have a history, and all truths need to be put into their historical and cultural context. Rightly understood, an acknowledgment of the role that subjectivity plays—what I would call a "soft" postmodernism—helps avoid both the pretensions of total objectivity and a paralysis of relativism. In other words, we don't know enough to be dogmatists, but we know enough not to be skeptics.

Both the empirical method and "hard postmodernism" tend to separate religious desire from religious traditions; that is, they separate spirituality from religion, especially religions that value reason and affirm a normative revelation. In the United States, a rapidly growing number of persons describe themselves as "spiritual but not religious," people who say they believe but choose not to belong to a religious community. They are unaffiliated.[8] Those who are spiritual typically live that life apart from religious communities and communal practices. For many people in the academy, the most respectable choice is to be privately spiritual rather than publicly religious. Empiricism distrusts the nonverifiable religious dimension, while postmodernism opposes all universal claims, including especially those made by religion. This reduction of reliable knowledge to what can be empirically verified is especially unfortunate since Catholics are neither fundamentalists in their understanding of scripture nor empiricists when it comes to reliable sources of knowledge. Philosophically, the doctrine of analogy relies on reason to uncover truths that are beyond empirical and mathematical methods.

In recent decades philosophers like Calvinist Alvin Plantinga and Catholic John Haldane have used analytic philosophy to establish reasonable grounds for belief in God and the role of religion in education. Besides philosophy, narratives also convey truths about human lives that transcend the empirical and cannot be measured mathematically. Literary classics, theologian David Tracy has shown, communicate timeless truths that shed light on how we are to live. In short, there are many more rigorously reasonable avenues than empiricism and postmodernism that lead to reliable knowledge that can be shared by a community.[9]

Besides cultural and epistemological limits, a third reality profoundly affects the shape of the modern university: our neoliberal economy. As much as we would like to believe that our students come to the university in search of wisdom and a liberal education, the vast majority come so that they might get a good job. The number of liberal arts majors compared to students who major in the professions continues to drop nationwide. And while it is undeniable that capitalism generates wealth and has lifted more people out of poverty than any economic system, the wealth it generates remains concentrated in the hands of only a few.

In a commercialized culture, everything can be monetized, even religion. Consider this interesting example. Charles Sheldon, a Congregational minister born in 1857, started writing stories for his congregation in Topeka, Kansas. In 1897, a series of those stories appeared in a book entitled *In His Steps*, which, after the Bible, was the best-selling book in the United States for sixty years. It was translated into twenty-one languages. Sheldon, however, received practically no royalties because he forgot to copyright the book, which quickly became "public domain." The subtitle of that book was "What Would Jesus Do?"

A century later, marketers figured out how to transform that question into money. They used it to produce initialed backpacks, Bible covers, pens and pencils, magnets, balloon whistles, T-shirts, markers, necklaces, and skateboard keychains, to name only some of the items. They created a website, wwjd.com, and a WWJD CD. These details indicate two things: first, most religious practice in a consumer society are inextricably enmeshed in an economic web, and second, those who have criticized the WWJD marketing movement as a trivialization of religion definitely have a point.[10]

Given all these obstacles—the relegation of religion to the private sphere, the power that the scientific method has exercised over the multiple forms of knowledge, the protest against metaphysics exemplified more recently by postmodernism in the West, and the pervasive consumerist ethos in our culture—it has become more and more difficult to relate Jesus to a Christian university in any meaningful academic way. Though less than 150 years ago all colleges and universities in the United States were religious, will today's few remaining religious colleges and universities also soon become secular? And if they do, aren't Catholic universities fighting—if they are fighting—a losing battle?

There are good reasons, then, to ask whether today Jerusalem has any place in Athens. In a culture that is secularized, in disciplines that remain isolated from one another and that mostly limit their work to what empirical tests can verify, in disciplines that doubt objectivity, and in an age in which religion is considered by most to be nonintellectual and best kept to oneself, why would anyone think that Jesus should have anything to do with the university, even with the Christian academy? To accommodate ourselves to modern academic culture, we have split our lives in half: the public side, which is secular, rational, and scientific, and the religious side, which is not intellectual and remains mostly private and personal.[11]

Rethinking the Question: Three Theological Responses

As the beginning of this chapter, I suggested that asking what Jesus would do might not be the most helpful way to phrase the question. Formulated that way, the question runs a double danger: first, it tends to reduce Christianity to a "personal" (mostly private) relationship between Jesus and the individual believer, leaving out the community of believers; second, it suggests that we should be able to answer the question simply by looking at what Jesus did as recorded in the New Testament. It leaves out all the centuries between then and now, centuries filled with great thinkers, great saints, great builders, artists, and important learning. We need, I believe, to pose the question in several other ways. Besides asking "What would Jesus do?," we should also ask an even more fundamental question: "Who is Jesus?" We should also ask how Christians have addressed the basic issues of human life since the first century. What did Jesus in fact do? What have Christian believed, learned, and done over the centuries? What mistakes have they made? What went wrong and how was it corrected? What contributions can they make to the common good in a pluralistic, commercialized, and individualist society?

Knowing who someone is helps us imagine what that person might do in a given situation. We say, "I can picture so-and-so doing that!" The scholastics believed that *actio sequitur esse*: what a person does flows from who that person is. At the same time, people's actions, as moderns believe, can shape who they are, and the way people live can deeply influence what they think and what they are able to see. In short, we come to know who Jesus is by coming to understand not only what he did but also what he and his followers do now.

For centuries, believers have repeatedly asked what Jesus would do, posing that question in different cultures at different times in different ways in the face of different challenges. Taking into account the historical record, believers have guided their lives by what they believed Jesus would do. Their practices, thoughts, and writings constitute the Christian tradition, that is, a history of many examples of discipleship, thinking, and creativity in art, music, architecture, and spirituality. Their lives and work offer important insights that help us think about what Jesus might have to do with the contemporary university, even though there were no universities for the first 1,200 years of Christianity.

Understanding the Christian Life Today

In thinking about Jesus and his teachings, Catholicism has come to stress several insights of particular value for the entire human community. I will limit myself to three: a communitarian ethic, a sacramental sensibility, and the dignity of the human person.

Faculty often have difficulty creating forms of genuine community at their universities. In this struggle, they rarely attempt to do so on any explicitly religious grounds. But at Catholic universities, where does a sense of community come from? Can that sense of community be attributed mainly to the fact that many of our colleges and even universities are small, compared to state universities? Can it be attributed to the fact that at some of our universities most of the students are residential? Or is it that some parts of the country are known for their sense of hospitality? The answers to all of these questions can shed light on the question of the sources of community on Catholic campuses.

A sense of community should draw strength from a communitarian ethic characteristic of Catholicism. Over against a highly individualistic culture, Catholicism stresses community more than most Protestant traditions, though the congregations of many Protestant churches are small enough to support a strong sense of community. "We are all one body," Catholics sing at the Eucharist, echoing the words of Paul in his letter to the Corinthians. When knocked down on the road to Damascus, Paul heard a voice that said, "Saul, Saul, why do you persecute *me*?"—not "Why do you persecute my followers?," but "Why do you persecute *me*?" In Matthew 25, Jesus tells his disciples very simply that when they feed the hungry, visit the sick, give to the poor—whatever they do to others, they actually do to Him. Catholic social teaching stresses the common good. From his Polish experience, Saint John Paul II borrowed the word "solidarity" and defined it as a firm and persevering determination to commit oneself as part of a community to the common good, that is to say, to the good of everyone and of each individual.

But thinking first in terms of the community does not come easily to Americans. In his 1985 book, *Habits of the Heart*, sociologist Robert Bellah and his associates described the advanced state of individualism in the United States that weakens the sense of community. The authors used "language" as a metaphor, the first being the language of utilitarianism and expressive individualism, and the second being that of biblical and civic-republican. Both languages, Bellah thought, exaggerate our individualism. Commenting on Fr. Andrew Greeley's writings about the Catholic imagination,[12] Bellah wrote about a "cultural code" determined in large part, he explained, by the Puritans, and especially Roger Williams, and then passed down through successive generations to our own. In the words of Seymour Lipset, Americans are "the only North Atlantic society whose predominant religious tradition is sectarian rather than an established church." For Americans, religious freedom is fundamental, as is "the sacredness of individual conscience in matters of religious belief." When our culture joins such striking religious individualism to the idea of economic freedom, regard for the common good and the building of community, Bellah concludes, practically drops off the American radar screen.[13] Our individualistic culture poses great challenges, especially to Catholics.

Besides the importance of a communitarian ethic, another resource more directly rooted in Catholicism is that of sacramentality. In ordinary day-to-day life, Christians should be able to see images and reflections of the divine. A meal with others becomes a communion with them, preparing lunches for one's children becomes Eucharistic, making up after a serious misunderstanding becomes an act of reconciliation, and deep friendships teach us about a God who is love. The writings of Ron Hansen, Flannery O'Connor, and André Dubus convey that sacramental sensibility.

Bellah also argues that the influence of Protestantism, and particularly Calvinism, has made it nearly impossible for us to understand reality sacramentally. Though not a Catholic himself, Bellah thought that an absence of a sacramental sensibility greatly impoverishes the Christian life. He placed the blame on two Protestant ideas:

The Reformers, fearing idolatry and magic, attacked the doctrines of transubstantiation and other Catholic practices. Afraid of the idea of the sacred in the world, they, in effect, pushed God out of the world into radical transcendence. With the doctrine of predestination Calvin . . . described a God who had preordained everything that can occur before the beginning of time. It was natural for some philosophers and scientists to move from that idea to a deterministic physical universe without a personal God at all.[14]

If God is only radically transcendent, according to Bellah, affirming the incarnation becomes impossible. To do so would be idolatry; it would be worshipping a physical image. A God who is only transcendent becomes totally other, a reality above and beyond and removed from the ordinary and from human relationships; this is the God of the Deists. If, however, the Word became human flesh and blood, then the human things of this world can be more readily seen as carriers of the divine, and the material realities of this life, ordinary bread and wine, for example, can be an encounter with the divine. Bellah concluded that it is not surprising that highly individualistic Americans have a hard time understanding sacramentality. He borrowed a phrase from fellow sociologist Robert Wuthnow, who wrote that Americans make only "loose connections" with others.[15]

If God never sat at a table hungry, never enjoyed an evening with friends, never wept at a friend's death, then indeed it becomes more difficult to picture the divine presence in human and ordinary terms. If Bellah is right, then one of the reasons for our inability to understand sacramentality may be not only our individualism but also the way we have removed God from the human and day-to-day events of our lives.

Building a community and doing so in a university comes more easily to people who have a sacramental sensibility, since all of reality has been touched by God through the incarnation. As stated in Colossians (1:15–16), "Jesus is the image of the invisible God, the firstborn of all creation, for in him all things in heaven and on earth were created, things visible and invisible." Moreover, sacraments are celebrated in community; it is impossible to celebrate a liturgical sacrament by oneself. People who make only "loose connections" don't celebrate sacraments well. It is possible to read the Bible and pray alone, a practice that more Catholics should embrace. On the other hand, a communitarian ethic and a sacramental sensibility reinforce each other: the former stresses that every person, especially when in communion with others (for Christians, God is a communion of three persons), is made in the image and likeness of God, and the latter stresses that not just interpersonal realities but also ordinary events and material things are laden with the presence of God.[16]

In view of the belief that people are created in the image and likeness of God, and belief in the transforming power of a sacramental vision, the Orthodox and Catholic Churches, and to a lesser extent the Episcopal Church, have nurtured traditions of mysticism, since they believe, unlike some Protestant traditions, that even sinful human beings can truly become holy. God is transcendent but also Emmanuel, God who is with and in and among the people. It should be obvious that all this emphasis on the sacramentality of all creation makes it possible for believers to see their work—whatever their academic work, be it studying the galaxy or plotting the genome—as connected in some way to the things of God, as graced.

Besides the communitarian ethic, Catholicism's incarnational emphasis also distinguishes Christianity from Judaism and Islam. All three religions believe

Because life is sacramental, the work of the univ. is

in the doctrine of creation, but only Christians believe that the Word became flesh. It is difficult to separate a Christian sacramental sense from a belief in the creation. It is even more difficult to separate the dignity of the human person from the belief that Jesus is what Christians claim him to be: human and divine. Indeed, I have already alluded to the incarnation several times. The late Cardinal George wrote, "In Jesus Christ, God has become a creature, without ceasing to be God and without compromising the integrity of the creature he becomes." The Council of Chalcedon taught that Jesus was "fully divine and fully human, the proximity of the former enhancing and not excluding the dignity of the latter." To believe in the incarnation is to acknowledge that truth—saving and transforming truth—is accessible within history, is present in interpersonal encounters. The poet Gerard Manley Hopkins explains how believers encounter Jesus in many ways in and through daily experiences:

> I say more: the just man justices;
> Keeps grace: that keeps all this going graces;
> Acts in God's eye what in God's eye he is—
> Christ. For Christ plays in ten thousand places,
> Lovely in limbs, and lovely in eyes not his
> To the Father through the features of men's faces.[17]

Despite how close the incarnation brings God to Christian believers, we should be careful about speaking about the truth as though we grasp it fully, lest we become like Tertullian, who thought that once he had accepted revelation he no longer needed to search or to ponder. Rather, recall that St. Paul reminded us that even the brightest of us only see "through a glass darkly." It is almost as though Jesus, in assuming human form and living the life of a carpenter, and then an itinerant preacher, heeded the advice of the poet Emily Dickinson, who knew that it was important to

> Tell all the Truth but tell it slant—
> Success in Circuit lies
> Too bright for our infirm Delight
> The Truth's superb surprise.
> As Lightening to the Children
> With explanation kind
> The Truth must dazzle gradually
> Or every man be blind.—[18]

The reality of the incarnation does not bowl people over or force them to their knees in submission, but rather invites them on a journey within a community of faith that continues to search all of creation for a deeper understanding of the truth. To be confident that meaning and truth can be found within our history may seem naive, even deluded, given the magnitude of the tragedies in the last century—the wars, the Holocaust, the savageries of genocide and ethnic cleansing, terrorist acts, and forced migrations of refugees, to say nothing of natural disasters such as hurricanes, earthquakes, fires, and tsunamis, as well as a pandemic. Indeed, we need community. We need to find and live a deeper truth. Christians believe that Jesus himself suffered violence, was executed by the state, and yet rose from the dead and ever since has been found graciously present, the poet tells us, in many forms and under many guises.

A Catholic university should root itself in the awareness of God's sacramental presence in our world. Catholic ways of understanding that presence are inescapably incarnational, rooted in persons who have a God-given dignity. Lived rightly, that sensibility embraces everything, which means that Jesus and the university welcome all comers, all who search for the truth of things. As the theologian Brian Daley put it: "For the university, dedicated as it is to studying all aspects of human and natural reality, all the strategies and ramifications of human thought, faith in the Incarnation provides both a goal and a sense of companionship for our wonder: this world is a holy place, a shrine of meaning, because God has made it His own."[19] For Catholic Christians then, the chasm between their academic work and their personal faith need not exist.

Conclusion

I have tried in this chapter to offer several theologically based reflections on three central affirmations of Catholicism—its emphasis on the communitarian ethic, sacramentality, and the dignity of the human person—all affirmations that should provide a rich context and profound vision to inform the work of Christian believers in the academy. My purpose in speaking theologically about these things is that I believe that conversations about the mission and identity of a Catholic university would be enriched if such affirmations motivated our academic work and informed the questions we ask. For those members of the Catholic university who are not Christian and those who are not religious, I hope that these reflections give some understanding into how Christians can undertake serious intellectual work without ever feeling that what they are about is somehow other than a Christian calling. We have a lot more to go on than asking only "What would Jesus do?"

The Yale philosopher of religion Louis Dupré, one of my best teachers, made a plea for increasing our capacity for wonder and deepening our appreciation of transcendence. I have stressed the importance of the Incarnation. What Dupré called for is a Marian attitude of faith and wonder. He wrote:

> What is needed is a conversion to an attitude in which existing is more than taking, acting is more than making, meaning more than function—an attitude in which there is enough leisure for wonder and enough detachment for transcendence. Culture requires freedom, but freedom requires spiritual space to act, play, and dream in. The space for freedom is created by transcendence. What is needed most of all is an attitude in which transcendence can be recognized again.[20]

The Gospel of John states that "the truth will make you free" (8:32). Harvard still uses as its logo *Veritas*, or truth, a word that a century ago the university proudly stated was *pro Christo et ecclesiae*, for Christ and the church. Harvard no longer states what the truth they seek is for. Perhaps at Harvard, Jerusalem has been replaced by Athens. In a Catholic university, truth is for Christ and the church, but also for all of humanity, especially those who are poor and in need. If we affirm the importance of wonder and reverence, we will in no way lessen our obligation to concern ourselves with the existential ramifications of what we study, for what we are about in a Catholic university, our teaching and research, must contribute to the building of a more just society. In a Catholic university, Jerusalem and Athens contend with each other. The presence of Jesus both comforts and challenges, heals and provokes, affirms and transforms. Thinking and believing should enrich each other. So should the relationship between Jerusalem and Athens.

2

Mary and the Intellectual Life

Introduction

At the beginning of chapter 1, "Jesus and the University," I asked, if Jesus were to seek a position in a Catholic university, where would he most likely want to be? By the end of that chapter, I never really did say where I thought he would be found. Instead, I devoted most of the chapter talking about the deleterious effects that scientism, commercialism, individualism, and the privatization of faith have had on the academy. While I am not very confident that I handled well the issues related to the topic of Jesus and the academy, a similar concern that motivated me to write that chapter—namely, that Christian academics at Christian colleges and universities often have trouble making any connection between Jesus and their intellectual work—has motivated me to write this chapter also.

Here I want to explore a similar question: does Mary, the Mother of Jesus, have anything to do with the intellectual life of Catholics? Should she? I ask these questions not just as a person who is a member of a religious order, the Marianists, dedicated in a special way to Mary's mission of making Jesus known, loved, and served, but also because the questions themselves intrigue me. I am unaware of any articles or books that would help me to answer these questions. As a consequence, this chapter has to be exploratory.

Few people link Mary and the intellectual life. Some years ago, a senior colleague and history professor at the University of Dayton[1] had heard that I planned to write on this subject. He asked me, "What does a teenage Jewish girl in a backwater of the Roman empire know about the intellectual life?" Fair question. What, indeed, did she know that would help us today? And who was she and what did she do? This chapter proceeds as follows: First, I discuss what we know about Mary's life in ancient Palestine and how mothers educated their children then. I then sketch several historical developments in Christianity, briefly mentioning some writings and sculptures relevant for our inquiry in the late Patristic and medieval periods, especially the matrilineal education of Jesus as exemplified in the late medieval St. Anne Trinity, and then the premodern period. Finally, I will describe how, beginning only a century ago, women have changed university life, which up until then had been almost exclusively a male bastion. Finally, I will offer some reflections on how faculty at a Catholic university might

The Future of Catholic Higher Education. James L. Heft, S.M., Oxford University Press. © Oxford University Press 2021. DOI: 10.1093/oso/9780197568880.003.0003

find it valuable to think about Mary, the Mother of Jesus, and what she might contribute to our work of education.

The Historical Mary

In an address that she gave in 2009 at the University of Dayton when she received the Marianist Award, Sr. Elizabeth A. Johnson, C.S.J., spoke about the historical Mary, about what it meant then to be a young Jewish mother raising a child.[2] I note here, as Prof. Johnson did then, that the New Testament does not give us much information about the historical Mary.[3] However, we do know that Mary was the Mother of Jesus and that she and Joseph raised him in Nazareth. And while it is undeniable that the lack of information about anyone creates lots of room for imaginary projection, not all projections are distortions. You only have to visit the University of Dayton's Marian Library and look at its nearly three thousand crèches to see how imaginatively people from around the world have represented or, better, "enculturated" the setting, persons, and animals present in the stable at Bethlehem for the birth of Jesus.

The New Testament portrait of Mary allows us to think of her as a teacher and even as a source of wisdom for Jesus. In particular, we read in Luke 2:40 that the child Jesus "grew and became strong, filled with wisdom." Again, in Luke 2:52 we read that Jesus "increased in wisdom." And in between these two verses, we have the story of Jesus at the age of twelve sitting in the Temple, where he amazed the scholars of the law with his knowledge.

The first chapters of Luke and Matthew exemplify the literary form of *Midrashim*, that is, imaginative but not imaginary reflections that help Christians understand better theological truths about Jesus. *Midrash* appears arbitrary to us moderns who think that the meaning of a text can only be found in the literal sense of a passage based on documentable history. However, in a culture not as preoccupied with the literal sense, the practice of *Midrash* "was not regarded as arbitrary but as necessary."[4] In that light, the child Jesus in the Temple is also not arbitrary or without significance for believers today.

What can we learn from these writings? First, the education of children was the primary responsibility of the mother. There were probably few if any local schools then, at least for ordinary people; just about every child was, in current terminology, "home-schooled." Mothers were expected to teach the children their culture and their religion. Unlike today, culture and religion were not separate but intimately related, and had very much to do with the pursuit of wisdom. At the age of thirteen, boys were turned over to their fathers to be taught a profession. So, at the age of twelve, Jesus was still under the tutelage of his mother.[5] The first lesson, then, is that Mary taught her son about his culture and religion. She also taught him, it can be inferred, the wisdom he had acquired by age twelve.

In several ways, the scriptures make clear the prominence of Mary in the early life of Jesus. For example, in the story about Mary and Joseph finding Jesus in the Temple, Luke refers twelve times to the parents of Jesus. Yet, when the couple finally finds Jesus, it is not Joseph but rather Mary who tells him that "your father and I have been searching for you in great anxiety" (2:48). Beverly Gaventa, a Princeton biblical scholar, thinks that the usual English translation, "in great anxiety," of the Greek word *odynoun* "fails to capture the poignancy" of the word. It would be better, according to Gaventa, to say that "your father and I have been searching for you and have been greatly anguished."[6] Note that it is not Joseph but Mary, his principal educator in his religious life, who expresses the anguish that both she and Joseph experienced. In today's language, we could picture Mary scolding Jesus: "What were you thinking? Didn't I raise you to be more thoughtful of others?" That she was responsible for his education is also suggested by another New Testament text (Mark 6:2), where we read that the people of Nazareth, after listening to Jesus speak in their synagogue, were amazed at his wisdom. They asked if he was not the son of Mary—suggesting again, perhaps, that her role as the educator of her son was what was ordinary, even if her son was not.[7] It might also be the case that, since in a patriarchal culture the son was always referred to as the son of his father, the opponents of Jesus would not mention his father to suggest that Jesus had another unknown father, that he was a bastard.

Should we assume, as some early Christians did, that since Jesus was the Son of God that his wisdom was not really taught to him by Mary but rather somehow mysteriously infused into him directly by God? This assumption would violate Christian teaching—namely, that Jesus, though divine, is also truly human. Recall that the early Gnostics gave little value to material reality but taught rather that salvation was only a spiritual reality for the intellectual elite, for those who "know" (*gnosis*). They taught that Jesus came *through* Mary, like water through a pipe, the pipe having no effect on the water. Orthodox Christians countered this way of thinking by stressing the full humanity of Jesus, affirming in the Creed that Jesus came "of" or "from" (*ex Maria*) Mary, not just passed through her.[8] The theologians of the early church also stressed the real humanity of Jesus by citing the text from Galatians (4:4) that he "was born of a woman, born under the law"—that is, he was born naturally, like any other human being.[9]

I might also mention here the debate over whether Jesus had siblings. In the Marcan text to which I referred in the previous paragraph—the one in which the people of Nazareth were asking where Jesus got all his wisdom—those same people also asked if James, Joses, and Judas were his brothers, and referred to his sisters as well. Whether Mary had other children has been debated among

Christians. The Catholic Church teaches that these others were Jesus's cousins; it is still customary in some parts of the Middle East to refer to cousins as one's brothers and sisters. The Orthodox Church teaches that they are Joseph's children by a previous marriage, and many Protestant churches teach that they are the natural children of Mary and Joseph. Whichever tradition one accepts, it is obvious that Jesus was not raised as if he were an only child. And if all of these cousins or half-brothers and -sisters or siblings were living in the same area, in the same village, or in the same cluster of one- or two-room houses, then Jesus was raised in a community or in an extended family, where the women shared a wide range of responsibilities, none more important than the education of the children.

One final point about the historical Mary. There were no books then. There were, of course, parchment scrolls. Common people, however, were unlikely to possess them. And even if they did, it is unlikely that they could read them (though we know from several Gospel texts that Jesus was able to read—which raises an additional question: who taught him to read?). Jesus was educated in an oral culture, which for us moderns is hard to understand, flooded as we are by print, easily accessible books and libraries, to say nothing of the endless flow of printed and visual information accessible on the internet. On the other hand, recall how many people today, especially younger people, seem to be able to remember and repeat by heart the lyrics of dozens of songs. How do they do that? By listening to them repeatedly. And it is not just the repetition of the words, some of which rhyme and are repeated, but words that are wedded to music with a beat and a memorable melody. In an oral culture, people entrusted with education passed on their culture through stories, songs, and poems, made even more memorable, especially in the children's religious education, by joining them to rituals, songs, and prayers.[10]

The Wisdom literature of the Old Testament teaches that wisdom is learned at home: "the home may be regarded as perhaps the original site of wisdom teaching, before and after such teaching became professionalized among the sages."[11] It is therefore quite reasonable to think that Mary, the teenage Jewish mother in a rural village in the backwater of the Roman Empire, taught Jesus his culture and religion, and indeed helped him grow in wisdom, by means of highly sophisticated and pedagogically effective forms of oral culture.

The Wisdom Literature

What are some of the most important themes of the Wisdom literature of the Old Testament? That literature includes Proverbs, Job, and Ecclesiastes, but also, from the Apocrypha, Ecclesiasticus (or Sirach) and the Wisdom of Solomon.

What is so unusual about this literature is that unlike the Pentateuch (the first five books of the Bible) and the prophets, which concentrate on the God of the history of salvation, these books describe what it means to be an educated person. As Roland Murphy, the Old Testament scholar explains, what is typically Israelite and Jewish is not to be found in these books: "There is no mention of the promises to the patriarchs, the Exodus and Moses, the covenant and Sinai, the promise to David (2 Sam. 7) and so forth."[12] Rather, the Wisdom literature is really about education. It has to do with how to educate and bring up children.

Murphy thinks that describing wisdom as a woman, that is, as "Lady Wisdom," is "the most striking personification in the entire Bible."[13] When speaking about Lady Wisdom, Christians are tempted to imagine an actual person, something that Jews would be unlikely to do, especially because of the strict monotheism that characterized their beliefs in the postexilic period. Christians tend to think of wisdom as a gift of the Holy Spirit. Since the fourth century, Christians began to speak of Mary as a source of wisdom, and later even as the Seat of Wisdom. Proverbs 8 is a key text for the personification of what Christians would later call Lady Wisdom. In Proverbs 8, Lady Wisdom stresses the honesty and integrity of her message; she teaches truth and justice (8:7–8).

The Wisdom literature taught that creation, being the work of the Creator, reflects the Creator (Wis. 13:5). It follows, then, that the more that God's creation is studied, as we do scientifically in the university, the more we come to an insight into who God is. We can discover a certain order in creation. If we are able to decipher that order and live according to it, we will reflect wisdom, which brings happiness with it. To ignore nature, or worse, to plunder it, destroys the sense of God.

Catholics call the ability to see God and God's hand in all things sacramentality. As a university community, it is important to realize that learning about creation implies learning from others who have spent their lives learning about creation—learning from their wisdom as well. According to the Wisdom literature, wise people in Israel spoke with wise people elsewhere in the world and learned from them even about God and creation. Why would they do that? Perhaps because they realized that wise persons who use their intelligence to understand the world and their place in it contribute to everyone's understanding of creation and its author.[14] The author of the book of Wisdom assures everyone that to seek wisdom is more important than seeking gold and silver, since wisdom makes them friends with God (7:14).

The wisdom literature offers important lessons for educators. When a child is born, the work of education begins; otherwise, a child will lack a language and other important human skills for learning and friendship. Therefore, educators, first the mother and father and extended family, can be understood as collaborators with God in the work of creation. I am speaking here not only of the

How is this diff. from Providentialism?

various human arts, like music and architecture, but also, and especially, about that masterpiece of creation that is the human being. In other words, educators share in God's project of creation. The book of Wisdom (11:24–25) tells us that God willed creation out of love. If God acted out of love, then educators should also love their students and celebrate their very existence. In a defining moment in human history, Mary, God's friend and collaborator, consented to, and yes, even desired the very existence of Jesus when she said to the angel Gabriel, "yes," *fiat mihi*, "let it be done unto me." Mary becomes the Mother of Jesus and, as a consequence, his first and most important educator. Mary's contribution to the mystery of redemption did not end with Christmas. It extends well beyond that momentous birth. Marianist biblical scholar Fr. Rossier offered an interesting way to think about Mary as an educator when he wrote: "the parallel between Mary and an educator is strengthened by the fact that she is the only mother in human history whose child existed before being conceived in her womb; likewise, an educator agrees to collaborate in the education of a child—a student— who has already existed before their first encounter."[15]

Before moving on to two other historical points, we may ask why this Wisdom literature is personified as feminine, as Lady Wisdom. After surveying the scholarship, Roland Murphy concludes that no satisfactory answer exists. He is not persuaded by the argument that wisdom is personified as a woman simply because the Hebrew noun *hokmah* is feminine. Nor does he believe that the Wisdom literature was developed mainly to educate young men. In Israelite society the education of young men by women says something important about the role of women, though that fact has been passed over for centuries by male biblical commentators. Murphy thinks we still have many unanswered questions about how to understand Lady Wisdom as she appears in the Wisdom literature.[16] Despite no satisfactory answer to that question, Mary, whom Christians called the Seat of Wisdom, educated Jesus.

The second point, important for anyone associated with the Marianist Family, is that Blessed William Joseph Chaminade (1761–1850), the founder of the Marianists, commented a great deal on the Wisdom literature. In the first volume of the two-volume collection of his writings about Mary, Chaminade actually quotes the Old Testament (276 times) more than he does the New Testament (245 times). He is especially fond of the wisdom literature, citing texts from Psalms 45 times, Proverbs and the Song of Solomon 35 times each, and the book of Sirach 47 times.[17] Chaminade wrote about Mary as the Mother of Wisdom, which indeed she was, since Christians, following St. Paul, believed Jesus to be the Wisdom of God. Drawing also on texts from the New Testament, especially the Gospel of John and the book of Revelation, he developed a profound Marian apostolic spirituality focused on the formation of lay leaders and institutions for social change. Chaminade and the Marianists have dedicated themselves to creating "family spirit," a point to which we will return later. But before that, I want to describe the central role that women, as an embodiment of wisdom, played in the lives of two famous men.

A Philosopher and Poet Led by Wisdom

Boethius (480–524), a philosopher, theologian, and Roman governor, wanted to translate Plato and Aristotle into Latin and comment on their significance for Christianity. This project was cut short when he was arrested, perhaps for treason, and put in prison. While awaiting execution, he wrote his most famous work, *The Consolation of Philosophy*. The book is structured as a dialogue between him and a mysterious woman, whom he describes at the very beginning of his book as standing above his head, "having a grave countenance, glistening clear eye, and of quicker sight that commonly Nature doth afford." To Boethius, she exhibited "unabated vigor" and in her right hand "held certain books, and in her left hand . . . a scepter."[18] She tells Boethius, who is in tears, that he should not think that "Wisdom hath been exposed to danger by wicked men."[19]

An extended philosophical dialogue follows between Boethius and this mysterious woman who, frequently drawing upon the philosopher Plato, explains to Boethius why good people suffer evil, why God's providence can be trusted, and what a wise person should seek. She reminds him, perhaps recalling that Mary, the Mother of Jesus, pondered many things in her heart, that "wisdom pondereth the event of things," and that he should not impatiently demand immediate resolution to his problems.[20] She assures him that she will carefully attend to his education.[21] At one point, Boethius addresses her as the "nurse of all virtues."[22] Boethius's book exercised profound influence in the following centuries. For our purposes, I simply wish to point out how, once again, a woman, with a book in her hand, instructed a man about what is most important in life.

We find a similar personification in Dante Alighieri's (1265–1321) classic, *The Divine Comedy*, which he divided into three parts: *Inferno* (hell), *Purgatorio* (purgatory), and *Paradiso* (paradise). Describing life as a journey, Dante passes through hell and purgatory and arrives finally in paradise. He does not make the journey alone. Virgil, who lived before the Christian era, was a poet whom Dante admired. Virgil, representing reason, assists him at the beginning of his journey and leads him in the midst of the darkness of hell. But it is Beatrice, not Virgil, who leads him into paradise. She leaves her seat (Seat of Wisdom?) in heaven to guide him on his journey. Beatrice, whom Dante had in real life actually met when they were both nine years of age, became for him for the rest of his life the center of his affection and desire. She educates him in the truths of the faith, building on the foundation of reason that Virgil taught him. Dante is drawn to

Beatrice's wisdom; at one point in his journey, Dante, overwhelmed by Beatrice's beauty, is rebuked by her. She instructs him to contemplate instead divine beauty. She instructs him in the truths of the faith and, as the embodiment of wisdom, leads him into paradise. When Virgil hands Dante over to Beatrice, the transition is seamless. There is no need for Dante to make a "leap of faith." Reason and faith are intimately related.

Both Boethius and Dante personify wisdom as women. Boethius is in prison awaiting execution, and Dante in hell experiencing condemnation. To their immense relief, both are assisted by Lady Wisdom, who instructs and leads them to the meaning of life and to the beatific vision.

Women, Education, and Universities

So far we have considered the historical Mary and the role that women in Israel played in educating their children. Then we described the importance of the Wisdom literature and the way it influences the education of children. We also looked briefly at two classics in Western literature, one philosophical and the other poetic, in which men were saved by the ministrations of women who embodied wisdom.

Now I want us to consider two other historical developments that influence ways in which we might imagine the relationship of Mary to the intellectual life. The first takes us to the late medieval period when the cult of St. Anne appears prominently in art and statuary. Already in the middle of the twelfth century, in the western portal or entrance of the Chartres cathedral, we find an image of a woman who represents Grammar, or *ars grammatica*, which was the first subject that students all over Europe had to learn in their newly founded universities. Enter that same cathedral and one also finds in the great northern window an image of St. Anne and her child Mary.

The four Gospels do not tell any stories about St. Anne; rather, stories about her are found in the apocryphal Protoevangelium of James, which does not have the same authority as the canonical Gospels. Nevertheless, it provides us with some interesting examples related to our topic. According to the Protoevangelium, Anne and her husband, Joachim, had no children. When an angel visited them and told them they would have a child, Anne told the angel that she would dedicate the child, boy or girl, to God. Joachim wanted the child to be brought up in the Temple when she turned two years old. Anne persuaded Joachim to wait till their daughter was three. In the Temple she was taught to read. From the eighth to the tenth centuries, priests in the Byzantine traditions preached sermons that described Mary, the Mother of God, as possessing the wisdom of Athena.[23] In the thirteenth century, St. Albert the Great, the teacher of Thomas Aquinas, taught that Mary had been a master of the seven liberal arts. In that same thirteenth century, artists created a stained glass window in Chartres that portrays Mary sitting with four other students learning from a teacher.

By the fourteenth and fifteenth century, we find dozens of images, stained glass windows, and statues that depict St. Anne, often with book in hand, teaching Mary, sometimes as an infant or as a child, and sometimes as the young mother of Jesus. Mary often has a book in her hand, as she passes on to Jesus what she has learned from her mother, Anne, Jesus's grandmother.[24] Many of these artistic renderings portray Mary learning very much like the children who were then being taught in the monastic schools of the twelfth century. In all of these works, the book that St. Anne holds is open, unlike the closed book that appears in most art portraying other saints.

All of these matrilineal trinities underscore the simple incarnational truth that Jesus was educated by a woman who was educated by a woman. Whether Anne or Mary could actually read is not the point, nor should we be concerned about the historical truth of St. Albert's pious opinion. The point is that Christians in the Late Middle Ages understood that the wisdom that Jesus embodied came to him through human means, certainly specially graced human means—through Mary, whose primary responsibility was to educate Jesus in his Jewish culture and religion of her day. I would suggest, then, that in this context when we think of Mary, we think of education.

A second, and more recent historical development I want to mention is the entrance of women into higher education. We know that some women, in the early medieval times, were literate, especially those who were monastics, for example, Hildegard of Bingen (1098–1179). And then, in the sixteenth century, there was also the daughter of Thomas More, Margaret, whose fluency in the Latin language was well known. While monastic schools from the sixth century on admitted boys, most boys for most of history received no formal education until the nineteenth century. Women's academies date from the seventeenth century, but again, they could be attended only by the daughters of the affluent. In the mid-nineteenth century a number of women's colleges were established in the United States. It was not until the beginning of the twentieth century that women in any numbers began to be admitted to universities.[25]

At the beginning of the twentieth century, only 1% of the US college-age population, nearly all males, attended colleges and universities. It was not until 1920 that women in the United States won the right to vote. And it was not until after World War II that they were allowed in the Catholic Church to study theology at the graduate level. This would not have happened without the leadership and courage of the visionary Sr. Madaleva (1887–1964), who founded the Graduate School of Theology at St. Mary's in South Bend, Indiana. In his 1963 encyclical, "Peace on Earth" (*Pacem in terris*), published shortly before he died, Pope John

XXIII identified the women's movement as one of the major movements of the twentieth century, a "sign of the times." He wrote, "Since women are becoming ever more conscious of their human dignity, they will not tolerate being treated as mere material instruments, but demand rights befitting a human person both in domestic and in public life."[26]

I realize that much of this history may already be familiar to the reader. What may be less known, however, is the significant impact that Walter Ong, S.J., the 1989 recipient of the Marianist Award, gives to the presence of women in the universities. Ong claims that education in the West, especially Catholic education, was *agonistic* until the 1960s, when it became largely coeducational. He refers to this change as an "in-depth revolution" that has remained mostly overlooked. By *agonistic*, Ong means that a certain enmity existed between the teacher and the (male) student. The subject matter was organized as a "field of combat, to purvey, not just to test, knowledge in a combative style."[27] The Latin word *campus* refers to a staging area for the Roman armies just before they marched in parades. The medieval universities stressed the importance of formal logic, held debates, and taught rhetoric. Students were taught to defend theses through oral argument. Disputed questions formed an essential part of the curriculum.

The structure of the question in Thomas Aquinas's *Summa* begins with objections to a thesis, followed by an answer with proof, and finally gives a response to the objections. Oral skills favored polemics, or arguments. Plato, if you recall, opposed writing, because it detracted, he thought, from the primary goal of education—to become a public speaker, a debater. Public speaking was highly prized; elocution contests continued at many major universities until after World War II. The learning of the Latin language had become a sex-linked language, a sort of puberty rite that marked a boy's exit from his family and entrance into the tribe. Today, about the only remnant of the *agonistic* character of the medieval university is the defense doctoral students are expected to give of their dissertation before a board of examiners composed of university professors.[28]

In the 1960s, according to Ong, all these agonistic practices rapidly disappeared, almost overnight, when women began to enter universities in greater numbers, especially in Catholic universities, which originally were intended only for men. The following things happened when women arrived:

(1) Latin was dropped, first as a means of instruction and then as a required subject; (2) the agonistic thesis method of teaching was replaced by less combative methods; (3) written examinations were substituted for public oral disputations and examinations; and (4) of course, physical punishment was minimized or suppressed.[29]

Catholic seminaries preserved the *agonistic* culture the longest; there, the culture of Latin and learning philosophy and theology in Latin persisted relatively intact in some places until the late 1960s. During a two-year period, from 1967 to 1968, St. Louis Divinity School ceased using Latin as a language of instruction, dropped the method of using theses for instruction, dropped staged disputations and oral exams as integral parts of the curriculum, and admitted women.[30] Ong believes that these were not four unrelated changes; he believes that they were all of one piece. Other cultural and historical factors were also surely in play—such as the trauma of two world wars, the Holocaust, the upheaval over the Vietnam War, the attack on the Western canon of literature, and the movement for greater "relevance" in the 1960s.[31] Whatever the causes of these deep changes in higher education, the entrance of women played a key role.

If this collapse of an agonistic tradition of education were not enough, consider also the profound change represented by the sixteen documents of Vatican II (1962–1965) in the early 1960s, a time of considerable optimism in the Catholic Church in the United States. None of the council's sixteen documents, though written in Latin, contains a single *anathema sit*, or condemnation. Vatican II has been called a pastoral council. Some conservative critics have argued that this means that nothing really changed since no new dogmas were proclaimed. But "man does not live by dogmas alone," to paraphrase scripture. One has only to read Jesuit historian John O'Malley's recent book, *What Happened at Vatican II?*, to realize that very much indeed has changed.[32] And while it is true that no new dogmas were officially proclaimed at Vatican II, several dogmatic teachings underwent important developments that opened avenues for ecumenism, interreligious dialogue, religious freedom, and significant changes in the way liturgy is celebrated.

In another book, *Four Cultures of the West*, O'Malley says more about the significance of the change in language at Vatican II.[33] Before Vatican II, conciliar documents typically adopted a "prophetic" style and language, often condemning teachings and practices that their authors opposed. The documents of Vatican II are written in a more open and noncombative style, a style similar to a homily or a commentary. Although O'Malley doesn't use the same words as Ong in describing these changes, both point to major cultural changes that supported them.[34]

What, then, might be the importance for higher education of this major cultural change? Consider first that a shift from the argumentative and debate (eristic) style of communication to one of face-to-face listening and understanding will foster community and friendship. Scholars have studied the extent to which social media and cable television contribute to polarizations of many sorts. Debate has its value, especially when people learn how to think about a topic from different perspectives. But the kind of debate that politicians, for example, engage in creates little confidence that either much genuine listening or under-standing has been achieved. Debates isolate participants. Scholars have also studied the extent to which addiction to social media, especially among ado-lescent women, increases the frequency of depression.[35] In short, real human contact as opposed to only the virtual (what one philosopher has described as "excarnation"[36]) connects people more than it isolates them.

Second, the art of dialogue increases respect and understanding. I will always remember a colorful banner created by Sr. Corita Kent that read, "To understand is to stand under which is to look up which is a good way to understand."[37] In chapter 12 on liberal education, I suggest that humanistic learning within a reli-gious context develops reverence. It also enhances one's awareness of how much of life is a matter of receiving thoughtfully what is offered respectfully. Nietzsche once wrote that "the trick today is not arranging a festival but finding people who can enjoy one."[38] The Catholic tradition welcomes ritual and celebration. The center of Catholic life is giving thanks for the many gifts received, the first among them God's love in Jesus Christ. A Catholic university that does not find ways to strengthen attitudes of respect, reverence, and gratitude would also find it diffi-cult to draw its members to thankful worship, literally, the Eucharist. Ritual, art, music, and dance should be central to Catholic higher education.

At the beginning of this chapter, I noted that almost nothing has been written about Mary and the intellectual life and that, as a consequence, what I would have to say about the subject would be largely exploratory. Summing up what I have written so far, I do believe that the emphasis on Mary as a teacher of wisdom and as someone who learned from her mother and passed on what she learned to her son Jesus, the entrance of women into higher education, and the profoundly dif-ferent tone that the bishops (yes, all males, and yes, still writing in Latin) used in writing the documents of Vatican II are all somehow related.

Suggestions for Thinking about Mary Today

Given these reflections, how might we profitably think about Mary and Catholic university education today? First, it seems counterintuitive that since Vatican II Mary has played an ever-increasing role in ecumenical and interreligious dialogues. I say counterintuitive because in the 1950s Mary was a point of deep division between Protestants and Catholics. But the bishops of Vatican II, in-stead of devoting a separate document to Mary, decided by a narrow vote to in-clude what they wanted to say about her in the document on the church, *Lumen Gentium*. In essence, this decision placed Mary not above nor apart from, but right in the middle of the people of God, where she became the "faithful dis-ciple," to use the title of a book by Marianist Fr. Bertrand Buby,[39] or, to express it another way, she became *Truly Our Sister*, the title of another book by Prof. Elizabeth Johnson.[40]

Since the council, there have been fruitful dialogues about Mary among Lutherans, Roman Catholics, and even Evangelicals. Chiara Lubich, founder of the Focolare Movement, officially named the Work of Mary, made interfaith relations one of the movement's most important initiatives. The response by members of other religions to Lubich's initiative has been extraordinary. Instead of beginning with a focus on doctrines, Lubich focused on the love of Jesus, who comes to us through Mary.[41] Besides this interfaith outreach, the movement, in the name and under the banner of Mary, has also established throughout the world "little cities" with training programs and economic cooperatives that help the poor but still make a profit.

As I mentioned earlier, Blessed Chaminade, over a hundred years before Chiara Lubich's Work of Mary, recognized the need for lay leadership and dedicated himself to the formation of lay communities of faith that foster holiness and a sense of mission, or what we might call today an environment for human flourishing. He drew directly upon the French School of Spirituality with its Christo-centric focus and fostered freedom from prescribed methods of personal prayer. Echoing the words of Mary, Chaminade encouraged everyone to do whatever the Lord Jesus asks. The Focolare Movement and the Marianist Family have much in common and would benefit by closer ties.

Mary also seems to be a bridge between Christianity and Islam. The Qur'an mentions Mary by name thirty-four times, though usually as the Mother of Jesus, not the Son of God. But it also presents her as a model and affirms her virginal conception of Jesus. One Sunni scholar, Yusuf Ali, says of Mary, "Chastity was her special virtue: with a son of virgin birth, she and Jesus became a miracle in all nations."[42] Still another striking example: only 7% of the population of the war-torn island of Sri Lanka (total population nearly twenty million) is Christian, but during the feast of the Assumption in 2009, over five hundred thousand people, including tens of thousands of Buddhists and Hindus—who fought against each other in the civil war—together thronged peacefully the roads to Madhu to honor the Mother of Madhu, represented by a five-hundred-year-old statue of Mary that miraculously escaped any damage during the previous quarter century of war. With thousands of these pilgrims singing "Ave Maria," one Tamil woman, who lost two of her sons in the war and had a third still missing, said, "The Virgin has brought us together. She has given us hope. It is now up to us to live together."[43] Who could have guessed a century ago that the Mother of Jesus would be such a magnet and force in ecumenical and interreligious activities?

These remarkable developments deserve more extensive research and theological reflection. They certainly caught the attention of the editors of *National Geographic* magazine, who in their December 2015 issue published a cover story on Mary, "The Most Powerful Woman in the World," replete with magnificent pictures capturing her global influence. That several Marianist scholars are quoted in the article is a source of pride for me.[44]

Second, returning to the discussion of the historical Mary, I think that careful historical studies keep our feet on the ground. That is to say, while projection has its place, we need to pay special attention to what we can learn from history about Mary. Jesuit Hans Kolvenbach remarked that for real solidarity to take place, more than concepts are needed. Solidarity with others also requires personal connections—both concepts and connections. In the past decades, we have benefited greatly by intertestamental studies that have given us a much better grasp of the times and places in which Jesus and Mary lived. These studies help us to connect with them as they lived their lives. Historical studies have helped us refrain from idealizing them, robbing them of their Jewishness and their humanity.

Recently, two women writers have drawn attention to the consequences of losing a sense of the particular within human experience. Mary Gordon, a Catholic novelist, believes that abstraction is one of the twin dangers of religious ways of thinking (the other is dualism). By abstraction, she means the "error that results from refusing to admit that one has a body and is an inhabitant of the physical world."[45] In a similar vein, the Episcopal priest Barbara Taylor Brown rejects "any religious definition of goodness that leaves the body behind." She states that God knew that the Word had to become flesh, since "the disciples were going to need something warm and near that they could bump into on a regular basis, something so real that they would not be able to intellectualize it and so essentially untidy that there was no way they could ever gain control over it."[46] No one knew the body of Jesus better than his mother, who nursed him, changed his diapers, and embraced his beaten dead body at the foot of the cross. A historically and biblically rich understanding of Mary inoculates us against the danger of abstraction, another word for gnosticism. Christian intellectual life ought to be embodied. Academics are not just bodiless minds or brains on a stick. Therefore, we should not ignore gender if we wish to understand the intellectual life, especially today.

Rowan Williams, the archbishop of Canterbury, noting that Jesus especially welcomed children, asks how those who do theology can afford to work in spaces where women are absent and children hidden away.[47] In the nineteenth and well into the twentieth century, the tendency to relegate women to domestic, private, and nonintellectual roles has made it difficult for many women to fare well in the academy. According to scholar Jennifer Popiel, we tend to think of Mary as nonintellectual "because we've inherited a tradition in which women and nurturing are 'obviously' private and therefore non-public, non-civic, non-intellectual."[48] Thanks to the women's movement, laywomen and men are now studying theology together, often with their children in tow. The theology that is being written in such environments is different than what was written in male celibate communities. This is not to say that such theology is, for that reason alone, going to be better theology—I think it is too soon to tell since we have been working in this new human environment now for only a few decades, and then only in a few Western universities.

Perhaps I should make explicit here something that until now has been only implicit. When we think about Mary and the intellectual life, we can look to the experience and wisdom of men as well as women. Speaking of the "genius of women" would make more sense if the Vatican also spoke of the "genius of men," though both phrases suggest that all men and women are the same, which certainly is not the case. I am not suggesting that a greater awareness of Mary's importance in academic work can be found in some special "feminine" approach to intellectual work. Remember that the idea of wisdom as feminine has been used as an image of Jesus as well as of Mary.[49] Tradition has called Jesus the Wisdom of God.

Nevertheless, significant changes are afoot. Theologians today employ many methods for doing theology and take up many themes in fresh ways—I am thinking here not only of theologies of sexuality and simplicity but also environmental and liberationist themes. Many of these works explore how to live as committed Christians in a pluralistic and consumerist society, and in a world where the gap between the very rich and the poor ever widens.[50] How to live is certainly the preoccupation of the Wisdom literature we have been discussing. A careful study of the times and places of the lives of Jesus and Mary makes the Gospel commitment to the poor and to women and children clearer, especially since throughout history they are the ones who bear the worst brunt of war and violence.

Conclusion

As I now conclude this chapter, I am concerned that these reflections may appear to the reader as scattered. My intention, however, has been modest. If I have been able only to raise issues that emphasize the importance of understanding Mary and her continuing influence in the world, then I am satisfied. The themes I've touched upon—the historical Mary, the wisdom literature, the need that a great philosopher and a poet had for women as wisdom figures, the role of women in education of children and more recently their impact on the shape of higher education—need further reflection. There is good reason to think that continued study of Mary has a place in the intellectual life of a university, certainly at a Catholic university, especially when the intellectual life is understood as rooted in history, in traditions of wisdom, and with a commitment to the poor and the marginalized. Perhaps, after all, a peasant teenage woman who spent most of her life in a backwater of the Roman Empire has something to teach us about what we might most value about the intellectual life—a search for wisdom.

A university is centered on the intellectual life, which for Christians means seeking wisdom—something more than learning a trade and receiving a credential. We need to look to the figures who embody this for us and ask ourselves what a university might look like that takes seriously the vision of Wisdom personified in the text (7:7–11) from the book of Wisdom:

> I prayed and prudence was given me;
> I pleaded, and the spirit of wisdom came to me.
> I preferred her to scepter and throne,
> and deemed riches nothing in comparison with her,
> nor did I liken any priceless gem to her;
> because all gold, in view of her, is a little sand,
> and before her, silver is to be accounted mire.
> Beyond health and comeliness I loved her,
> and I chose to have her rather than the light,
> because the splendor of her never yields to sleep.
> Yet all good things together came to me in her company,
> And countless riches at her hands.

3

John Henry Newman in Context

Introduction

I have chosen John Henry Newman as my third "north star," mainly because of the vision he has for what a university should be. Jesus and Mary never addressed this question. Newman, who believed in Jesus and was devoted to Mary, did and with great eloquence. But even more than his mastery of rhetoric, Newman's emphasis on the importance of the integration of knowledge (wisdom) and formation of students (holiness)—two imperatives that most of today's universities have forgotten—should be essential features of education in a Catholic university. This chapter examines Newman's times and his vision for a university education. Though there are great differences between university education in England in the mid-nineteenth century and in the United States today, I argue that Newman's thought is still relevant, especially given the need today for an integrated vision for a college education, for the liberal arts, and for the moral formation for students. I begin with a sketch of Newman's life.

Newman: The Unwelcome Convert and Unusual Catholic Saint

Newman's long life spanned most of the nineteenth century. Born into an Anglican family of bankers in London in 1801, he underwent his first conversion at the age of fifteen, one that made him during his teenage years a devout evangelical who had come to two "absolute and luminously self-evident beings, myself and my creator."[1] He enrolled at Oxford, was ordained an Anglican priest in 1825, and three years later was appointed chaplain of St. Mary the Virgin Church in Oxford. He held that position until 1843 when, as a consequence of his studies of the first five centuries of Christianity (the "Patristic" period), his doubts about the apostolicity of the Church of England led him on October 9, 1845, to be received in the Roman Catholic Church. After studying for a year in Rome, he was ordained a Catholic priest in 1847 and returned to England to found an oratory, a small community of priests, in Birmingham.

For most of his adult life, he was not trusted by most Anglicans, especially when he led the Oxford Movement well into the 1830s; for them, he sounded too

The Future of Catholic Higher Education. James L. Heft, S.M., Oxford University Press. © Oxford University Press 2021.
DOI: 10.1093/oso/9780197568880.003.0004

"Roman." Nor was he trusted after 1845 by Catholics because his writings did not sound scholastic enough. Historian Frank Turner explains that during his Anglican years, Newman

> had been the chief disruptive academic personality in Oxford. In point of fact, John Henry Newman had been the kind of faculty member whom every university administrator dreads, trustees deplore and fail to understand, and more staid alumni find embarrassing, but whom students and the young among the faculty and alumni cheer toward further extravagances.[2]

As a Catholic, Newman continued to be a source of disruption for most Catholic theologians because of the way he approached the religious issues of the day. Newman's own archbishop and later Cardinal Manning found Newman difficult and overly sensitive. He wrote about Newman to a friend in Rome: "I see much danger of an English Catholicism, of which Newman is the highest type. . . . In one word, it is worldly Catholicism, and it will have the worldly on its side, and will deceive many."[3]

In a more positive light, English theologian Nicholas Lash described Newman a century later as a gifted controversialist who sought "to prove by persuasion rather than to persuade by proof."[4] Newman paved the way for a different kind of theology and created an understanding of the church that was widely embraced by the bishops at Vatican II. In 1975, Pope Paul VI told the participants in a Newman symposium that

> many of the problems which he treated with wisdom—although he himself was frequently misunderstood and misinterpreted in his own time—were the subjects of the discussion and study of the fathers of the Second Vatican Council, as for example the questions of ecumenism, the relationship between Christianity and the world, the emphasis on the role of the laity in the Church and the relationship of the Church to non-Christian religions.[5]

Well before Newman died in 1890, Pope Leo XIII recognized Newman's religious genius and made him a cardinal in 1879, over the objection of Manning, who himself privately thought Newman to be a heretic. According to Newman, the reception of the red hat lifted forever a cloud that had been hanging over him. Toward the end of his life, he continued to write, mainly revising and polishing for republication many of his forty books.

On January 22, 1991, Saint Pope John Paul II recognized Newman for his heroic virtues and named him "venerable." In 2001, he expressed the hope that Newman, a "sure and eloquent guide in our perplexity," might soon be declared "blessed," the step before finally being declared a saint. The pope explained that

Newman had created "a remarkable synthesis of faith and reason." Because of the rich interplay of that synthesis, Newman, according to John Paul II, avoided both rationalism, which rejected "authority and transcendence," and fideism, which "turns away from the challenges of history and the tasks of this world." Fideism, according to John Paul II, ends in a "distorted dependence upon authority and the supernatural."[6]

On September 19, 2010, in Birmingham, England, Pope Benedict XVI beatified Newman, remarking that though Newman did not die a martyr, he should still be recognized as one:

> [Newman] bore eloquent witness to [the Lord] in the course of a long life devoted to the priestly ministry, and especially to preaching, teaching, and writing. . . . In Blessed John Henry, that tradition of gentle scholarship, deep human wisdom and profound love for the Lord has borne rich fruit, as a sign of the abiding presence of the Spirit deep within the heart of God's people, bringing forth abundant gifts of holiness.[7]

On October 13, 2019, Pope Francis canonized Newman in a ceremony held at the Vatican. He noted that Newman gave great importance to consulting the faithful, the dignity of each individual's conscience, the recognition that the doctrines of the church evolve, and that theologians' needed "elbow room" in their work. That Pope Francis—who himself consults the faithful regularly, especially most recently on the subject of marriage, believes that the church should help form but not replace conscience, and promotes open and vigorous discussion of difficult issues—canonized Newman should come as no surprise. Some bishops, such as Bishop Robert Barrron, are already calling for Newman to be named a doctor of the church, a title given to only a few saints who have made major contributions to the church's understanding of its faith.

Newman's canonization would have been unimaginable one hundred years ago. At that time, some of his critics associated many of his writings with "modernism," a movement that attempted to bring the church into a closer relationship with the modern age. Modernism was roundly condemned by Pope Pius X's 1907 encyclical, *Pascendi dominici gregis*. Newman's writings on the importance of the laity, his attention to religious psychology in making the act of faith, and his conviction that doctrine develops over time rendered him suspect of modernism. Even though Newman's reputation enjoyed a renaissance later in the twentieth century, some scholars still, for various reasons, not only disagreed with some of his key ideas but also actively opposed his canonization. Obviously, and as far as I am concerned happily, they did not prevail.[8]

The Reception of Newman's *Idea*

Newman's writings on education were not as suspect as some of his other writings. In fact, his major lectures on university education, collected in a volume entitled *The Idea of a University*, went relatively unnoticed when first published. In the United States, from the 1920s to the 1960s, a period the historian Philip Gleason referred to as the "Golden Age of Newman's *Idea*," Newman was often quoted by leaders of Catholic education, as well as by the famous reforming president of the University of Chicago, Robert M. Hutchins. But it is unlikely that *The Idea* actually shaped most of the priorities of Catholic educational institutions. Nonetheless, it has reaped great accolades, none more eloquent than that of the late and distinguished historian of Christian doctrine Jaroslav Pelikan, who wrote that Newman's *Idea* was "the most important treatise on the idea of a university ever written in any language."[9]

But can such praise for Newman's *Idea*, even one so graciously given by a scholar as eminent as Pelikan, actually stand? Some scholars argue that what passed for education in the middle of the nineteenth century bears no value for today's universities; others think that Newman never had to face the complexities of a modern university. Take, for example, the view of J. M. Roberts, who served as the vice chancellor of the University of Southampton and then the warden of Merton College at Oxford. He believes Newman's ideas about university education need to be kept in the nineteenth century, when they were written, and where they made sense. Roberts explains that

again and again . . . Newman's assumptions reveal themselves to be so different from ours, the background against which he writes is so utterly removed from our own, the universities of his day . . . so unlike ours, either in their business or their ethos, that we cannot expect him to speak to our specific needs.[10]

It is, of course, true that in Newman's time, only the elite went to the university, and all of them male, although small women's colleges were founded at Cambridge in 1869 and 1870, and at Oxford in 1879. At that time, England did not support the commitment to "mass education" as the United States did, especially after the Civil War. Before that war, the elective system with majors and minors had not yet been created, nor did the social sciences exist as we know them today. Nor did American educators believe then, or for that matter now, that every student should study the liberal arts before undertaking any professional education.

And what about those critics who claim that Newman never faced the challenges that university administrators face today? Though he admired Newman's *Idea*, Fr. Theodore Hesburgh, the long-time president of Notre Dame,

wrote in 1962 that Newman provided little guidance for today's university presidents: "it *is* easier to write about what a Catholic university should be than to
create and administer one in reality."[11] Frank Turner writes that Newman did
not have a faculty that was unionized, a board of trustees, a large and powerful
alumni group, government regulations, or big-time athletics. If all these specific historical differences were not enough to render Newman's vision of education irrelevant, the former president of the University of Rochester, George
Dennis O'Brien, dismissed Newman's *Idea* as "a favorite text for commencement
genuflections to ideals" but a vision of the university that has enjoyed "no institutional realization." Like Hesburgh, O'Brien wrote that Newman offers no advice
on the fundamental issue of who makes what decisions. Any president who today
sets out to reform a real university, O'Brien explains, needs "to persuade a suspicious faculty, a restive alumni body, a bottom-line board of trustees, and a tran-
sient population of adolescents."[12] And if all these criticisms are not enough to
make Newman's vision of education irrelevant, what should we make of the fact
that after only four years as president, Newman resigned? Should the ill-fated
Catholic University of Ireland then be remembered, as Ian Ker suggests, "only
because of the book to which it gave birth?"[13] In the face of all these criticisms,
it must be asked, then, whether the conclusion inevitably follows that Newman's
Idea, apart from its rhetorical beauty, has never amounted to much, simply because the university he described, was called upon to found, and then tried to
lead, turned out to be irrelevant for educational leaders today.

There is still another factor we should keep in mind before I make a case for
Newman's continued relevance. We need to be aware of just how much change,
since Newman wrote his *Idea*, that higher education in the United States has
undergone. In 1862 the federal government established land grant institutions,
expanding access to a large population for practical education, agriculture, and
the mechanical arts. Then, in the mid-twentieth century, shortly after World War
II, the government began pouring money into universities for research. At about
the same time, community colleges appeared and multiplied, and for-profit
institutions, like the University of Phoenix, began enrolling thousands of mostly
nontraditional students.

The Catholic community of the United States, now less than 7% of the world's
Catholics, established and sustained a very large number of colleges and universities, not for the elite, but mostly for immigrants. But since the 1950s, the
steady flow into Catholic higher education of postsecondary students has by the
twenty-first century included more women than men, most of them middle and
upper middle class, as well as a more diverse student population than ever before.
In effect, over the last 150 years, higher education in the United States has been
deregulated, and Catholic higher education changed significantly. No longer are
these universities a sort of finishing school for elite males.

Despite the differences in time, country, and the shape and mission of higher education in the United States from mid-nineteenth-century England, I believe that Newman's *Idea* remains relevant. Moreover, the challenges that Newman faced in the 1850s were, in fact, every bit as formidable as, and in some ways even more formidable than, those that face a typical president of a Catholic university today. Newman had to deal with a divided board of trustees composed of bishops, protect the academic freedom of professors, manage the animosity of the Irish against the British, deal with increasing competition, and persuade a skeptical Irish public of the value of a Catholic university. Despite these challenges, I will argue that some of Newman's central insights into the purpose of education remain especially important for Catholic colleges and universities today.

Newman's Difficult Situation

Before arguing for the continuing relevance of Newman's vision for a university education, I want to take a closer look at some of the specific challenges he faced. Until the middle of the nineteenth century, Ireland could boast of only one college, Trinity, established in 1591. A British statute of 1637 required all students to attend worship services and partake in communion according to the Anglican practice, and that all the fellows take "an oath against popery (the *Pontificia Religio*)."[14] Two centuries later, after ignoring the plight of the Irish people during their devastating potato famine, the British government, under the leadership of Sir Robert Peel, decided in 1845 to establish three Queen's Colleges located in three cities: Belfast, Cork, and Galway. These were to be nonsectarian colleges, that is, colleges that, in the language of that time, offered "mixed education" for both Catholic and Protestant students. Since no theology would be taught, both Catholics and Protestants could attend these colleges, the government believed, without compromising their religious convictions. There would be no religious tests for matriculation nor religious requirements for graduation. Shortly after the government announced this plan, the Catholic bishops of Ireland met to decide how to react to Peel's initiative, a plan "pregnant," they thought, "with danger to faith and morals" of Catholic young men.[15] Within two years, Pope Pius IX supported them in their opposition to mixed education and instructed them to condemn the entire initiative. All the Irish bishops did not agree with the pope, though in public they kept a united front.

In 1851, Archbishop Cullen, recently returned from thirty years in Rome where he had served as the rector of the Irish College, invited Newman to come to Dublin to present several lectures against the mixed education initiative. Cullen also invited him to establish a Catholic university and be its first rector. After some reflection, Newman accepted these invitations and in the spring of 1852 presented five public lectures in Dublin. By the time Newman resigned as rector in 1858, he estimated that he had crossed the Irish Sea more than fifty times.

Consider some of the personal challenges Newman faced. First, he was not an Irishman, but an Englishman, and though he shared the language with the Irish, he did not share their culture. Second, he was a recent convert, still distrusted by members of the Catholic hierarchy. Third, he had to speak to several different audiences, some of whom disagreed with each other. For example, some bishops favored the mixed education scheme, thinking that it was, under the circumstances, the best they could do, while others wanted a seminary—not a university—for laymen. All along Newman wanted a real university where different ideas would be debated and people would freely pursue their thinking and research. And all this Newman was expected to accomplish in a conservative Catholic nation that had never felt the need to found a Catholic university.

If that were not enough, many of the most prosperous Irish businessmen preferred to send their sons abroad to be educated in England and in Europe. A *Catholic* university was not that important to them. Most of these Irish leaders, with the suffering and starvation caused by the potato famine (1845–1848) fresh in their memories, had trouble seeing any use for a liberal education; they wanted their sons to learn how to be successful businessmen. All along, Newman believed that he was founding a university for English-speaking Catholics, not just Irish Catholics, a conviction not shared by many in his Irish audience. As one scholar put it, "The Irish were too Irish to desire an education that should turn out an Irish replica of the 'English gentleman.'"[16]

It gets worse. Newman's superior, Archbishop Cullen, often refused to answer Newman's letters and requests and, behind his back, criticized him to Roman authorities. Cullen didn't allow Newman to hire his own staff.[17] His "board of trustees" was divided but not open about it; they were, to use a psychological phrase, "passive aggressive." How well would today's presidents of Catholic universities be able to lead if their board chair didn't trust them, was incommunicative, and secretly criticized their leadership to the local bishop? In short, Newman lacked the backing of his board chair and was unsupported by a divided board. Taken together, they radically reduced his freedom to create the university he envisioned.

When his successor as president of the fledgling Irish Catholic University, a Jesuit priest Bartholomew Woodlock, asked for advice, Newman wrote: "It is my duty, when you, as head of the University, ask my mind, to give it, and I do so, but I don't wish what I say repeated." After assuring Woodlock that there was indeed talent sufficient to "accept the great venture of a real Catholic University," he felt it necessary to add, "On the other hand, it is *essential* that the Church should have a living presence and control in the action of the University. But still, till the bishops leave the University to itself, till the University governs itself, till it is able to act as a free being, it will be but a sickly child."[18]

And there was still another, more personal challenge that weighed heavily on Newman at this time. Since August of 1851, he faced a criminal charge for libel. Giancinto Achilli, an ex-Dominican priest, had been sentenced to imprisonment by the Roman Inquisition for sexual immorality, including assault. Achilli escaped Italy, converted to Protestantism, and was running around England attacking the Catholic Church. Relying on statements given him by his own bishop Ullathorne, Newman attacked Achilli in print. When charged with libel, Ullathorne couldn't verify his sources. Although found guilty of libel in January of 1853, Newman was fined only a small amount in lieu of some time in prison. Public sympathy sided with Newman, but the personal toll on him was great.[19]

When all this was going on, Newman somehow found the strength and the presence of mind to deliver his lectures on the idea of a university. It should not be surprising, then, to learn that by his own admission, he found the writing of these lectures the most difficult task he had ever undertaken. Even though they seemed to have been well received in Dublin, he complained that writing them had "oppressed me more than anything else of the kind in my life.... I am out on the ocean with them, out of sight of land, with nothing but the stars," and again, that the lectures were "the most painful of all" that he ever wrote.[20] In the 1859 preface to the book version of his lectures, he, in the third person, wrote: "They [the lectures] belong to a time, when he was tried both by sorrow and anxiety, and by indisposition also, and required a greater effort to write, and gave him less satisfaction when written, than any of his Volumes."[21]

In summary, then, while the specific challenges that Newman faced in the 1850s were not exactly the same as those that face presidents today, they were every bit as formidable as, and perhaps even more formidable than, those that today confront most presidents of even small colleges. Newman possessed a lot of grit and demonstrated heroic resilience. It remains, however, to ask whether his *Idea* constitutes a legacy that we should seek to keep alive and hand on today. To proceed with this analysis, a diagnosis of our situation today will make it more possible to answer that question in an informed way.

The Commercialization of Higher Education

Elsewhere in this book, I have written at greater length about the danger of the "commercialization" of Catholic higher education. Here, I would like to explain how commercialization marginalizes liberal education.

The "prestige ratings" published annually in *Newsweek* and other popular media outlets depend primarily on quantitative measurements: acceptance rates, endowments, library holdings, and teacher-student ratios. When I first moved to Los Angeles in 2006, I was struck that every week the *Los Angeles Times* published a list of how much money movies grossed at the box office. People, especially those involved in fundraising, now described as "advancement officers," speak of persons according to their "net worth." College degrees are valued by most consumers according to how much graduates will get paid. In a highly commercialized world, parents are relieved when their sons and daughters choose majors that will secure them viable employment. In the midst of a commercialized culture that quantifies and monetizes everything, how does one go about making a compelling case for the importance of the liberal arts?

By contrast, in Newman's day, commercialization had not yet redefined the purpose of education. As long as a university education was reserved mostly to a few men of elite standing in society—men who did not worry that much about making a living—it could focus, as it did, mainly on the classics. The proper preparation for one of the professions was typically acquired after graduation, on the job, as an apprentice, in the field. At least until the early twentieth century, moral education constituted an integral part of campus life, imparted especially through the small residential colleges typical at Oxford, but also in small colleges in the United States.[22]

Another major force for commercialization in US higher education grew out of World War II when the government directed increasing amounts of federal money to universities willing to undertake research that served the needs of the military and the economy. Many of the country's leading research universities now rely heavily on such funding. The vast majority of Catholic universities today receive only a fraction of the amount of government funding that the nation's major research universities do. Nevertheless, a few Catholic universities do receive enough government funding to require a serious examination of whether they too have become servants of national economic and military priorities.

The disparity in faculty salaries also indicates the commercialization of higher education. If some graduates with degrees that garner higher salaries make more money than graduates in the humanities, so do their major professors. Berkeley historian David Hollinger cites a study that documents the vast differences in the professorial salaries. The difference, according to Hollinger, gives "compelling evidence that the gap is closing between what universities value and what is valued in the commercial marketplace." At its worst, factors outside the academy determine the salaries of professors. One only needs, Hollinger continues, to see the disparity among faculty salaries in the fields of economics, business administration, law, biotechnology, and computer science. At the same time, those faculty whose careers are the most fully centered in the universities, and who have the least opportunity to generate private income through consulting and other outside activities, are the ones to whom universities pay the least.[23]

These economic disparities make it more and more difficult for faculty at a single university to agree on a common mission for their institution, a mission that has already been shaped, fragmented, and even balkanized by market forces. As a consequence, academic disciplines operate apart from, if not in direct competition with, each other. Is it possible, given such powerful economic pressures, for faculty to come together and agree upon a distinctive mission of the university that goes beyond meeting the priorities of the government, private business, and a preoccupation with their graduates getting well-paying jobs? To shape the university's mission from the inside presupposes that the faculty possess at least some autonomy from external forces, not only the government, but also sometimes accrediting agencies that often act like lobbies that enhance their professional units, such as law, business, engineering, and education. The liberal arts, with very little external support, search for a home in fragmented curricula and balkanized universities.

Even liberal arts colleges, as distinct from universities, are increasingly pressured to prepare their graduates for a profession. In a highly commercialized culture, students think of general education programs as courses that they need to "get out of the way" so that they can get on with their "real" education. How many students at Catholic universities would sign up for courses in theology and philosophy if not required to do so?

In Newman's day, the first forces of commercialization were already afoot in England to push higher education into its current instrumental role. London University was founded in 1826 as a secular alternative to the religious universities of Oxford and Cambridge. Newman caricatured the type of education offered there as a bazaar where various products were available to meet all interests, but with little or no connection between them. Their students, Newman lamented, rarely interacted or formed communities. Instead, what Newman wanted was a university that was a home, a "mansion house, of the goodly family of the sciences, sisters all, and sisterly in their mutual dispositions." It is only when education becomes part of a "goodly family"—that is, when a community seeks an education that shapes a student's ability to think critically through regular person-to-person (not virtual) conversations with peers and faculty—that students are truly educated. He spoke with great affection of a college as an *alma mater*. Addressing faculty and administrators in a sermon, he asked: "Is it not one part of our especial office to receive those from the hands of father and mother, whom father and mother can keep no longer? Thus, while professing all sciences, and speaking by the mouths of philosophers and sages, a University delights in the well-known appellation of '*Alma mater.*'"[24]

Newman and Liberal Education

In contrast to a commercialized university, a "mansion house" creates an environment where liberal education can flourish. Newman's *Idea* offers a comprehensive and integrated understanding of the purpose of a university education. To provide a coherent and compelling vision for the academy was no small achievement, even then; the challenge now is even greater. Only a few educational leaders, such as Robert Hutchins and Mortimer Adler, both at the University of Chicago, attempted to implement Newman's vision of a liberal education, mainly through the great books curriculum. Few presidents leading our major universities today actually articulate an integrated vision of what a university education should be—that is, a vision of liberal learning rather than commercialized professional courses, advertised and sold with current buzz words like innovative, entrepreneurial, creative, diverse, inclusive, dynamic, and transformative.

It is not commonly known that although Newman located liberal education at the very heart of a university education, he never excluded professional education as part of the curriculum. In fact, he was proud of the School of Medicine at his newly founded Catholic university. He valued professional education, but not in isolation from the liberal arts:

> If then I am arguing, and shall argue, against Professional or Scientific knowledge as the sufficient end of a University Education, let me not be supposed . . . to be disrespectful towards particular studies, or arts, or vocations, and those who are engaged in them. In saying that Law or Medicine is not the end of a University course, I do not mean to imply that the University does not teach Law or Medicine. What indeed can it teach at all, if it does not teach something particular? It teaches *all* knowledge by teaching all *branches* of knowledge, and in no other way.[25]

If a professor of medicine or geology were to teach outside of a university, he or she would become, according to Newman, nothing more than a professor of medicine or geology. Inside a university, however, such a professor would come to understand where his or her subject stood in relation to all the other subjects, and from that understanding would gain from those other subjects "a special illumination and largeness of mind and freedom and self-possession."[26]

Liberal education was not, according to Newman, a superficial knowledge about a lot of things. Intellectual dilettantes, in his estimation, were capable only of "viewiness," a mental state that enfeebled the mind. He commented that "an intellectual man, as the world now conceives of him, is one who is full of 'views' on all subjects . . . of the day. It is almost thought a disgrace not to have a view at a moment's notice on any question."[27] One thinks of today's pundits commenting on "breaking news," immediately and endlessly. Rather, real knowledge for Newman is a certain formation of the mind, a capacity to "do philosophy," which requires the ability to put things in order and relate them as they should be related. Again, an integrated university education forms habitual ways of thinking:

> The result is a formation of mind, that is, a habit of order and system, a habit of referring every accession of knowledge to what we already know, and of adjusting the one with the other; and, moreover, as such a habit implies, the actual acceptance and use of certain principles as centers of thought, around which our knowledge grows and is located. Where this critical faculty exists, history is no longer a mere story-book, or biography a romance; orators and publications of the day are no longer infallible authorities; eloquent diction is no longer a substitute for matter, nor bold statements, or lively descriptions, substitute for proof.[28]

Newman's liberally educated person habitually thinks carefully and critically. Again, in his own inimitable words:

> It [a university education] gives a man a clear conscious view of his own opinions and judgments, a truth in developing them, an eloquence in expressing them, and a force in urging them. It teaches him to see things as they are, to go right to the point, to disentangle a skein of thought, to detect what is sophistical, and to discard what is irrelevant. It prepares him to fill any post with credit, and to master any subject with facility.[29]

A university that commits itself to a strong liberal arts core, to close curricular connections between colleges of arts and sciences and the professional schools, and to preparing its graduates not only for their professions but also even more for living their lives carefully, faithfully, and thoughtfully—and that has a faculty that embraces these commitments—will offer an education that does much more than prepare students for entry into the marketplace. Agreement about the importance of liberal education will not by itself radically alter salary policies set more by the market than by the intrinsic value of the subjects studied. Such an agreement should, however, help faculty come to a clearer sense of the deeper purpose of education and extend to the professors of the humanities the curricular space, respect, and support they deserve.

Newman and Student Formation

Given the different versions of the moral life, many Western democratic societies have reduced morality to individual consent; there are no longer right and wrong actions, just actions that you give consent to, or that you and someone else mutually agree upon. If sex with someone is consensual, it is morally acceptable, even good. To presume today to offer a moral formation to college students strikes many as quaint or presumptuous: quaint because it is believed to be hardly needed for mature college students, and presumptuous because "everyone knows" that, to begin with, morality is only a matter of personal opinion, purely subjective rather than objective. Therefore, morality is personal and no one should prescribe it for someone else. The university mission, so the argument goes, needs to be about intellectual development and research, not moralizing.

Clark Kerr, an influential voice in the development of the University of California networks, once described Newman's education vision as "bucolic," as representing "the beautiful ivory tower of Oxford as it once was," relevant only for elite undergraduates who live in small colleges.[30] Kerr favored the German model of education, especially on the graduate level, a model he believed was more dynamic and relevant than that offered by the liberal arts college. Kerr's preferred vision of education applied not only to graduate students but also to undergraduates. His university bore no responsibility for the moral education of the students. The university was no longer expected to act *in loco parentis*. Kerr's university would not be called an *alma mater* but rather, in Newman's description, a bazaar.

The argument against teaching morality at a university was put even more bluntly by John Mearsheimer of the University of Chicago, who famously proclaimed that "elite universities," the supposed model for all other universities that crave recognition, are not immoral but amoral. In other words, they have no business giving students any moral guidance: "Universities do not have a moral agenda and do not give students moral guidance, because that would involve preaching about values, and that is an enterprise that holds hardly any attraction for modern universities."[31] Instead, Mearsheimer asserts, universities should be about the business of teaching "critical thinking." I will talk more about the limits of critical thinking later in this book.

Newman would be aghast with Mearsheimer's vision of education. Newman stressed the importance of the moral formation of students, both undergraduate and graduate. His vision of moral education depended in large part on the role of college as distinct from the role of the university. Each college was a small academic society in which students lived, ate, prayed, played, studied, and socialized. Tutors, typically Anglican celibate clergy, lived in the college, where they met regularly with the students. Newman distinguished between the college and university, picturing their relationship as complementary:

> A University embodies the principal [sic] of progress, and a College that of stability; the one is the sail, and the other the ballast; each is insufficient in itself for the pursuit, extension, and inculcation of knowledge; each is useful to the other. . . . The University is for theology, law, and medicine, for natural history, for physical science, and for the sciences generally and their promulgation; the College is for the formation of character, intellectual and moral, for the cultivation of the mind, for the improvement of the individual, for the study of literature, for the classics, and those rudimental sciences which strengthen and sharpen the intellect.[32]

Newman believed that the close personal relationships between students and their mentors who shared life in smaller residential colleges were the incubators of needed moral maturity. Newman considered college-age men no longer boys but not yet men. Mega universities, by their sheer size, militate against moral formation, especially when they leave students to figure out on their own what is moral and immoral. Newman believed that in small residential colleges, friendships with other students and intergenerational conversations with tutors formed students morally. He also believed that "the right relations between the various disciplines [could] be made to fall into place in the minds of undergraduates, by a constant process of discussion and dialogue."[33]

A Catholic philosophy of education does not separate into distinct compartments of learning and moral formation. To educate the "whole person," it is necessary to pay attention to the moral habits that students develop. Catholic philosopher Bernard Prusak, consistent with Newman's vision of moral formation, notes that the work of faculty and the moral formation of students are inextricably linked: "Defining commitments, bonds of affection, moral development and experience, depth of self-understanding, and spiritual maturity all bear on students' capacity to know. They inform the mind, we might say, so that it can receive information."[34]

A similar argument is made persuasively by Lutheran educator Mark Schwehn. In an article exploring the relationship between faith and learning, love and understanding, Schwehn explains how truth is primarily relational, not propositional; it follows, then, that the deepest experiences of truth are encountered in and through love. He calls for the development of a theology of Christian higher education that ponders "the interplay between Christian friendship and

Christian charity on the one hand, and the pursuit of truth and understanding on the other." Developing this distinctive vision of education is, Schwehn continues, "a first step toward a systematic consideration of relationships among Christian spiritual virtues and intellectual virtues."[35]

For Newman, an integral part of moral formation required intellectual formation. He believed that theology and a philosophical sensibility were central to a liberal education. As already mentioned, philosophy, in Newman's view, was not an academic discipline as much as it was a way of thinking while studying all the disciplines. In this sense, philosophy helped students learn how to think, ferret out assumptions, and make an argument; it forged connections with all the other subjects. Philosophy in this sense ends dilettantism.

Theology, however, played an important but different role than philosophy. Theology was not like any other subject. It had a special nature and role. It did not dictate the content of all other subjects, but put them in proper relationship. When theology is absent from the curriculum, Newman writes, some other subject fills that vacuum and assumes its role. If commercialization fills that vacuum, the purpose of education changes dramatically. The study of theology, however, helps students understand what subject should receive the greatest attention, and where that subjects fits in with an overall understanding of the nature and limits of all knowledge. Both theology and developing a philosophical habit through study and personal meetings with mentors and fellow students in residential colleges constitute for Newman how a true liberal education imparts both a moral and intellectual formation.

The commercialized and secular university curriculum banishes theology. Newman warned that "the systematic omission of any one science from the catalogue prejudices the accuracy and completeness of our knowledge altogether, and that in proportion to its importance."[36] Anticipating the specialization and fragmentation of the modern university's curriculum, Newman wrote:

> Divine truth differs in kind from human, but so do human truths differ in kind from one another. If the knowledge of the creator is in a different order from knowledge of the creature, so in like manner metaphysical science is in a different order from physical, physics from history, history from ethics. You will soon break up into fragments the whole circle of secular knowledge, if you begin the mutilation of the divine.[37]

Obviously, universities that enroll thousands of students and arrange lectures for hundreds of students packed into large auditoriums make it nearly impossible to realize, physically and spiritually, Newman's vision of education and the moral formation of students, especially when there are no smaller college communities in which students and mentors live and learn together. Smaller Catholic colleges and universities, however, with largely residential populations have the best chance of bringing Newman's vision to life.

Newman's contributions to a Catholic vision of education are not limited to his commitment to liberal education and student formation. Another of his important contributions is his understanding of the critical role theological work plays within the church and his description of the relationship that ought to exist between theologians and bishops. I treat those contributions in chapter 13 in this volume.

Conclusion

As different as our times are from those of Newman, his vision of a Catholic university remains in many ways compelling, and in some ways, for Catholic colleges and universities, absolutely necessary. It is true that he understood the university as a place for men only, did not give sufficient emphasis to research for undergraduates, and offered little practical guidance to administrators and faculty who are called to lead universities. Nevertheless, Newman understood what should be at the heart of Catholic education—a strong liberal arts education with a special place for theology and for the formation of intellectual habits. His canonization underscores for our own age his importance as a religious writer and thinker. In summary, his vision of a university education places at its center the liberal arts, philosophical habits, theology, and moral formation—a vision especially important in an age of the commercialization of the university.

PART II

THE UNIVERSITY AND THE CHURCH

In 1979, St. John Paul II published *Sapientia Christiana*, an apostolic constitution that described the nature and mission of seminaries and pontifically chartered Catholic universities (like the Catholic University of America), over which bishops have direct authority. It did not apply to the many Catholic universities in the United States that from the late 1960s had established lay boards of trustees that exercise genuine fiduciary responsibilities. In 1990, he published an apostolic constitution, *Ex corde ecclesiae*, the first papal document devoted explicitly and extensively to the nature and mission of nonpontifically chartered Catholic universities. There can be little doubt that given the sweeping changes issued by the Second Vatican Council (1962–1965), along with the increasing secularization of the culture and the professionalization of the academy, the Vatican felt the need to offer some guidance to the leaders of Catholic colleges and universities.

Many academics today sharply distinguish between the church and the university. They like to repeat George Bernard Shaw's quip that a "Catholic university" is an oxymoron. In other words, the intellectual freedom a university requires is made impossible by the authoritarianism of the church. But the title of the pope's 1990 document suggests that the Catholic university grew from the very "heart of the church" and therefore remains intimately linked with the mission of the church. What should be the nature of that "link"? In the following chapters, I argue that the link between the university and the church is not an oxymoron, but rather a redundancy, though not an identity. A Catholic university must be catholic, but it is not a parish.

Three chapters in this section of the book deal directly with the reception, criticism, and expectations of *Ex corde ecclesiae*, including its recommendations that theologians ask for the *mandatum* from the local bishop and that universities should evangelize. I devote a separate chapter to the inevitable tensions that have arisen and continue to arise between bishops and theologians, in particular over academic freedom. I begin this section, however, with an analysis of the cultural context in which the relationship between the church and the university plays out.

4

Secularization and Catholic
Higher Education

Introduction

People concerned about the future of Catholic higher education in the United
States have asked themselves whether Catholic colleges and universities are now
at the same point in history that major mainline Protestant colleges and universities were one hundred years ago. In other words, are the leading Catholic colleges
and universities about to lose their Catholic identity and mission, separate themselves from the church, and become secular universities? This question raises
still other questions: How valid is this parallel between the Protestant universities of the early twentieth century and the Catholic universities of today? How
different now is the culture in the United States from that of the pre–World War
I era? Has the European sociologists' classic thesis elaborated over one hundred
years ago that secularization inevitably follows from modernity, turned out to
be true? Scholars have weighed in on these questions and, not surprisingly, have
not reached a consensus. In this chapter, I wish to review and comment on what
some others have said about these questions and then offer my own response to
the question: are the major Catholic universities, despite John Paul II's 1990 apostolic constitution on Catholic higher education, despite mission effectiveness
officers, and despite required theology courses and campus ministry programs,
nonetheless on the verge of secularizing themselves?

The Classic Secularization Thesis: Revisited

What is the classic secularization thesis? Hugh Heclo, professor of public affairs at George Mason University, described it this way: "A hundred years ago,
advanced thinkers were all but unanimous in dismissing religion as a relic of
mankind's mental furniture."[1] Thinkers like Max Weber, Sigmund Freud, John
Dewey, and others assumed that the consequences of modernity—that is, the
consequences of capitalism, industrialization, the bureaucratizing of businesses,
democracy and pluralism, and the dominance of scientific and technological
ways of understanding all aspects of life—would not only marginalize religion

The Future of Catholic Higher Education. James L. Heft, S.M., Oxford University Press. © Oxford University Press 2021.
DOI: 10.1093/oso/9780197568880.003.0005

but also eventually make it simply disappear as a vestige of the past. Religion, they explained, depended on supernatural revelation, miracles, and religious authority, all of which are based on and generate superstition. Modern science, by contrast, encourages questioning, recognizes no authority without empirical verification, and, unlike dogmatism, is self-correcting. Science equipped scholars, they believed, with a method vastly superior to religion for developing reliable knowledge.

In the spring of 1966, when I was finishing my first year of teaching religion at a Catholic high school in Cincinnati, the cover story of *Time Magazine* asked in bold print, "Is God Dead?"[2] One of my more clever students asked me, "If God is dead, do we still have a subject for this course?" I remember telling him that I thought the so-called "death of God" theologians featured in the cover story were revealing more about American culture, about some Christians, and perhaps even about their own spiritual experience than they were about whether God was alive or dead. Five decades later, I still think that.

But even then, various movements in the culture signaled that religion was anything but dead. In the 1970s and 1980s, evangelical Christians exerted considerable political leverage in the United States, while Catholics in Poland united to topple the communist government. Ayatollah Khomeini's Islamic revolution took the Carter administration by surprise. We continue to face various international conflicts fueled by the potent combination of political and religious objectives. In other words, religion has returned in some parts of the world, if it ever really had left, as a powerful public and political force.

In an important book-length study, sociologist José Casanova presents five case studies spanning three continents that clearly documented the resurgence of religion in the public sphere. He concludes that the expectation of various eighteenth-century Enlightenment thinkers that religion should disappear, and the late nineteenth-century classical secularization theory that accommodated that expectation, was obviously, by the late twentieth century, as yet unfulfilled.[3] Thus, the classic secularization thesis has proven neither inevitable nor accurate.

How, we might ask, could so many sociologists and other intellectual elites have been so mistaken? Perhaps it is because, as Casanova explains, they had indiscriminately lumped together three dimensions of secularization that should have been kept distinct: secularization as differentiation of the secular spheres from religious institutions (which Casanova finds to be unambiguously true), secularization as decline of religion (which he shows is unproven as an overall explanatory theory), and secularization as marginalizing religion to a privatized sphere (which he demonstrates to be false).[4] No doubt, modernity has beaten up on religion. But because of that fight, sometimes brutal, modernity has also purified religion of some of its pretensions.[5] In the West, for example, Catholicism now recognizes the autonomy of science, defends the separation of church and state, and affirms religious freedom. Who would have predicted one hundred years ago that a Polish pope, St. John Paul II, would be one of the world's leading defenders of human rights and a major promoter of dialogue between world religions?

Perhaps the most important contribution to this discussion has been made by another Catholic thinker, philosopher Charles Taylor. In his major study, *A Secular Age*, he has rethought the entire phenomenon.[6] Catholic philosopher Alasdair McIntyre, not noted for giving out many accolades, wrote that Taylor's book is "a highly original contribution," that "there is no book remotely like it," and that "no summary could communicate Taylor's extraordinary skill."

Taylor opens his first chapter with this striking question: "Why was it virtually impossible not to believe in God in, say, 1500 in our Western society, while in 2000 many of us find this not only easy, but even inescapable?" If modernity beat up on religion, religion pushes back to remove modernity's suffocation of the transcendent. Taylor explains it this way. In answering his question, he does not accept the "subtraction stories" that claim that science and modernity have simply rendered religion irrelevant. Nor does he believe that the intense religiosity of the Middle Ages would have continued had it not been for some philosophers who put reason in the place of faith. He believes that although our own age suffers from an "exclusive humanism" that suffocates the transcendent, important initiatives—such as human rights, freedom of conscience, and philanthropy—have nonetheless flourished and can be considered authentic expressions of the gospel. He concentrates less than Casanova on the public force of religion, analyzing instead the impact of our own times on the experiences of individual believers, who in the midst of massive religious pluralism no longer believe or doubt, but doubt while believing. It is much more difficult today to identify with a religion and embrace its communal practices. As a consequence, individuals are now forced to discover the spiritual dimension in personal and authentic ways in their ordinary life. In short, religion has not disappeared but has become a personal spiritual journey for individuals who no longer consider themselves religious.[7] Though a challenging read, studded with neologisms ("social imaginary," "buffered self," and "the nova effect"), Taylor's book makes a major contribution to understanding what it means to believe in a secular age and how secularization might be understood.

Secularization and the Academy: A Review of the Literature

Has the return of religion to the public sphere, or as a form of personal spiritual seeking, affected all segments of modern culture? Assuming that Casanova, Taylor, and others are basically correct in their conclusion that the classic theory of secularization has turned out to be false, what impact has the return of religion, both as a personal spiritual journey and as a public force, had on the American academy? According to a growing number of authors, very little. That is, unlike most Americans who claim that they are religious, or at least in some sense spiritual, most academics, as academics, are by contrast highly secular. Sociologist Peter Berger put it in a rather striking way by suggesting that if India is the most religious country in the world and Sweden the least, then the United States is a nation of Indians ruled by Swedes.[8] In other words, the power elites in the United States, and especially the cultural elites, including most of the faculty in our leading universities, are secular, whereas the majority of ordinary people remain quite religious. Taylor also thinks that most academics are Swedes, to use Berger's typology, who habitually exclude religion as irrelevant in fields such as the natural sciences, social sciences, history, philosophy, and psychology. As a consequence, "unbelieving sociologists of religion often remark how their colleagues in other parts of the discipline express surprise at the attention devoted to such a marginal phenomenon."[9] Several excellent Protestant evangelical colleges, such as Calvin, Wheaton, and Hope, however, are clear exceptions to the pervasive secularization of the academy. That they are colleges and not universities shows, perhaps, how difficult it is to sustain an overall Christian vision when an institution is deeply committed to doctoral education in fields other than theology and theological ethics.

The Declensionist View

Scholars give various explanations for this American anomaly of the "secular academy" in the midst of a religious society. Nevertheless, more scholars than Berger and Taylor have documented the secularism of the academy. I will mention here only three: George Marsden, James Burtchaell, and Philip Gleason.[10]

Marsden, an evangelical Christian and once a history professor at the University of Notre Dame, documented in a widely debated book published in 1994 the transformation of evangelical Protestant colleges first into mainline Protestant universities and then into secular institutions in which any religious influence was confined to chaplaincies or divinity schools, neither of which played a key role in the "real" business of the academy. The combination of the rapid rise of modern science and the accommodations made by inept but well-intentioned presidents—mostly clergymen until about 1900—effectively excised Christian scholarship from the university. Marsden wrote nothing about Catholic colleges and universities because he thought they had little to do with shaping the standards of the major universities of the country.[11]

Burtchaell, a Catholic theologian and one-time provost of Notre Dame, surveyed in his 1988 book, *The Dying of the Light*, seventeen church-related institutions from seven different denominations, three of which were Catholic. He came to the same conclusion as Marsden. He located the driving forces of secularization in the explanatory power of science and well-intentioned presidents who, again unwittingly, facilitated the secularization process of their institutions. He traces successive revisions of university mission statements that ended up uniformly vapid, banal, and clothed in a "stupor-inducing vagueness."[12] It is one thing that these statements did little to inspire; what was worse was that they, along with the presidents who wrote them, lost their capacity to direct the mission of the institution. Burtchaell traces the debilitating consequences of the decision of many Protestant colleges to transcend denominational differences and become "nonsectarian." These institutions shifted their emphasis from doctrine to morality, then from morality to manners, and finally from manners to accepting the academic priorities of the pace-setting secular research universities like Stanford, Johns Hopkins, and Harvard. For most of these once religiously affiliated institutions, a form of nonintellectual pietism rapidly morphed into a rationalism indifferent and even hostile to revealed religion.[13]

Finally, Phillip Gleason, professor emeritus of history at Notre Dame, published in 1995 a magisterial history of Catholic higher education. He is not as committed as Burtchaell to arguing that Catholic colleges and universities are on an inevitable trajectory toward secularization. Nevertheless, he describes how their condition in the turbulent decade of the 1960s severely weakened their sense of Catholic identity. These institutions, he wrote, were crippled by "a lack of consensus as to the substantive content of the ensemble of religious beliefs, moral commitments, and academic assumptions that supposedly constitute Catholic identity, and a consequent inability to specify what that identity entails" for their practical functioning.[14] Built on the foundation of Thomistic philosophy during the first half of the twentieth century, the articulation of their Catholic mission collapsed like a house of cards blown over by the winds of Vatican II. In an unpublished paper read at the 1999 International Federation of Catholic Universities conference held in Ottawa, Gleason found little to cheer about in Catholic colleges and universities since the 1960s due to a "combination of religious, professional and practical factors" that has "produced . . . a hollowing out of the Catholic character of the faculty, in numbers, self-identification, and group morale."[15] Thus, according to Gleason, the old paradigm of Catholic identity largely fell apart in the 1960s and has attenuated ever since. Despite all these signs of declension, he remains hopeful that Catholic colleges and universities will not inevitably be on a path to complete secularization once followed by so many formerly Protestant institutions.

A More Positive Assessment

Historian David O'Brien reads the current state of Catholic higher education more positively. Author of the 1994 book *From the Heart of the American
Church*,[16] O'Brien is aware of the dangers of secularization. Yet, he sees Catholic
higher education at a new point of maturity, possessing a greater capacity for
scholarship, and strengthened by the growing number of dedicated lay academic
leaders and scholars. As O'Brien sees it, all of these developments augur well for
the future of Catholic higher education. Catholic colleges and universities in   ✳
the United States have blended a Vatican II sense of Catholicism with some of
the best achievements of American higher education and culture. Rather than
walking down the same path that the mainline Protestant schools did one hundred years ago. O'Brien applauds Catholic higher education's advocacy of social
justice and lay leadership.

　　Historian and Ursuline Sister Alice Gallin also pointed to a number of positive post–Vatican II achievements. After serving for nearly fifteen years as the
executive director of the Association of Catholic Colleges and Universities,
she published a series of important books on Catholic higher education, all of
which concentrate on developments since Vatican II.[17] In an important 1999
essay, she directly addresses the question of whether Catholic higher education is on the same path of secularization that major Protestant schools were
one hundred years ago.[18] Her analysis offers an insightful comparison between
the history of Protestant and Catholic colleges. Sr. Gallin develops her analysis
by describing five similarities between Protestant and Catholic colleges and
universities, and then five differences. First, both announced their founding
purposes as the moral development of youth, the formation of leaders for their
churches, and the importance of the liberal arts. Second, they both changed
as their churches changed (Catholics need to recall in the 1960s, the dramatic
changes of Vatican II in the understanding of the role of the laity, the importance of ecumenism and interreligious dialogue, the affirmation of religious
freedom, and the return to scripture and history as a key part of its theological
and pastoral agenda). Third, the leaders of both institutions, personally committed members of their churches, made changes in the relationship with their
churches that they hoped would strengthen their institutions academically.
Fourth, both were affected—but in different ways—by the separation of church
and state (major Protestant universities were an integral part of the dominant
culture and enjoyed support in many ways that Catholic schools, founded as an
alternative to that culture, did not). Fifth and finally, both had to struggle with
how to balance their specific religious mission and attachment to a single faith
community with the growing pluralism and secularity of their clientele and
main financial supporters.

✳ must distinguish btw. these & posit that
cath. will look diff. in univ) then
in colleges (see p. 74)

On the other hand, Sr. Gallin explains that there were and are significant differences between the situation of major Protestant universities and Catholic universities. First, the dramatic shift in relationship to the church took place at very different times. For Protestant universities, the move away from their founding churches happened when science was rapidly gaining prominence. By then, at most mainline Protestant schools, faith became a moral attitude severed from doctrine and intellectual development. Science rapidly filled the doctrinal void and became the main producer of reliable knowledge. At that time, American Catholic institutions had largely insulated themselves from the power of the sciences and did not distinguish themselves with research in scientific or, for that matter, most other fields of knowledge. Instead, they taught immigrants their tradition rather than attempt to produce new knowledge. For the most part, Catholic institutions, disrespected by the dominant Protestant culture, maintained a countercultural stance, emphasizing philosophy and religions courses, and preparing immigrants for the professions.

Second, Protestant colleges originally had a direct link to the church, received financial support from it, and prepared ministers to lead the church. Nearly all Catholic colleges, however, were founded by religious orders and received no financial help from bishops, who typically preferred, especially after the Civil War, to educate their future priests in seminaries not connected to Catholic universities. Moreover, the religious orders, whose members lived on campus and provided the leadership of the colleges, constituted the official link, albeit only an indirect one, with the hierarchy. The dramatic growth in student populations during the 1950s and 1960s challenged the religious leaders to think about how their colleges could remain Catholic if they did not remain in full control. By the late 1960s, the number of religious began to decline dramatically, professional standards for faculty increased, institutional complexity intensified, and, as a consequence, both the role of the religious and institutional identity became less clear.

Third, in the late nineteenth century, liberal Protestants readily supported an increased scope for scientific research and its quest for "objective" knowledge. In giving more support to science, they increasingly limited the role of religion as an integral part of the education they offered. When Catholic institutions made their biggest changes in the 1960s, a "takeover" by science was not a major threat. At that point the contested issues were faculty governance, lay leadership, academic freedom, and institutional autonomy. The leaders of Catholic universities, until then almost exclusively members of the religious orders that founded the universities, had some tense conversations with their bishops. On their campuses, they had to deal with an increasingly well-educated and diverse lay faculty whose religious and theological background rarely matched their academic sophistication.

Fourth, by the middle of the twentieth century, very few of the formerly mainline Protestant schools had any relationship with their founding church. Consequently, no church authority prevented them from adopting the patterns and principles of the secular academy. Shortly after Vatican II, bishops continued to make statements, hold discussions, and pose pointed mission and identity questions to the leaders of Catholic colleges and universities. Moreover, in the United States, the Association of Catholic Colleges and Universities provided the opportunity for the presidents of Catholic colleges and universities to come together and, as a group, think through questions of mission and identity. The presidents also debated the scope of the bishop's authority in relationship to the newly appointed lay boards of trustees and to academics, mainly theologians, who were perceived to have departed from proper Catholic teachings. Protestant institutions lacked both church leaders with the authority to press questions and a national organization to help them address their challenges as a body.

Fifth and finally, Catholic institutions retained to the present, though in a less extensive way than before the 1960s, undergraduate requirements for philosophy and theology. Only in the 1950s did Catholic colleges and universities begin to form faculties of theology. Until then, only seminarians studied theology; lay students were taught mainly Thomistic philosophy and some religion courses that stressed apologetics, that is, ways to defend the Catholic faith in an increasingly secular culture. Nearly all formerly Protestant institutions had long since dropped such requirements that, even when they did exist, took the form of courses in moral philosophy and Bible study. Today, it would be fair to say that most theological research and teaching in the Catholic world are no longer done in most seminaries, but in Catholic colleges and universities, where mainly Catholic laity, married and single, explore theological questions using a wide variety of methods.

After making these mainly historical comparisons, Sr. Gallin concludes with a call for more scholarship distinctively rooted in Catholic intellectual traditions. She believes that the late entry of Catholic colleges and universities into the academic mainstream has been in many ways a blessing, for that delay has allowed them to avoid, until recently, the danger of being swept up in various powerful currents of secular culture, especially the dominance of science and graduate education. So, if one posed the question to Sr. Gallin, "are Catholic colleges and universities moving in the same direction as the mainline Protestant schools were a century ago?," her answer would be, I believe, a qualified "no." Is she right?

Is Secularization Likely?

As I begin my own analysis, I think it is important to realize that the factors that need to be weighed are both multiple and complex. For example, it would be wise, especially today, to avoid any overly sharp distinctions between Protestants and Catholics. Sr. Gallin's historical comparison of them focuses on their history and location in the culture. Theologically, today, there are some major and significant differences, but there are also some important shared beliefs and ways of thinking—for example, beliefs in the divinity and humanity of Jesus, in the Trinity, in the doctrine of creation, and, to varying degrees, in the importance of both faith and reason—all of which have consequences for educational institutions, at least for those that take those religious traditions seriously.[19]

In the first part of this chapter, we evaluated the secularization thesis that had to do with an analysis of the evolution of Western culture. It is time now to look a little more closely within the academy and examine how the methodologies embraced by scholars, often seemingly unaware of their epistemological consequences, excluded theology as a legitimate academic discipline. Historians John Roberts and James Turner, in their coauthored book *The Sacred and the Secular University*, concluded that two disciplinary approaches contributed significantly to the exclusion of not just theology but even the study of religion from many secular universities: methodological naturalism in the sciences and historicism in the humanities. While the former "tended only to exclude religious belief from knowledge, historicism actually tended to explain it away."[20] Both scholars regret the exclusion and dissolution of religion, but neither believes the eviction of religion from the academy was simply a conscious plot by nonbelieving academics or by presidents enamored of science.

Of course, science need not be an enemy of theology. To the extent that science tells us true things about physical reality, it is a very good thing, and that in the most deeply theological sense. But as the sole paradigm for all knowledge, it is inadequate. And yet, even within its own sphere, certain understandings of the scientific approach run the risk of constricting our thinking in such a way that we ask only those questions that we believe we can answer, or that we have the means to answer. As British theologian Denys Turner put it, we will ask only "sensible questions whose route to an answer is governed by agreed methodologies." Turner worried, as I also worry, that in our universities there is the danger that "we will reverse the traffic between question and answer so as to permit only such questions to be asked as we already possess predetermined methodologies for answering, cutting the agenda of questions down to the shape and size of our given routines for answering them."[21] Were we to ask only such questions as we can answer, then we would spell the death not only of the humanities but also of all our disciplines, and certainly the death of a Catholic university, where questions even about God should be asked.

If at the turn of the nineteenth century Protestant schools were particularly vulnerable to the presumed power of scientific explanations, Catholics have never had quite the same conflict with science. Whether this is because, as Sr.

Gallin explains, Catholic colleges and universities in 1900 were not involved that extensively in scientific research or because they were less likely to take the Bible literally and more likely to give reason a significant role in extrapolating the meaning of the Christian life, Catholics overall have done a better job in figuring out how the work of scientists and theologians might mutually enrich each other. The biggest challenge for Catholic colleges and universities today comes from a lack of understanding and appreciation of the Catholic intellectual tradition, the commercialization of the academy, and the extensive reach of a local and international market economy.

A third complexity, often overlooked, is the great diversity of institutions in higher education. David Riesman and Christopher Jencks published a very influential book entitled *The Academic Revolution*.[22] Despite its title and date of publication (1968), the book was not about the cultural upheavals of the late 1960s. Instead, it described the significant consequences of the professionalization of the academy: increased faculty authority over hiring and curriculum, a greater emphasis on externally funded research and publication, less attention to undergraduate education, and the decrease in the authority of presidents and boards of trustees. Recent studies, however, have shown that while such a revolution may have taken place in major research universities, the same cannot be said of all smaller private four-year institutions, and certainly not of the fastest-growing sector of American higher education in the last thirty years, namely, community colleges. Professors at research universities publish most of the books and journal articles. When they write about education, they often write about institutions like their own, leaving the impression that all colleges and universities neglect undergraduates, emphasize research more than teaching, and are governed by faculty.[23] The actual state of higher education in the United States is more complex.

Fourth and finally, among the subset of the two hundred or so Catholic colleges and universities in this country, considerable diversity may be found. It is worth noting that American Catholics, who make up only a small percentage of the world's Catholics, have established nearly 20% of the world's Catholic colleges and universities. A few of them have substantial endowments that support strong centers of graduate education and enjoy some of the acceptance and recognition that elite secular universities have. However, the vast majority of Catholic colleges and universities are not in that class, and some of them, perhaps a greater number than most observers realize, face financial crises on a regular basis.

Given all these complexities, is it possible to defend any generalizations about whether major Catholic universities will soon become secular institutions? I believe so. I shall, however, limit my observations to three. Given the great diversity of Catholic universities and colleges in the United States, my observations will apply mainly to well-established, or what I shall call major, Catholic colleges and universities.

First, along with Sr. Gallin, I believe that the most important internal resource for Catholic colleges and universities is their faculty. More specifically, I think it is critical that these institutions hire some faculty who are knowledgeable about Catholic intellectual traditions, along with other faculty who want to explore how their research and the curriculum can be distinctive in ways that give their graduates what might be called in our market economy a "competitive edge." I devote a separate chapter to the hiring and developing of a distinctive faculty and curriculum.

No doubt, certain religious traditions, if strengthened, might not enrich the intellectual life as Catholics would typically understand it. Academic leaders who set out to strengthen Catholic intellectual traditions need not resort to "faith tests" in the hiring process. Nevertheless, they should search for faculty who have an intellectual grasp of Catholicism, as well as welcome persons of different faiths and even no religious faith who can affirm the importance of liberal, scientific, and professional education and who understand the significance of research that examines ethical and religious perspectives. In other words, Catholic universities need faculty who believe that a religious university makes a valuable contribution to the pluralism of American higher education. Therefore, in a Catholic university understood in this way, that is, as an "open circle," people of different religious perspectives can contribute to the mission and identity of a Catholic university. As true as this openness is for the type of faculty Catholic universities should welcome, I believe that if one can't find any Catholic intellectuals at a Catholic university, that university will have a difficult time being Catholic in any meaningful sense. William Portier's description of Catholic intellectuals is helpful:

> Catholic intellectuals, as opposed to intellectuals who happen to be Catholic, might be inclined to think and inquire the way Catholics are accustomed to pray and worship. They would be the bearers of a tradition, a language and a conversation, that was there before they got there and which it is their calling to pass on to the next generation in a way analogous to the way it was passed on to them. Like the rabbis, they would be inclined to think about new things by reading and talking about familiar and proven old texts in different ways. It would be important to them to insist that they were only saying for a new time what those before them had said. They would want to teach the young to think and talk and write this way, in the waters of tradition.[24]

Portier's description of Catholic intellectuals applies especially to faculty in the humanities, and among them, particularly to philosophers and theologians.

what about cath. univs. that have medical schools — are they not being catholic?

Catholic intellectuals in the sciences and social sciences would draw on the religiously grounded doctrines of creation and incarnation, the nature of the human person and community, and ethical and religious dimensions of political power, as I explored the importance of these themes in the first chapter of this book. Besides these academic disciplines, what should be said about the professional schools such as business, engineering, medicine, and law? At their best, they build bridges between the arts and sciences on the one hand and the worlds of commerce and the professions on the other. A great deal of thought should continue to be given to what needs to be done so that Catholic universities are intellectually distinctive.

The Church's Global Perspective

If my first consideration for keeping Catholic universities Catholic—the necessity of Catholic intellectuals—is persuasive, my second consideration will likely be less persuasive, at least for many people in today's academy. I believe the Catholic Church itself must continue to play a key role in helping Catholic colleges and universities remain Catholic. Remember that the Catholic Church is arguably the world's largest international, multicultural, and diverse organization in the world. Only two institutions have survived in the West from the Middle Ages to the present: the papacy since the beginning of Christianity and the university since the twelfth century. Recall that the Catholic Church has been doing philosophy, theology, and moral analysis for two millennia. Given the width of its embrace and the depth of its history, the Catholic Church has the internal intellectual cohesion to be a critic of society—a role academics themselves should play. Over the past one hundred years the Catholic Church has elaborated an extensive body of teachings that address directly issues of international justice, the rights of the poor and the elderly, medical and legal ethics, universal health care, the death penalty, abortion, and the environment. Scholars at Catholic universities may well disagree with some or much of the moral reasoning embodied in these teachings, but if they ignore them, they will be without an essential resource for doing well the work they are called to do as informed critics of society.

This second consideration—the understanding of Catholic tradition, the hierarchy, and its teaching authority—has itself undergone considerable development. Through a long and difficult worldwide conversation, the leaders of Catholic higher education and the bishops worked out, especially during the 1980s, a more careful understanding of the authority of the church in relationship to the mission and identity of Catholic universities. That understanding is officially expressed in John Paul II's 1990 apostolic constitution on Catholic higher education, *Ex corde ecclesiae*.

Catholics acknowledge that the hierarchy of the church as an international authority can determine what is and what is not Catholic. Of course, some of these statements turn out to be inadequate, even wrong, but at best they are arrived at slowly and only after sufficient consultation with the entire church. The international character of the Catholic Church helps Catholic educational institutions in a particular country to be less controlled by local cultures, be they political or academic, or even ecclesiastical, than if there were only national. An expression of that globally distinctive vision for Catholic higher education may be found in *Ex corde ecclesiae*'s affirmation of the importance of the relationship between knowledge and conscience:

> It is essential that we be convinced of the priority of the ethical over the technical, of the primacy of persons over things, of the superiority of the spirit over matter. The cause of the human person will only be served if knowledge is joined to conscience. Men and women of science will truly aid humanity only if they preserve the sense of the transcendence of the human person over the world and of God over the human person.[25]

It may seem ironic, but truly Catholic colleges and universities, committed to such a distinctive vision, may actually be well positioned to help modernity save itself. José Casanova, whose book on the public role of religion I referred to earlier, argues that public religion actually can promote the best of modernity in three ways:

> (1) When religion enters the public sphere to protect not only its own freedoms but all modern freedoms and rights and especially the right of a democratic civil society to exist against an absolutist, authoritarian state; (2) when religion enters the public sphere to question the absolute autonomy of the secular spheres and their claims to be free from extraneous ethical and moral considerations; and (3) when religion enters the public sphere to protect traditional social patterns and loyalties from administrative or juridical state penetration. In doing all three of these things, religion brings the issue of normative values into the public realm for the self-reflection of modern discursive ethics.[26]

One of the privileges a college or university has is bridging the world of reflection and politics. Casanova's positive analysis of the role public religion can play in the social and political orders describes in a compelling way one of the contributions Catholic colleges and universities can make to the countries in which they are located. Charles Taylor's analysis of North American culture is greatly enhanced by his deep familiarity with the social sciences and ethical theories. For a Catholic university to be truly "catholic," it must retain its international relationship to its global character, in the church.

Lay Leadership

Third and finally, there is the transition to lay leadership. A recent widely cited survey, at least in the circles of Catholic higher education, indicates that few lay presidents have much theological background; many have degrees in education. Only 45% have any religious education beyond high school, and of the 25% who underwent any religious "formation," nearly all of them were former priests or religious, who themselves will soon retire from administration. The survey reports widespread agreement that inadequate preparation of lay leadership presents a problem for the future of Catholic higher education.[27] It should be admitted, however, that a number of priests and religious, despite extensive theological and religious formation, were not good presidents. Some theologians have made very incompetent presidents. Yet, if lay presidents who lack theological background learn from others at their institution who have it, their presidencies can strengthen the Catholic mission and identity of their institutions. The best situation, of course, is lay leaders who grasp what a Catholic intellectual life is. One does not have to be personally a Catholic to appreciate and advance Catholic intellectual traditions.

A second problem is preparing for the succession of leadership. Too many religious orders have only recently begun to prepare the way for lay leadership at the institutions they have founded. There seems to be several reasons for this delay. One is the general ambivalence, if not distrust, many academics have toward any faculty member who announces that he or she aspires to be in academic administration. Faculty are suspicious of individuals who appear to be singled out and groomed for leadership. As understandable as this reaction might be, it ignores important lessons from the history of higher education. Great universities have great academic leadership. When such leadership falters, the best of the faculty are able to go elsewhere; the mediocre faculty remain. And their mediocrity gradually envelops the entire institution. To avoid such situations, Catholic colleges and universities should cultivate and prepare scholars for leadership in their institutions.

There is still one more reason some religious communities have taken little initiative to prepare well the next generation of lay leaders. Religious seldom mention it publicly. Many religious are simply grieving, not just because of the departure of many religious classmates in the late 1960s and 1970s, classmates who now could be shouldering with them the responsibilities and challenges of leadership. They are also grieving because young new members are not joining their orders and embracing the way of life that they have lived and loved, and that has over the years benefited so many people. For some religious, to launch a major effort to form lay leadership feels like an admission of defeat, and even the death of their beloved orders. Like some aging childless couples, some religious have difficulty rejoicing in a new generation that is not "their own." Whether we understand fully what the Holy Spirit is doing in the church, and I for one do not, lay leadership needs to be formed and welcomed by everyone, most of all by religious, who have contributed so extensively to the education of so many of the laity in the United States.

For most Catholic families seeking a Catholic college education for their sons and daughters, the presence of religious and priests was a visible sign that the institution was Catholic. While every religious and priest on the faculty and staff did not foster a vital intellectual life, their presence did ensure parents that their children would interact with people who had dedicated their lives to Christ, the church, and the gospel. Given the decreasing number of priests and religious in higher education, we need to ask what the visible signs and practices should now be to make clear that the college and university is Catholic. How will the research agendas, the curricula, the campus and liturgical life, art, and music make Catholicism evident in the new era that we are entering?

Conclusion

Let us return now to the question we posed at the beginning of this chapter: will the major Catholic colleges and universities remain Catholic? I answer yes, but very much on the condition that faculty develop vibrant forms of Catholic intellectual life; that the institutions maintain a real but appropriately autonomous relationship with the Catholic Church as a whole; and that the current leaders within these institutions, lay or religious, prepare well future leadership—scholars and not just administrators—to guide them into the future. I do not say that these three are the only conditions; I do say, however, that they are among the most crucial conditions for sustaining and strengthening Catholic colleges and universities now and in the future. Who knows, such vibrant Catholic colleges and universities may well help to add to the rebirth, already being experienced in recent years, for the very religious orders that founded them.

5

A University That Evangelizes?

The Vision of *Ex corde ecclesiae*

After years of consultation with leaders of Catholic higher education and bishops, St. Pope John Paul II published in 1990 an apostolic constitution on Catholic higher education, *Ex corde ecclesiae*.[1] Familiar as the document has become to many leaders in Catholic higher education, its robust vision deserves a closer examination. So do the challenges it presents, one of which I wish to focus on in this chapter: the expectation that Catholic universities should evangelize. Should a Catholic university in the United States evangelize? And if so, how should evangelization itself be understood?

Before trying to answer these questions, a short introduction to the apostolic constitution and the efforts of the US bishops to implement it would be helpful. The constitution is divided into two parts, with the first section describing the identity and mission of a Catholic university, including its mission of service, while the second proposes several general norms for implementation. In early 1991, the National Conference of U.S. bishops established a committee of several bishops and eleven consultants, eight of whom were Catholic college or university presidents, to determine how to implement the document.

During the fall of 1994, the implementation committee asked the consultants and the bishops to discuss several themes featured prominently in the constitution: Catholic identity, *Communio*, the relationship of faith and culture, pastoral ministry on campus, the relationship between the diocesan bishop and the Catholic college or university in his diocese, and the legal issues involved in the implementation of *Ex corde ecclesiae*. Five additional issues were proposed for local dialogues during the spring of 1995, one of which concerned evangelization as it is presented in paragraphs 48–49 of the constitution.

As part of the dialogue, the Board of the Association of Catholic Colleges and Universities (ACCU) asked Fr. Leo O'Donovan, SJ, then president of Georgetown University, and me, then provost of the University of Dayton, to explore this topic and how it should be understood at a Catholic university. We divided our reflections into four parts: first, a clarification of the meaning of the word "evangelization" for Catholics in the United States; second, a brief description of the various meanings of the word "evangelization" as it is used by *Ex corde*; third, *Ex corde*'s description of the unique contribution a Catholic university makes to the

The Future of Catholic Higher Education. James L. Heft, S.M., Oxford University Press. © Oxford University Press 2021.
DOI: 10.1093/oso/9780197568880.003.0006

church's mission of evangelization; and fourth, in light of the aforementioned parts, a brief response to the discussion questions provided by the *Ex corde* implementation committee. What follows is a summary of what Fr. O'Donovan and I presented to the ACCU board. I have since included references to some more recent developments that pertain to this topic.

Evangelization and North American Culture

The church has committed itself to evangelize ever since Jesus commanded his disciples (e.g., Matt. 28:18–20) to go forth to all lands preaching the Good News. Different periods of history—the preaching of St. Paul; the sixth-century mission of monks that converted, among other peoples, the English and the Irish; the evangelization of the New World in the sixteenth century; and the call to send missionaries throughout the world during the twentieth century—all these successive waves of apostolic activity have spread the gospel, despite the ill treatment of nonbelievers and especially Jews, throughout the Western world. In 1976, in his letter *Evangelii nuntiandi*, Pope Paul VI offered the church a masterful presentation on how the church's mission of evangelization should be understood in the last phase of the twentieth century.

Though the work of evangelization is thus integral to the mission of the church, the word "evangelization" is not. It is in certain respects foreign to American Catholics. Until the early seventies, the word was used mainly by Protestant evangelicals and fundamentalists who typically understood it as an aggressive style of presenting the gospel to all who had not yet accepted Jesus as their "personal Lord and Savior." From the early eighties to the present, Protestant evangelists have made extensive use of radio and television and called everyone to accept Jesus. Today, North American Catholics, in general, do not think of themselves or their priests as evangelizers. Catholics seem more at home with priests who "give sermons," give "witness" to their faith, and provide a good example by the way they live their lives. Catholics are more comfortable with a laid-back approach captured in the saying "Preach the Gospel at all times, and if necessary, use words." If you ask most Catholics about their faith, they will try to explain it. However, they will not begin conversations, especially with strangers, asking them if they have accepted Jesus.

The Catholic view of evangelization involves not only good example and preaching but also, more importantly, liturgical rituals and the sacramental life. Moreover, for Catholics, the life of faith involves more than a personal conversion; for many, it involves the transformation of communities and the critique of culture, or, to be more precise about the United States, the critique of many diverse cultures—a clarification that should be kept in mind throughout these reflections. For example, drawing on both papal and Episcopal teachings, Catholics in the United States have been called to oppose the death penalty, to recognize the sanctity of human life from conception to natural death, to criticize economic policies that oppress the poor, to protect the environment, to welcome immigrants, and to reject every form of racism, sexism, and anti-Semitism. For Catholics, then, evangelization, despite the foreign ring that the word itself has, is a rich and multifaceted reality and embraces a wide range of social initiatives.

Ex corde ecclesiae and Evangelization

At the very end of the apostolic constitution, Pope John Paul outlines in two paragraphs a notion of evangelization as it should be understood and practiced by Catholic universities. He speaks of the Catholic university's contribution to the church's primary mission: "to preach the Gospel in such a way that a relationship between faith and life is established in each individual and in the sociocultural context in which individuals live and act and communicate with one another" (par. 48). Evangelization affects, therefore, not only individuals but also the communities in which they live. In fact, the radical nature of the gospel may be expected to lead to a confrontation with those aspects of people's lives and culture, "upsetting . . . humanity's criteria of judgment, determining values, points of interest, lines of thought, sources of inspiration and models of life, which are in contrast with the Word of God and the plan of salvation" (par. 48). John Paul II is actually quoting Pope Paul VI's 1976 encyclical *Evangelii nuntiandi*.

But the process of evangelizing people and cultures is not merely a matter of confronting the sinful practices of a culture; it is also a matter of benefiting from the good elements that all cultures possess. In particular, paragraph 44 of *Ex corde* explains that the Catholic university assists the church by enabling it to come to a better knowledge of diverse cultures, to "discern their positive and negative aspects, and to develop means by which it can make the faith better understood." Moreover, it adds that the gospel is lived by people "who are profoundly linked to a culture, and the building up of the kingdom cannot avoid borrowing the elements of human culture or cultures" (again, citing Pope Paul's *Evangelii nuntiandi*).

Over the last several decades, the bishops of Latin America have led an important, if at times controversial, discussion on the relationship between evangelization and culture, first at Medellin (1968), then at Puebla (1979), then at Santo Domingo (1992), then at Aparecida (2007), at which the then archbishop Bergoglio and later Pope Francis played a key role. Pope Francis's encyclical *Evangelii gaudium* laid out his vision of the church's mission, drawing heavily from both Pope Paul VI and St. John Paul II. These statements offer striking insights into some of the best ways to express the complex relationship between a vital gospel faith and human culture. St. John Paul II frequently emphasized that any time a religious tradition sets itself apart from what is human and from the culture of human beings, it robs faith of its appropriate clothing and context. When speaking to the intellectuals, students, and university personnel in Medellin in 1986, he described faith without culture as "a decapitated faith," a faith in the "process of self-annihilation."

In summary, then, a full Catholic understanding of evangelization includes multiple dimensions, both personal and communal, both critical and appreciative of the cultures in which it takes place. The process of sharing the faith is complex, requires patient discernment, and calls for neither the complete denunciation nor the full approval of any culture.

The Unique Role of the Catholic University

Ex corde ecclesiae develops a rich appreciation of the nature of a university. As the very first paragraph put it, the university "has always been recognized as an incomparable center of creativity and dissemination of knowledge for the good of humanity" (par. 1). Its fourth paragraph speaks of "a kind of universal humanism" by which "a Catholic university is completely dedicated to the research of all aspects of truth in their essential connection with the supreme Truth, who is God." As a consequence, a university must pursue "every path of knowledge." Especially important is the assistance the university can offer the church in understanding and influencing the nature and direction of modern science (see pars. 7, 45, and 46).

Finally, *Ex corde ecclesiae* stresses that the church believes in "the intrinsic value of knowledge and research" (par. 15). Affirming that all truth is ultimately one, that the truth is the only sure road to freedom, and that Jesus is the Truth, John Paul II related intimately the search for understanding and discovering God. A Catholic university, then, is well positioned to emphasize neglected aspects of evangelization, especially the necessary relationship between a serious intellectual life and a mature Christian faith, as well as the relationship between the communities of inquiry and of belief.

After an introduction to the constitution from the pope himself, the document itself is divided into two parts. The first part treats the identity of a Catholic university, stressing not only its nature and objectives but also its reality as a scholarly community in which faculty, students, and administrators participate in an important mission related in an integral way to the mission of the church. Two of the articles in this first part of the constitution (which runs from paragraphs 12 to 29) are particularly important. Paragraph 13 is taken directly from the 1972 statement of the Second International Congress of Delegates of Catholic

Universities held in Rome, "The Catholic University in the Modern World." It stipulates that every university, if it is to be Catholic, must have the following essential characteristics:

1. A Christian inspiration not only of individuals but also of the university community as such.
2. A continuing reflection in the light of the Catholic faith upon the growing treasury of human knowledge, to which it seeks to contribute by its own research.
3. Fidelity to the Christian message as it comes to us through the church.
4. An institutional commitment to the service of the people of God and of the human family in their pilgrimage to the transcendent goal that gives meaning to life.

Given these four essential characteristics of a Catholic University, *Ex corde* describes in paragraph 15 the types of research that a university with such characteristics carries out:

1. The search for an integration of knowledge.
2. A dialogue between faith and reason.
3. An ethical concern.
4. A theological perspective.

Thus, paragraph 13 seems to identify major defining characteristics of a Catholic university, while paragraph 15 offers a list of assumptions and practices that should be embraced in research undertaken at such a university. Obviously not all departments of a university, nor all faculty members, will embody all the practices outlined. But it would be reasonable to expect that they will be recognizable generally in the work of the faculty.

At the beginning of the second main part (pars. 30–49) of the constitution, which treats the Catholic university's mission of service, the constitution describes in paragraph 30 the purpose of any university as the "continuous quest for truth" and its dissemination, but adds that a Catholic university fulfills this purpose with its own specific characteristics: (1) service to church and society, (2) pastoral ministry, (3) cultural dialogue, and (4) evangelization. This list of essential characteristics is hardly exhaustive, especially given the great diversity of Catholic colleges and universities worldwide.

In any event, at the heart of each of the four special purposes of the Catholic university is the existential uniting of two orders of reality: "the search for truth and the certainty of already knowing the fount of truth" (par. 1). Christians may well *believe* that all truth is ultimately one in God and that through *faith* they truly know the "fount of truth." But Christians must likewise acknowledge their necessarily limited grasp of that truth and continue their effort to integrate their diverse perceptions of it. Furthermore, as classic Thomistic studies have proven, belief in God is not entirely, or even primarily, an intellectual matter. Still less does it bestow upon believers the ability to articulate fully what they affirm through faith. In recent years, members of the scientific community have become increasingly aware of how their measurements are often only approximations of the realities they study. Likewise, Christians through the centuries have learned in many painful ways that the eyes of faith, as St. Paul so clearly and strikingly stated, see only "through a glass darkly."[2]

In addition to pastoral ministry and evangelization, "service" and cultural dialogue are considered special responsibilities for a Catholic university. How can service and cultural dialogue be essential parts of the way a Catholic university enters into the process of evangelization? It may be helpful here to recall the famous statement in a document entitled "Justice in the World," issued by the 1971 World Synod of Bishops:

> Action on behalf of justice and participation in the transformation of the world fully appear to us as a constitutive dimension of the preaching of the Gospel, or, in other words, of the Church's mission for the redemption of the human race and its liberation from every oppressive situation. (par. 6)

Since 1971, serious theological analyses and criticism of this Synodal statement have helped us avoid limiting the mission of the Catholic Church to the promotion of a social gospel focused on resolving political and social problems. Nevertheless, keeping in mind such criticism, the 1971 Synod's more inclusive understanding of evangelization clarifies how the following research themes, mentioned in *Ex corde* and integral to so many research programs at Catholic universities, can be understood as part of the university's efforts at evangelization:

> The dignity of human life, the promotion of justice for all, the quality of personal and family life, the protection of nature, the search for peace and political stability, a more just sharing in the world's resources, and a new economic and political order that will better serve the human community at a national and international level. (par. 32)

All professors, including those who are not Catholic but understand and respect the Catholic mission of the university (par. 27), can commit themselves to such research. For the Christian believer, such research affirms the dignity of the human person and is able to develop "a true Christian anthropology, founded on the person of Christ" (par. 33), an anthropology that by the time of the New

Testament already included several different but complementary ways of understanding both Jesus and the human person. At the same time, Christian anthropology, grounded on the mystery of the incarnation, is important to more than believers, since the full sense of Christ, who is the head of a community, embraces the whole human family. Such efforts constitute part of the unique contribution of the Catholic university to the mission of the global church.

The cultural dialogue that is open to all human experience includes, according to *Ex corde*, matters such as "the meaning of the human person, his or her liberty, dignity, sense of responsibility, and openness to the transcendent. To a respect for persons is joined the pre-eminent value of the family, the primary unit of every human culture" (par. 45).

There will be, of course, still other important issues that must be addressed, such as the environment; the rapid developments in genetics, neuroscience, and technology; and the difficult questions surrounding global economics, poverty, immigration, the environment, and population, just to mention several pressing issues. In fact, paragraph 45 singles out as an area of particular interest modern science. All of these issues raise complex questions about the relationship between faith and reason and require not only knowledge of theology but also an understanding of modern science, along with various epistemological questions raised by different approaches to understanding reality.

Ex corde describes pastoral ministry as the integration of religious and moral principles *with* academic study and nonacademic activities through prayer, sacraments, and various forms of religious outreach. In its treatment of pastoral ministry, it recognizes that some members of our university communities may not share the Catholic faith and that pastoral ministry must be provided in a way that respects their beliefs. Indeed, the extensive development of campus ministry programs on American campuses with many significant outreach movements and, on a growing number of our campuses, staff from other Christian denominations and even other religions may constitute a special contribution of the church in America to the implementation of *Ex corde ecclesiae*. This unique contribution, however, requires a more serious examination of the relationship between campus ministry and the role of the faculty, to which I devote a separate chapter in this book.

It may also help to contrast the life of Catholic parishes and Catholic universities. Catholic parishes devote most of their time to the direct evangelization of their members, who in turn reach out to meet the spiritual and material needs of people beyond the parish. Surely, reflection on living the faith in today's culture goes on continuously in the life of parishioners, particularly as they seek to understand how best to live the gospel faithfully in their families, communities, and professions.

Catholic universities, on the other hand, focus directly on understanding, developing, contributing to, and critiquing many fields of knowledge, which, taken together, not only constitute our modern culture but also include cultures of people from other parts of the world, both now and in the past. The life of an academic community draws nourishment by setting aside time to learn what it does not know and to discover what has never been known. The mission of a Catholic university, then, requires discovering and sharing that knowledge. In the heart of a Catholic university, as *Ex corde* states, there will be a desire to integrate all such knowledge, exploring its ethical consequences from various theological and philosophical perspectives that respect the power of both reason and faith so as to enter into the deepest dimensions of every academic discipline. Indeed, the Catholic Church does its thinking wherever thoughtful Christians live out the gospel: in workplaces, homes, chanceries, soup kitchens, and rectories. But in the Catholic university, faculty and students devote the major portion of their days to research and learning all that is worth knowing so that such learning, appropriated in the light of the gospel, might benefit everyone, especially the poor and the needy.

In summary, then, when *Ex corde* develops the unique role of the Catholic university, it includes a wide range of intellectual and religious initiatives and responsibilities that require a broad understanding of "evangelization." While the Catholic university, especially through campus ministry programs, undertakes the direct pastoral ministry of preaching and celebrating the sacraments in much the same way as the parish does, it also makes, as a university, a unique contribution to the process of evangelization by its work of research, teaching, and dialogue with all facets of modern culture.

However, obstacles to evangelization remain. Paragraph 18 of *Ex corde* describes effectively the vision needed to overcome the resistance to evangelization typical in our culture: its technocratic paradigm (to quote Pope Francis), its preoccupation with commercial gain, and its marginalization of the poor and immigrants. The document boldly proclaims that if the pursuit of knowledge is not rooted in the formation of conscience and exercised with practical wisdom, the common good will not be served.

None of us lives apart from or above our culture. Therefore, each of us has to deal with the challenge of making sure that what is most important actually guides us in our research and teaching. To the extent that our colleges and universities are able to articulate this vision, and then win the support of the university community in the effort to realize the vision more fully, that community will make sure that supportive structures are in place and sustained. Such structures make it more likely that the university will hire individuals who support the mission and appropriately draft guidelines for promotion and tenure activities, as

well as budget decisions that reflect the centrality of the dialogue between faith
and cultures.

Conclusion

In view of an understanding of evangelization drawn from *Ex corde* and
presented in this chapter, is it possible for us to imagine that a Catholic university
could be expected to be a part of the church's mission to evangelize? The answer
is definitely yes, as long as we understand that evangelization in the university
context is not proselytization, that it respects the integrity of the academic disciplines, focuses on the search for truth in its research and teaching, gives special
attention in its research and teaching to expanding knowledge that serves the
common good, and keeps moral and religious questions in the awareness of the
faculty. If it does these things, I see no reason that a Catholic university should
not be an agent of evangelization. At a Catholic university, even the campus ministry programs, which evangelize in a more direct fashion, should nonetheless
take advantage of their location in a university context where, more than in a
parish, their programs explore in a more explicit way the relationship between
faith and reason.

6

Ex corde ecclesiae and the *Mandatum*

Introduction

For almost a full decade, the American bishops and leaders of Catholic universities wrestled with how best to implement the 1990 document, *Ex corde*. In 1999, after the Vatican rejected their first proposal, which was written with a pastoral emphasis and stressed the importance of dialogue, the bishops were directed by the Vatican to draft a second proposal with more explicit requirements, some of which had been included in the revised code of church (canon) law published in 1983. The Vatican approved their second proposal but unilaterally added three expectations: (1) that half the faculty as well as the board of trustees should be Catholics, (2) that the president should make explicit his or her commitment to Catholicism, and (3) that Catholic theologians teaching courses in Catholic theology should request a *mandatum* from their local bishop. This last expectation caused some of the greatest concern, even though in subsequent years it has turned out not to be a major problem. Nonetheless, the matter of the *mandatum* deserves careful reflection, not least because it affects how theologians are expected to understand their work in the university and the church.

First, some background is in order. There are more than 180 dioceses in the United States, and of those, 101 have at least one Catholic college or university, and one has eleven! Roughly 85% of all Catholic colleges and universities are east of the Mississippi, and most of these are in the Northeast, where typically Catholicism has taken on a more conservative character than in the upper midwestern and southwestern parts of the United States. Only a few universities are well endowed; most are not. About half of these colleges were founded by women's religious congregations, most of which no longer exist or, beginning in the 1950s, have merged with men's universities. If you added together all of the endowments of all the women's colleges, they would not equal a fraction of Notre Dame's endowment.

Archbishop Pilarczyk and Theologians at Dayton

After the 1999 Vatican approval for implementation, the US bishops were asked to hold discussions with theologians about the *mandatum* at all these

The Future of Catholic Higher Education. James L. Heft, S.M., Oxford University Press. © Oxford University Press 2021. DOI: 10.1093/oso/9780197568880.003.0007

very diverse colleges and universities. At the time, I served as the provost of the University of Dayton, one of the ten largest Catholic universities in the United States, located in the Archdiocese of Cincinnati. I still taught one course each semester. The archbishop then was Daniel Pilarczyk, who had also served as the chair of the Episcopal committee charged with working out how to implement the *mandatum*. We invited him to meet with us. At the beginning of the meeting he said, "There is no debate as to whether or not we will have the *mandatum*. The question we are now facing is 'how best we can make it work.'" By nearly everyone's admission, the *mandatum* created an awkward arrangement in the American system of higher education. So the approach we adopted at the university (though some members of the Department of Religious Studies were skeptical) was to find some thoughtful and productive ways to work with this expectation of the Vatican.

Attended by nearly forty theologians, both full time and part time, the meeting with Archbishop Pilarczyk was both lively and respectful. The attendees were of different minds about the *mandatum*. A number supported it in principle but recognized that many practical difficulties remained. Some were undecided as to whether they would ask for it. Some thought it meant unacceptable control of theologians. Others, confident that they taught in communion with the church, nevertheless said they would not ask for one "on principle"; they thought the bishops should trust them to do what any thoughtful Catholic theologian should do.

At the beginning of the meeting, the archbishop briefly reviewed the proposed guidelines and opened the floor for discussion. An open, candid, and at times pointed give and take followed. Questions were posed, clarifications were made, and some important common understandings were reached. I took careful notes. What follows is a list of the questions that we raised and the answers given by Archbishop Pilarczyk.

1. What is the meaning of "full communion with the Church"? Answer: Theologians cease to be in full communion only when they deny obstinately a teaching that the church presents as infallible. For example, it is unlikely that a theologian would lose his or her mandate by questioning whether defining a dogma was timely, as Blessed John Henry Newman did on the matter of papal infallibility.

2. What about wealthy right-wing groups that use the media to attack theologians they believe have strayed from the true faith? Answer: Tenured professors, convinced of the scholarly validity of their work, should be able to stand up to the objections of right-wing vigilante groups (however, non-tenured faculty are more vulnerable and need protection).

3. What is the meaning of the new category of official teaching called "defin-itive" (created by the Vatican to describe its statement on the ordination of women), and must one accept all such teachings to be in "full communion with the church"? Answer: This is a complex matter and needs further study by theologians. Most of the theologians at the meeting, however, did not think that "definitive" teachings were infallible.

4. Should a university state in its statutes that a Catholic theologian should have a *mandatum*? Answer: Since the *mandatum* is a statement of a per-sonal relationship between the bishop and the individual theologian, the university is not required to put in its by-laws that all their theologians must request it.

5. If a theologian with a *mandatum* from one bishop moves to a university in another diocese, can the bishop in the new diocese revoke the *mandatum*? Answer: If a bishop in a different diocese or a new bishop comes to a dio-cese and decides to revoke a *mandatum* granted by his predecessor, that bishop must first enter into a canonical process and provide in writing reasons to support his action. In other words, the granting of a *mandatum* is a juridical act and can't be revoked without evidence of a canonical pro-cess. And of course, the theologian may appeal. Rogue bishops, smiled the archbishop, can be as much a problem as dissenting theologians.

6. Two final questions were raised. First, what constitutes a theological dis-cipline? Second, what about a theologian's personal life? Answer: If a pro-fessor does not teach Catholic theology (but instead teaches, for example, church history or world religions), a *mandatum* is not expected. Second, the *mandatum* refers to a theologian's teaching, not to his or her personal life, unless one's personal life can be interpreted as teaching—a distinction not always easily made. Ordinarily, a professor's behavior is to be governed by the university's own statutes; the *mandatum* has to do with teaching.

Following this discussion, problems remained in understanding how the *mandatum* should be applied. It was still not clear how church law, when it refers to certain subjects (e.g., dogmatic theology, moral theology), actually compares to the way in which some courses are typically designed in our universities. For example, is a course in the history of Christianity the same as a course in church history? Is Christian ethics the same as Catholic moral theology?

Nevertheless, the conclusions reached at that Dayton meeting encouraged most members of the Department of Religious Studies. Meetings held in other dioceses may or may not have gone as well. The possible lack of a consensus among bishops nationally remained a matter of genuine concern. Theologians at the meeting agreed that it was important for the bishops to work together to come to a common understanding of the conditions for granting and revoking the *mandatum*. But even if they succeeded in agreeing upon a common approach, practical difficulties continued to arise. The bishops agreed to review the entire situation in five years. Many bishops led these reviews, but only a few made them public; in general, things seem to have gone well, with an occasional dispute. There have been no public reviews since 2006, and if there have been any private ones since then, we simply don't know.

Possible Benefits of the *Mandatum*

The archbishop asked us to make the best out of a situation that the American bishops had tried to avoid by the way they had drafted their first implementation plan. One theologian, after our meeting with the archbishop, suggested that our task was to make lemonade out of lemons. Some of the theologians worried about a loss in their academic credibility if their academic work had to be approved by the local bishop. Some others felt that an appropriate academic freedom would be lost. Still others worried about the lack of sufficient protection for individual theologians. In subsequent conversations with some of my colleagues, I came to the conclusion that there actually were ways we could think about the *mandatum* that would make it a potentially positive arrangement, not only for the church, but also for theologians and Catholic universities. Let me suggest four possible positive developments.

First, a *mandatum* may make it possible to see that a certain form of "advocacy" may have a place in the classroom. Academics who oppose indoctrination and advocacy in the classroom have a point. When theologians, or any professor for that matter, restrict the subject matter to their own idiosyncratic interpretations, suppress legitimate criticism, make the course all about themselves, or introduce favorite topics irrelevant to the actual subject matter, we have an abuse of the trust placed in a professor. On the other hand, fear about theologians indoctrinating students rests on a double standard of evaluation. For example, committed and enthusiastic teachers of political science, biology, or English are delighted when students fall in love with the subjects they teach. They are thrilled when students decide to change their major because of a course they have taught—that is, change their major to the one that professor teaches. Dedicated academics take pride in teaching their disciplines. Why, then, should these academics object to theologians who also want their students to love theology and, even more radically, fall in love with God? Do they mistakenly assume that theologians who want to "astonish" their students will no longer foster an objective and critical understanding of religion? Love and critical judgment are not mutually exclusive. True love is bound not blind, as G. K. Chesterton once quipped. Love and enthusiasm for one's discipline is a legitimate form of advocacy. One possible positive outcome of the *mandatum* is that it might make clearer that all professors should be enthused about teaching and not confuse it with advocacy or, worse, brainwashing.

Second, instead of taking away from the "credibility" of theologians, the *mandatum* might well lead theologians to become advocates for more capacious methodologies that the humanities require, something I spell out in greater detail in chapter 8 on academic freedom. A more liberal and capacious understanding of academic epistemologies will benefit theologians, the rest of the faculty, and the academy in general.

Third, all faculty face the issue of their need for independence from forces outside the university, such as the power of major donors, accrediting agencies, and federal funding. Should the *mandatum* be seen as anything other than an additional inappropriate effort on the part of nonacademic bishops, individuals external to the university, to control theologians? Yes, this perception is quite plausible. However, I think that it is possible that the *mandatum* will contribute to greater due process in the relationship between theologians and bishops. It is to be expected that a genuine, if occasionally rocky, relationship with bishops is an integral part of a correct understanding of the nature of Catholic theology. Archbishop Pilarczyk explained that a bishop who revokes a theologian's *mandatum* is required to make a case in writing for his action. When the US bishops finally implemented *Ex corde* in 1999, they recommended the use of the 1989 US bishops' document for resolving disputes between theologians and bishops. That recommendation, like all recommendations, can be ignored, as bishops did twenty years later in the case of theologian Elizabeth Johnson, which I discuss in chapter 7. But many in the theological community supported Johnson and used the 1989 document to remind the bishops of the due process they had once agreed on. Progress over the past decade has been made. I point out several positive recent developments in chapter 7.

To the extent that theologians are in regular and fruitful dialogue with their bishops and bishops seek the counsel and guidance of theologians, an arbitrary revocation of a theologian's *mandatum* is unlikely. With more regular conversations with theologians, bishops will also not appear to be "external nonacademic agents" or, as historian David O'Brien once wrote, potted plants that appear on stage at graduate ceremonies. Instead, they will be pastors who remind theologians that theology needs to be attentive to the "joys and the hopes, the grief and the anxieties of the people of this age, especially those who are poor or in any way afflicted," and theologians will be scholars who will remind bishops of the breadth and depth and multiple legitimate interpretations of the faith.[1]

Fourth and finally, a theologian's request for a *mandatum* could make clearer than is presently the case the unique character of the Catholic theology as an academic discipline and the unusual scope that theologians must keep in mind as they go about their work. The great Protestant theologian Karl Barth once remarked that a theologian must have the Bible in one hand and the newspaper in the other. Barth is right, but the newspaper that Catholic theologians must read reports more than the local or even national news; it reports global news. The baseline, if you will, of Catholic thinking is global, articulated officially by church councils, and more recently by the Synods of Bishops. Part of a theologian's work is to apply those teachings to the local culture. To do that intelligently, the theologian must read the "signs of the times" in the light of the Bible or, more specifically, the Gospel. Not only theologians but also bishops should have the Bible in one hand and global Catholic thinking in the other. At the same time, theologians need to understand culture, discern what is good in it, and not hesitate to argue for the incorporation of the positive dimensions of culture, even if they call into question some of the current official teachings of the church.

Catholic theologians also need to pay attention to more than their local bishop. Just as professors of constitutional law keep an eye on Supreme Court decisions and political scientists and sociologists do their best to understand what is going on in society, so too must theologians try to understand how God is working within the global church. Ninety-nine percent of that global church is not ordained; their lived experience of the faith constitutes the indispensable basis for theological reflection. It is the global reality of the Church that in the long run, interpreted officially and authoritatively at an international church council, which offers a transnational and reliable interpretation of the faith as it evolves over time. Theologians pay attention to bishops, of course, but both bishops and theologians must pay attention to the *sensus fidelium*, the sense of the faith of believers throughout the world. Therefore, bishops, theologians, and the entire people of God contribute in different ways to understanding the faith, with bishops having the responsibility for its official expression, which even on the dogmatic level is open to revision but not reversal.

Who Should Know?

How should the president of a university answer prospective students and their parents if they ask, as some have, "How many of your theologians have a *mandatum*?" At the Dayton meeting, following the suggestion of the archbishop, the consensus about who should answer the question of whether a particular theologian has a *mandatum* is best left to the individual theologian. It also follows that if the *mandatum* is a statement of a personal relationship between the bishop and the theologians, bishops should not publish lists of theologians who have accepted the *mandatum*. Unfortunately, as noted earlier, if some theologians fear a loss of credibility if they acknowledge that they have requested and received a *mandatum*, others who refuse to say anything will be suspect for not requesting one. The decision to make public whether a theologian has a *mandatum* did not last very long. No bishop published a list. On the local level, some smaller and more recently founded Catholic colleges took pride in announcing to parents that all their theologians have *mandata* and assure parents that at their university theologians are happy to state publicly that they are obedient to the magisterium of the church.

On the other hand, there may be good reasons for a particular theologian not to ask for a *mandatum*, such as not being a Catholic or not teaching Catholic theology. And just because theologians do not have a *mandatum* does not mean that what they teach is not in full communion with the church. Teaching in full communion with the church is one thing; being recognized officially as doing so by the local bishop may be quite another. However, if no theologians at a Catholic university ask for a *mandatum*, the university may have, in my opinion, a problem. If no theologian desires to ask for a *mandatum*, it could indicate distrust between the theology department and the local bishop. That relationship needs to be positive and valued.

At the same time, even though a bishop may revoke a *mandatum*, he does not have the authority to fire a theologian or, for that matter, any professor at a Catholic university, unless that university is pontifically chartered. Again, if history is our guide, tensions and misunderstandings, not just between the bishop and the president of a university but also between the university and the wider community, inevitably arise and need to be handled with prudence.

Levels of Authority and Official Teachings

Most Catholics do not know that official teachings of the church are taught with different levels of authority. Many controversies have been about teachings that are not infallible; I don't recall in recent years any debate over the articles of the Creed. There have been continuing debates about the official teaching on birth control, homosexual marriage, and the ordination of women. But none of these teachings has been officially taught as infallible, though some theologians say that they are. So the question about the level of authority at which a teaching is taught is important.

In a report issued by the Catholic Theological Society of America, it was stressed that the "hierarchy of truths" should be kept in mind when evaluating the level of authority a teaching has. However, I do not think that the "hierarchy of truths" should be used in a discussion about the different degrees of authority of official church teaching. First, the context in which the Vatican II document

mentioned the "hierarchy of truths" had to do with theologians involved in ecumenical discussions. The bishops at the council were not talking about the
mandatum. Rather, they were recommending that Catholic theologians in ecumenical discussions should begin with what they hold in common with their
Christian dialogue partners (e.g., typically, Baptism and Trinitarian doctrine)
and only after an agreement on them is reached move on to areas where there is
likely to be less agreement (e.g., Mary and papal infallibility). Second, the council
assumed that the truths within this hierarchy are all *truths*, not teachings that
might turn out to be just badly formulated or even false. What is relevant for
theologians concerned with the reach of the *mandatum*, then, is not a "hierarchy
of truths," but rather whether certain teachings, especially those that are now
described as "definitive," are infallible. It is important to remember that the vast
majority of church teachings are not infallible, and even infallible dogmas are
historically conditioned in at least five ways.[2] It should also be remembered that
there is no infallible list of infallible teachings. There will always be some debate
on these issues among theologians.

It may be helpful to recall that medieval theologians created "theological
notes," a graduated list of the level of authority that particular teachings should
be understood to have. That list included both positive and negative notes. At
the bottom of the list are teachings that may be described as *tuta*, meaning that it
would not be imprudent to believe this teaching; then *probablilis*, the teaching is
probably true; then *sentential communis theologorum*, most theologians consider
this teaching to be true; then *theologice certum*, the doctrine is not yet explicitly declared to be true or necessarily connected with revelation but, in the more
or less unanimous opinion of theologians, its denial would involve a denial of a
truth of faith or indirectly threaten it; then *doctrina catholica* in the strict sense,
the doctrine is authentically taught by the universal or papal magisterium; then
fidei proximum, the doctrine is commonly considered revealed but not yet clearly
taught as a truth of revelation; and then *de fide divina*, the doctrine is clearly
contained in the sources of revelation.[3] The appropriate level of authority for a
teaching, if it can be agreed upon, should be kept in mind by both theologians
and bishops. It would be very useful for the theological community, in dialogue
with bishops, to construct a new list of such levels of authority, though reaching
a consensus would be, of course, a contested process, except for teachings professed in the Creed (though debates about how best to understand Jesus's "de-
scent into hell" continue). Archbishop Pilarczyk admitted that the meaning of
the Congregation for the Doctrine of the Faith's novel category—teachings that
are "definitive"—created more questions than it answered.

After presenting clearly the teaching of the church on this matter, could a
theologian raise questions respectfully about the persuasiveness of the reasons
given for preventing women from being ordained priests? St. John Paul II, with

the support of Cardinal Ratzinger, then the head of the Congregation for the Doctrine of the Faith, stated that the teaching banning the ordination of women is "definitive." Calling for the restoration of a system of "theological notes," theologian Nicholas Lash commented on the "definitive" claim in a way that brings some clarity to how the current debate might be handled:

> When . . . Pope John Paul II announced that the Church had no authority to ordain women to the presbyterate, and that the matter was not to be further discussed, two questions immediately came to mind: first, how does he know? (That is to say: what were the warrants, historical and doctrinal, for his assertion?); and secondly, what theological note should be attached to his assertion? In view of the fact that, so far as I know, the question has never, in the Church's history, come up for serious and close consideration, that note cannot be very high up on the scale. From which it follows that his further instruction that we must not discuss it lacks good grounds.[4]

If questions can be raised legitimately by theologians about the teaching banning ordination of women, it would not be at all improper to disagree with the claim that the teaching on priestly celibacy is ontologically grounded, as one cardinal and a retired pope recently argued. In short, restoring the understanding of different levels of authority for official teachings will bring some order and enlightenment to many current theological and disciplinary discussions in the church.

Most theologians agree that calling a press conference and orchestrating opposition to official teaching is not a responsible way to go about the necessary work of theological criticism. Forgoing that, what venues, then, do theologians have for raising critical questions in their writings, in their conversations with other theologians, and while they are teaching graduate students or first-year students? In 1990, Cardinal Ratzinger recommended in *The Ecclesial Vocation of the Theologian* that theologians discuss their concerns with their local bishops. But his recommendation would prevent theologians from talking with their peers in a variety of other settings—with colleagues in their department and at national meetings—or from raising questions in articles published in professional journals or as letters to an editor. Obviously, the press has access to theological conferences and can read journal articles. How to resolve these matters is, therefore, not readily apparent.

What is at stake here is the room necessary, the "elbow room" as Cardinal Newman once described it, for theologians to do their critical work. *Ex corde* does not exclude such work, nor do the proposed guidelines mentioned earlier. Theologians are required to present Catholic teaching accurately—a perfectly reasonable expectation. Theologians are still free to present other points of view as well, a necessary part of thinking through the Catholic faith. But again, may theologians not also offer arguments that criticize some official teaching not infallibly taught?

The very existence of such questions requires that the criteria for granting and especially withdrawing the *mandatum* should be based on an adequate understanding of the legitimate diversity within Catholic theology and the different levels of authority that specific teachings should have. Moreover, the process for making judgments about granting and withdrawing the *mandatum* should be applied consistently by all the bishops.

Diverse Reactions to the *Mandatum*

Some theologians have strongly opposed the *mandatum*. Chicago Loyola theologian Jon Nilson argued that the decision of the American bishops to require the *mandatum* presents Catholic universities with a stark choice—they will have to be either "sectarian" or "secular." He also described the American bishops as simply caving into the demands of Rome. He used the "doomsday" metaphor.[5] Two months later, theologian Monika Hellwig, then executive director of the Association of Catholic Colleges and Universities, offered a quite different appraisal. After a rapid sketch of the history of Catholic higher education in the United States since the 1950s, she concluded:

> Catholic higher education is alive and well in its corporate expression on our campuses—not everywhere, not always, not in every professor or administrator, but predominantly and very actively. Where the religious congregations are diminishing, a new generation of lay leadership has come to the helm with considerable energy, good will and sense of purpose and direction.[6]

The choice before Catholic higher education should never be between being secular or sectarian. That choice poses a false dichotomy. To agree with how Nilson posed those stark alternatives is to buy into a bad bargain that American culture has for years tried and continues to offer religious educational institutions—an offer that should always be rejected. A group of University of Dayton colleagues and I wrote the following unpublished response to Nilson's complaint that the US bishops simply caved into Rome by demanding the *mandatum*:

> A richer, more historically astute sensibility would place the contemporary situation in a wider context. The obligations of bishops to the Pope, of theologians to their faith traditions, of scholars to their disciplines and to the academy and to their students—these are complex relationships, full of

tensions and satisfactions and complicated motivations, subject, like all human relationships, to seasons and evolutions. Reductionist simplification does no justice to any of them.

We concluded our response as follows:

> If we can say to the bishops, as we should, that a university can be independent and fully American without the threat to its Catholic identity, we should be equally unafraid to say to the academy that accountability to a faith tradition poses no threat to our excellence as scholars and teachers. Even further, we should be confident about what we have to offer to the human community precisely because we distinctively connect religious and intellectual concerns.

At Holy Cross? [handwritten marginalia]

A Catholic university is composed of many more faculty than theologians. Therefore, the responsibility for sustaining a relationship between intellectual and religious concerns should never be the responsibility of the theology faculty alone, as important as theology is for a Catholic university. Unfortunately, theology faculties often have little influence in curricular turf wars and in many of the major budgetary and policy decisions of Catholic colleges and universities. They have few majors. Except for those majors, the rest of the student body spends little time studying theology. Theology courses usually constitute only two, and sometimes now only one, of forty courses students need for graduation. Claiming much more of students' curricula are business courses, the social sciences and science courses, and preprofessional majors. Equally painful for theologians and humanities professors is that development officers and administrators find it easier to raise money for sports, buildings, and professional education. It is rare that Catholic universities place the humanities at the core of a capital campaign.

When bishops concerned about the catholicity of a university focus only on theologians, they make it easier for the rest of the faculty to forget their responsibility for it. To be Catholic, a university needs more than Catholic theologians. It also needs business professors who can critique capitalism. It needs law professors who emphasize social justice and the common good; engineering professors who protect the environment; science professors who recognize the ever-present moral and religious issues inherent in their research, as well as the epistemological limits of the scientific methods they employ; and social science professors who understand the human person as both physical and spiritual, individual and communal; humanities professors who understand the depth of human existence, including the significance of love, commitment, and faith; and indeed, theologians who are in conversation with professors in all these disciplines. Above all, faculty in Catholic universities need to understand Catholicism as an intellectual tradition intimately related to and nourished by the faith of the entire church. Catholic universities need to do this within a community that welcomes not only Catholic intellectuals, without whom it is impossible to have a Catholic university, but also, as full and equal partners, faculty and staff of other faiths and even no religious faith who nonetheless support in various ways the mission of the university. A Catholic university should be an "open circle."

Conclusion

At the end of the day, however, the role of Catholic theologians in the university remains crucial. Theologians should not want to teach Catholic theology except in communion with the church, with or without a *mandatum*. Difficulties remain and will always remain. Dealing well with these difficulties calls for ecclesial common sense on the part of bishops as well as theologians. If in its tenor and substance the conversation held between Archbishop Pilarczyk and the theologians at the University of Dayton was any indication of how such difficulties might be addressed and worked through, theologians would have less difficulty accepting the *mandatum*. More important than debates about the *mandatum*, Catholic colleges and universities need not just faithful and competent theologians but also the entire faculty to collaborate in building a distinctive educational experience rooted in its Catholic intellectual and spiritual tradition.

7

Bishops and Theologians

Introduction

It should be expected that bishops and theologians sometimes do not get along. Bishops themselves, for that matter, don't always get along with one another; neither do all theologians. The relationship between bishops and theologians is different than that between bishops or between theologians. Bishops are responsible for preaching and conserving the faith, theologians for explaining, interpreting, and critiquing it. In a time of heightened polarization, like our own, disagreements within the church have at times become acute. Polarizations often end in standoffs, even schism. But can these disagreements be turned into dynamic tensions instead—that is, relationships that respect differences, welcome disagreements, and serve the common good of the church and society? This is the question I wish to explore in this chapter. I begin with a brief review of how this relationship between bishops and theologians has played out in certain periods of history, then describe how it has gone badly and how it has gone well. I conclude with a few suggestions that should help keep the relationship positive and fruitful.

A Brief History

Many of the great theologians in the early church were bishops who developed a theology deeply rooted in the pastoral issues they faced. One needs only to mention names such as John Chrysostom, Gregory of Nazianzus, Ambrose, and Augustine to discover the theological creativity of the patristic period. From the sixth century on, the theological work of monks such as John of Damascus, Anselm, and Bernard retained a pastoral dimension that focused on the spiritual and ascetical life, particularly of monks and nuns.

With the establishment of the universities in the twelfth and thirteenth centuries, however, a new form of theology, university theology, was added to the tradition of pastoral theology. In the universities, highly technical questions were debated and explored, such as the theological authority of the newly translated works of Aristotle and whether they should be added to, alter, or even correct the authority of the Bible. Theologians debated issues such as the doctrine of creation

The Future of Catholic Higher Education. James L. Heft, S.M., Oxford University Press. © Oxford University Press 2021.
DOI: 10.1093/oso/9780197568880.003.0008

and the role of natural law, not the pastoral topics on the minds of most laypeople and monks. Proponents of each approach often argued with each other, most eloquently, as in the case of the theologian Peter Abelard versus the great monastic leader Bernard of Clairvaux.

During the medieval period, few bishops were theologians. Theologians wielded great authority in determining what was acceptable theologically. Bishops, even popes, did not want to get on the wrong side of major theological schools. For example, in 1334, the Avignon Pope John XXII asked the theologians in Paris not to judge prematurely the orthodoxy of his sermons on the relationship of the body and soul after death.[1] He assured the theological community that he was speaking not as pope, but only as a private person exploring a debated theological issue. In a similar way, centuries later, Pope Benedict XVI explained in the introduction to his first book on Jesus of Nazareth that he had written it not as the pope but only as a private theologian open to criticism by other theologians.[2] But the twenty-first century is not the fourteenth. Unlike Benedict, John XXII faced a powerful theological guild that exercised considerable influence and did not hesitate to correct popes when they thought it necessary.

During the Protestant Reformation, Catholic theologians still played a key role in influencing bishops. At the Council of Trent, the bishops invited theologians of different schools of theology to examine and debate contentious issues in their presence. Only after listening to the theologians did the bishops discuss and draw their own conclusions.[3] The Reformation, however, profoundly affected the tone of theological work; it became confessional, defensive, and often adversarial.

Two centuries later, the French Revolution pushed the Catholic Church into an even more combative posture: now it had to face not only Protestantism but also the secularizing power of the Enlightenment. Those Catholic theologians who attempted to address in a sympathetic way the issues raised by the Enlightenment (e.g., the recognition of the historical character of doctrine, the importance of experience, and the role of the *sensus fidelium*) came under constant Episcopal scrutiny. From the first half of the nineteenth century through the Second Vatican Council, popes and bishops were determined not just to monitor the work of theologians but also control it. In 1863, Pius IX published what was called the "Munich Brief," in which he declared that bishops were not just to oversee the work of theologians, but also to direct it.[4] According to ecclesiologist Joseph Komonchak, "Under Gregory XVI and Pius IX, every significant attempt at an independent encounter between faith and reason, between religion and modern society came under suspicion if not outright condemnation."[5] Monsignor George Talbot, who served as papal chamberlain to Pope Pius IX, described Saint John Henry Newman as "the most dangerous man in England."[6]

The following year, Pius IX published the *Syllabus of Errors*, a sweeping condemnation of modernity.

One of the most significant ways that popes began to direct the work of theologians in the church was through encyclicals. For most of the history of the church, popes published only their rulings on various matters. They did not publish teaching documents or encyclicals. Beginning in the eighteenth century, all this began to change. Benedict XIV (1740–1758) and Pius VI (1775–1799) published, respectively, only one and two encyclicals. Pius IX (1846–1878) published thirty-eight and Leo XIII (1878–1903) published seventy-five, an average of three encyclicals a year. Historian John O'Malley comments that "even before but especially after the definition of infallibility, what popes said in their encyclicals tended to assume an irreversible quality."[7] This trend has continued to the present day and presents special difficulties when a pope through his encyclicals usurps the legitimate role that theologians should play in the life of the church.[8]

Before the nineteenth century, the word *magisterium* (from the Latin for "teacher") applied in different ways to the work of both theologians and bishops. Especially after the 1870 definition of papal infallibility, the word applied only to those who taught with public authority—namely, bishops. Theologians taught only as private persons, without an official role in shaping church teaching. Today, the word *magisterium* is used almost exclusively to describe the teaching authority of the hierarchy. These changes weakened the teaching authority of theologians and ignored the role of the laity in the discernment of the faith.

During the so-called Modernist crisis, theologians were required by Pope Pius X (1903–1914) to take an oath against Modernism. Pius X and subsequent popes believed that Modernism ceded too much ground to the temper of the times, particularly to modern rationality, radical biblical criticism, personal experience, science, and liberal democracy. In effect, Pius X had erected a wall between the church and the age. In the 1950s prominent theologians such as Yves Congar, Henri de Lubac, and John Courtney Murray were silenced and forbidden to publish. But in 1958 a new pope was elected, John XXIII (1958–1963), who, despite his advanced age, surprised the world when he called for an ecumenical council not to correct errors or define dogmas, but to renew the life of the church. At that council, bishops and theologians interacted more extensively and fruitfully than perhaps at any time in the history of the church. Bishops recognized the importance of the work of theologians, inviting them to the council to serve as theological advisers, including Congar, de Lubac, and Murray. Vatican II balanced Vatican I's emphasis on papal primacy and infallibility with a strong affirmation of collegiality among the bishops and of the *sensus fidelium* among the laity. Once again, theologians were encouraged by the bishops to pay closer attention to the experience of the faithful, as well as to work with other Christian scholars (Orthodox and Protestant) and Jewish scholars, and scholars even of still other religions.

This close collaboration between theologians and bishops seemed to usher in a new age of learning from each other. In 1966, Pope Paul VI (1963–1978) wrote:

> Without the help of theology, the *magisterium* could indeed safeguard and teach the faith, but it would experience great difficulty in acquiring that profound and full measure of knowledge which it needs to perform its task thoroughly, for it considers itself to be endowed not with the charism of revelation or inspiration, but only with that of the assistance of the Holy Spirit.[9]

In the years since Vatican II, the dynamic and positive relationship between bishops and theologians has suffered new strains and difficulties, with the work of theologians once again coming under closer Episcopal scrutiny, especially under the pontificates of John Paul II and Benedict XVI. But the situation of theologians seems to have improved under Pope Francis.

Characteristics of Dynamic Tension

What sort of interactions among the laity, theologians, and bishops will protect and strengthen the tradition of faith within contemporary Catholicism? How and to what extent should the experience of the laity be taken into account before doctrinal decisions are made? What happens when bishops overreach their authority, theologians question official teaching, and the laity are ignored? What practices need to be followed when controversies inevitably flare up between theologians and bishops?

The case of St. John Henry Newman is instructive. As a Catholic convert, he labored under the hostile suspicions of bishops and the Vatican. In the opinion of his prominent biographer, Ian Ker, Newman went on to make his "last great contribution towards a theology of the Church"[10] in the third edition of his "Lectures on the Prophetical Office of the Church." There Newman wrote about three "indivisible though diverse" offices in the church—teaching, rule, and sacred ministry. The church, he wrote, is at once

> a philosophy, a political power and a religious rite: as a religion, it is Holy; as a philosophy, it is Apostolic; as a political power, it is imperial, that is, One and Catholic. As a religion, its special center of action is pastor and flock; as a philosophy, the Schools; as a rule, the Papacy and its Curia.[11]

The laity along with their pastors is, according to Newman, where the faith is lived out. Newman grants to theology a "fundamental and regulating principle of the whole Church system," and adds that the church is in its greatest danger when the schools of theology are weakened or no longer exist. On the other hand, theologians cannot always have their own way; they can be "too hard, too intellectual, too exact, to be always equitable, or to be always compassionate."[12] Ordinary Catholics, by themselves, lapse into superstition, just as the hierarchy left to itself inclines to power and coercive control. When both the theologians and the bishops are attentive to the thought and practice of the laity, to the *sensus fidelium*, all three will relate in a dynamic way, even though they may not agree. In his groundbreaking essay "On Consulting the Faithful in Matters of Doctrine,"[13] Newman highlighted the critically important contribution to orthodox teaching that the laity made during the Arian controversy.

The role that the laity should play in influencing the formulation of correct teaching was stated clearly by Cardinal Basil Hume of England. At the 1980 Synod of Bishops on the Family, he stressed the need to consult the laity especially on matters of family and sexuality. He explained that the prophetic mission of husbands and wives is based on their experience as married people "and on an understanding of the sacrament of marriage of which they can speak with their own authority."[14] Both their experience and their understanding constitute "an authentic *fons theologiae* from which we, the pastors, and indeed the whole Church can draw." Because married couples are the ministers of the sacrament, Cardinal Hume continued, and "alone have experienced the effects of the sacrament," they have special authority in matters related to marriage. Hume's recommendation anticipated the surveys conducted by Pope Francis in preparation for the 2014 and 2015 meetings of the Synod on the Family. Though only a small number of the laity actually attended these meetings, the published results of the Synod on the Family, *Amoris laetitia*, clearly reflect a rich understanding of marriage and a deep pastoral sensitivity.

The sense of the faithful, as Newman has shown, will not necessarily support every current teaching of the hierarchy, any more than the bishops gathered at Vatican II supported the official church teachings then in force on the separation of church and state, religious freedom, and ecumenical and interreligious dialogue. Pope Francis once remarked that a good Catholic must *sentire cum ecclesiae*; that is, a good Catholic must *think* with the whole church, which, as mentioned in the previous chapter, does not mean thinking only with the bishops.

Newman's ecclesiology has continued to influence thinking about the church.[15] In a 1981 essay in *Concilium*, Fr. Avery Dulles stressed that all three offices in the church—the laity, theologians, and bishops—need to be open and receptive to each other. Channeling Newman's thought, Dulles explained that bishops, isolated from theologians and the laity, tend to "encourage passive conformity and blind conservatism." Bishops are then tempted to "suppress troublesome questions" and "avoid new and provocative issues such as, in our day, the changing patterns family life and sexual mores."[16]

During the first thirty years of his life as a Catholic, Newman suffered from overbearing Episcopal authority. It became almost unbearable shortly after the Vatican's definition of papal infallibility when some bishops, including Newman's own bishop Henry Edward Manning, described papal authority as unlimited. Newman wrote, "We have come to a climax of tyranny. It is not good for a Pope to live 20 years. It is an anomaly and bears no good fruit; he becomes a god, has no one to contradict him, does not know facts, and does cruel things without meaning it."[17] Pope Pius IX (1846–1878) would continue as pope for another eight years, one of the longest pontificates in history.

The hierarchy, of course, is not the only group that needs to be checked. Theologians, Dulles warned, also need to be checked because of "their love of speculation" and their inclination "to neglect the spontaneous piety of the people and the practical wisdom of the pastoral leaders." They become "infatuated with their own systems and neglectful of the beliefs and practices that do not fit harmoniously into their own mental categories." In the light of Vatican II, Dulles also noted that in distinct but not separate ways, bishops and theologians both have the responsibility to discern the faith of the church, including especially that of the laity who, day in and day out, live the Catholic faith in "the trenches." Dulles concluded that it is important that none of these three groups in the church should take over the specialization of the others or reduce the others to "innocuous servitude."[18]

In that same 1981 Concilium volume, Yves Congar contributed a final summary essay, in which he returned to Dulles's remarks about the balance that needed to be kept among laity, bishops, and theologians. One very important fact about the teaching authority in the church is, according to Congar, that both bishops and theologians are accountable to scripture, tradition, and the faith of the people. Everyone in the church, including bishops, is required to seek the truth. Congar argues that all theological research should focus not on infallibility, but on " 'life in the truth of Christ' (1 Cor. 12:3)."[19] He also wrote that when interpreting documents issued by the bishops, theologians should go "beyond a naïve reading" and offer instead a "maturely critical understanding and a rerendering that meets the needs of the educated world today."[20] Concerning the faith of the whole church, the sensus fidelium, Congar gives great importance to Christian practice, especially in situations where Christians suffer oppression and injustice, and above all to the witness of martyrs: "The blood of witnesses guarantees the seriousness involved."[21]

All three offices in the church are called to be obedient to the truth of the Gospel. It makes sense, then, for bishops to remind themselves and not just the laity and, especially, theologians—as is the custom in most Episcopal documents—to discern carefully the faith of the whole church, to be temperate and cautious in their pronouncements, to avoid scandal in their words and deeds, and, above all, to search for and be obedient to the truth.

The philosopher Alasdair MacIntyre famously described tradition as a social embodied and historically extended argument.[22] That a philosopher would describe tradition as an argument carried on among scholars is how philosophers seek the truth among themselves. However, the heart of a tradition is not found first in the intellectually precise formulations of doctrines wrought by scholars and bishops. In his study of the fourth century, Newman located orthodoxy in the "faith of uneducated men." He quoted the church fathers who believed that "the ears of the common people are holier than are the hearts of the priests." For him, tradition was "a profoundly democratic concept, which did not trickle down from theologians, popes, and councils to the people; but filtered up from the faithful (who are the Church) to become the subject matter for the speculations, controversies, and systems of the dogmatic theologians."[23]

Newman, Dulles, and Congar stress the democratic character of tradition and spell out the qualities of fruitful interaction among the laity, theologians, and bishops. All three theologians personally suffered times when these three dimensions did not retain a dynamic balance. But they also stress that such tensions should nevertheless be expected, even welcomed, and worked through.[24]

When Tensions Are Destructive

Having sketched how authority should ideally function in the church, we also need to understand how the relationship between theologians and bishops becomes dysfunctional. Newman, who lived through most of the nineteenth century, fought for greater freedom for theologians to do their work and, at a particularly difficult time in his life, once described, with perhaps some exaggeration, the inevitable tensions between theologians and bishops as an "awful, never-dying duel," or as a night battle "where each fights for himself, and friend and foe stand together."[25]

Aware of the length of time that Tridentine Catholicism held sway, historian John O'Malley described the period from the culmination of the French Revolution in 1789 to the death of Pope Pius XII in 1958 as the "long 19th century." Moreover, except for the work of theologians like Newman and Adam Möhler, theological creativity was the exception. In his private correspondence, Newman often complained about the overreach of the hierarchy. Explaining his reluctance to publish his own theological work, he wrote:

> As well might a bird fly without wings, as I write a book without the chance, the certainty of saying something or other (not, God forbid! against the Faith),

but against the views of a particular school in the Church, which is dominant. I cannot accept as of faith, what is not of faith; who can? I cannot, as I said before, work without elbow room. I cannot fight under the lash, as the Persian slaves. To be the slave of Christ and of His Vicar, is perfect freedom; to be the slave of man is as bad in the mind as in the body. Never, as I know, was it so with the Church, as it is now, that the acting authorities as [at] Rome . . . have acted on the individual thinker without buffers. Mere error in theological opinion should be met with argument, not authority, at least by argument first.[26]

The buffers to which Newman refers protect the ordinary give and take between theologians, free to write what they think and to criticize one another without the fear of immediate hierarchical intervention. Newman explained that the great theological vigor of the medieval schools depended on theologians who were allowed "free and fair play" and did not feel "the bit in their mouths at every word they spoke." As a Catholic, he often complained that bishops held theologians on a short leash. If theologians were to render a real service to their students and to the church, Newman insisted they needed "elbow room." He believed that spirited debate displaced weak arguments with stronger ones. Only when such disputes became dangerous for the whole church did Newman think that hierarchical intervention was appropriate, as it was in the seventeenth and eighteenth centuries, for instance, when the Jesuits and Dominicans were ordered to stop arguing with each other about grace.

Newman lamented that the great theological schools of Europe were destroyed by the French Revolution. To fill that vacuum, schools of one mindset were established in Rome.[27] There, the dominant school of theology, in its early formative stages, was manualist scholasticism, wooden summaries of St. Thomas constructed in question-and-answer formats, mainly designed for apologetic purposes. In Rome, many assumed it to be the only orthodox form of theology. Newman worked out of a different tradition—one grounded in the writings of the fathers of the church, sensitive to historical development, and often inductive, aware of the psychological and pastoral dimensions of faith. Representatives of manualism, which became even more dominant during the next century until Vatican II, were the very people who silenced Congar, Murray, and de Lubac in the 1950s. merton ?

A student of history, Newman knew that the relationship between bishops and theologians could be tense. He knew it in his own life as well. Occasionally, a bishop is a good theologian, but ordinarily not. As I mentioned at the beginning of this chapter, bishops and theologians have different tasks. In the last analysis, the faith of the entire church is strengthened by the work of theologians who have the freedom to explore and remain in dialogue and communion with their bishops.

* Is there genuine intellectual freedom in the church? ("elbow room")

Newman affirmed the importance of the university's appropriate relationship with the Catholic Church itself. He argued that the church is necessary for the integrity of the Catholic university:

> The university is a place of teaching universal knowledge. This implies that its object is, on the one hand intellectual, not moral. . . . Such is a University in its *essence*, and independently of its relation to the Church. But practically speaking, it cannot fulfil [*sic*] without the Church's assistance; or, to use the theological term, the Church is necessary for its *integrity*. Not that its main characters are changed by this incorporation: it still will have the office of intellectual education; but the Church steadies it in the performance of that office.[28]

Even over a century before the Vatican's apostolic constitution, *Ex corde ecclesiae*, Newman realized that the link between the church and the university was not direct control by the hierarchy. The university has an intellectual mission, and in that sense is independent of the hierarchy. He did not want the university to be a seminary or a convent. He wanted, as already mentioned, theologians to have "elbow room" in their work. *Ex corde ecclesiae* affirms that a Catholic university "possesses that institutional autonomy necessary to perform its functions effectively, and guarantees its members academic freedom," adding that the rights of both the individual and the community are kept within the truth and the common good.[29] Unless a Catholic university sustains an appropriate relationship with the church, the theological foundations of the Catholic intellectual life may crumble, as they already have at so many universities that originally were founded by Protestant Christians in the United States. Unless a core of the faculty at a Catholic university remains committed to the educational relevance of Jesus Christ and the Catholic intellectual tradition, the Catholic university's distinctive intellectual and existential dimensions will weaken and eventually disappear.

Ex corde ecclesiae does better in understanding the role of bishops than did the Irish bishops who asked Newman to establish a university. *Ex corde* does not claim for bishops any direct role in the running of Catholic colleges and universities, and grants to universities institutional autonomy and academic freedom, "properly" understood. Newman actually anticipated much of *Ex corde ecclesiae*. In fact, in some ways, he went beyond it.

Acquiring a Richer Understanding of the Catholic Dimension

The changes brought about by Vatican II were far-reaching: they affirmed the central role of the laity, opened dialogue with Protestants and followers of other religions, declared religious freedom, and recognized the inescapable effects of history on formulations of even infallible teachings. One would think with all these changes in official teaching that a new age of more fruitful collaboration between bishops and theologians had dawned, one when henceforth they would enjoy a dynamic and fruitful working relationship. But the theological messianic age has not arrived. Newman observed that church councils have "ever been times of great trial"[30] and that understanding them and implementing their decisions takes time, even a century or two. Tensions between theologians and bishops continue, some of which, unfortunately, could be avoided if due process were more closely observed.

The theological community in the United States has changed considerably since the time of Newman. Catholics have also experienced dramatic changes, especially in their numbers and sophistication. So have the religious orders that have founded most of the Catholic universities in the United States. In 1960, for example, there were 8,338 Jesuits in the United States; in 2011 there were 2,650.[31] In 1965 there were over 3,500 Marianists worldwide; now there are about 1,200. The typical pre–Vatican II core curriculum built on Thomistic theological and philosophical synthesis has collapsed. Now lay theologians vastly outnumber theologians in religious orders; they employ multiple theological methods. Theology has become highly professionalized, which has had both positive and negative consequences. Positively, its rigor has increased, but negatively its focus has become more specialized and in many instances has lost a pastoral dimension. Faculty and students are more diverse in their beliefs and ethnicity. And since the late 1960s, the governance of nearly all these institutions has been confided to lay boards of trustees, while faculty, who for the first time now has tenure, play an increasing role in academic governance. Some bishops worry about whether these institutions will remain or, even now, are Catholic.

Given all these dramatic changes, it is understandable why in the early 1980s the Vatican wanted to clarify the mission of these institutions. Published in 1990, *Ex corde* affirms that a Catholic university "possesses the institutional autonomy necessary to perform its functions effectively" (par. 12), At the same time, bishops have a responsibility to promote Catholic universities and should not be seen simply as "external agents" (part I, par. 28). Most significant for many leaders of these universities, bishops are not to "enter directly into the internal government of the university." I discussed more of the significance of *Ex corde* in the two previous chapters.

However, with regard specifically to theologians and bishops, *Ex corde* guarantees that the university has "academic freedom, so long as the rights of the individual person and of the community are preserved within the confines of the truth and the common good" (part I, art. 2; part II, art. 2, par. 5). Academic freedom is guaranteed to theologians as long as they are faithful to the "proper principles and methods" of their discipline. Since bishops are the authentic interpreters of the Word of God, Catholic theologians recognize and accept their authority in that role.[32] Finally, theologians who teach Catholic theology have been asked to request a mandate (*mandatum*) from the "competent ecclesial authority" (part II, art. 4, referring to Canon 812). Concerns remain. Komonchak worries about a juridical imbalance in *Ex corde* with regard to the relationship between bishops and theologians:

> To preserve the integrity of faith there is the requirement that Catholic theologians have a mandate from ecclesiastical authority, but to preserve the exigencies of reason, there is only the affirmation, in principle, of institutional autonomy and of academic freedom; no institutional safeguards of these are indicated.[33]

To correct this juridical imbalance, some Catholic scholars have simply adopted the American Association of University Professors' (AAUP's) definition of academic freedom, based as it is on a liberal theory of individual rights.[34] The AAUP focuses on the rights of professors, not on the rights of institutions to be distinctive. While there is much to be affirmed in that AAUP definition—especially the practices of due process and peer review—the freedom of Catholic theologians is exercised within, not against, the Christian tradition, respecting its dogmatic boundaries, even if those boundaries are revised. Theologians are part of a community, not just individual scholars. I have devoted chapter 8 in this volume to the complexities of academic freedom.

Catholic theologians need to be in communion with the whole church and in solidarity with its long and multifaceted tradition. But having affirmed that solidarity, it still must be asked whether theologians have sufficient protection for them to enjoy, in Newman's words, the necessary "elbow room" to debate theological issues. Komonchak asks why the principle of subsidiarity, invoked by the church to ensure the rights of the family and civil and cultural associations over against an imperial state, should not also be invoked to protect the appropriate autonomy of theologians.[35]

A Recent Test Case

The juridical imbalance that caused Komonchak to worry played out in the case of theologian Elizabeth Johnson and the US bishops' committee on doctrine. In Johnson's case, the bishops chose not to follow the due process procedures outlined in the 1989 document "Doctrinal Responsibilities: Approaches to Promoting Cooperation and Resolving Misunderstandings between Bishops and Theologians"—a document written by theologians, canon lawyers, and bishops and then approved by the National Conference of Catholic Bishops. Instead, the bishops' committee on doctrine decided to publish, without any prior conversation with her, severe criticisms of her 2007 book *Quest for the Living God: Mapping Frontiers in the Theology of God.*[36]

The theological community strongly criticized the bishops for not talking with Johnson before issuing their critique of her book. In response to this criticism, the bishops explained that the 1989 document was intended for the use of an individual bishop dealing with an individual theologian in his diocese. Johnson's case, they claimed, affected more than one diocese, so widely read was her book. I believe that the bishops, in retrospect, realized that they should have first talked with Johnson. Later, they issues a "pastoral resource" for bishops explaining their responsibilities as official teachers of the faith.[37] In it, bishops are encouraged to maintain a close relationship with the theologians in their diocese. Once again, however, the appropriate juridical protection for theologians was missing from the "pastoral resource." Without that juridical protection, the rights of theologians are too easily overlooked, such as, according to the 1989 agreement, "the right to a good reputation, and, if needed, the defense of that right by appropriate administrative or judicial processes within the Church" and "in cases of dispute the right to expect access to a fair process."[38]

A lack of due process assured by the bishops is not the only problem that increases tensions. Information technology and media outlets often misunderstand, distort, promote, and exaggerate controversies in the church. Drawing upon the work of numerous cultural critics, theologian Vincent Miller of the University of Dayton explores the impact of the media and consumer culture on the life of the church.[39] Miller contends that contemporary media facilitates the formation of like-minded enclaves and special-agenda organizations not limited geographically. Instead of sustaining "the complex orthodoxy and orthopraxis of a tradition," these groups gravitate around a single issue or a cluster of similar issues, creating a narrowly defined identity that empowers people in our diffuse society. There are very vocal groups of Catholics, for instance, focused on either prolife or social justice issues.[40]

Theologian Anthony Godzieba[41] explains how "digital immediacy" facilitates, to an unprecedented degree, the centralization and reach of papal authority (e.g., the Vatican website). He points out that many of the laity are religiously subliterate, unaware of the traditional criteria—such as a system of "theological notes" described in an earlier chapter—that theologians use for interpreting not only papal texts but also the entire tradition. These issue groups seem to have little time or interest for such careful analysis. Newman, who in his day had to deal only with newspapers, pleaded with bishops to be more patient with theological disagreements; he recommended that bishops allow a generous amount of time for theologians to work out their differences before intervening. In our age, digital and electronic media have largely replaced newspapers. Today we are bombarded with "breaking news," even when there isn't any. Exaggerations and distortions are common. Patience is nearly nonexistent. Media facilitates immediate Episcopal intervention and theological misunderstandings.

A Way Forward

Despite these challenges, there are some encouraging developments that make it more likely that the interaction of theologians, bishops, and the laity will result in a dynamic rather than destructive tension. I will single out only three.

First, in 2012, the Vatican's International Theological Commission (ITC) published a document entitled "Theology Today: Perspectives, Principles and Criteria" and in 2018 one entitled "Synodality in the Life and Mission of the Church." The ITC is composed of an international group of theologians appointed by the Vatican to study issues and report their findings to the Congregation for the Doctrine of the Faith. These two studies in particular, approved by the Congregation for the Doctrine of the Faith, are good news for several reasons. The 2012 document states that "the years following the Second Vatican Council have been extremely productive for Catholic theology" (art. 1) and praises the development of multiple theologies, because revelation is "too great to be grasped by any one theology" (art. 5). It affirms the historicity of revelation (art. 22 and 29) and the use of both historical-critical and theological methods of interpretation (art. 22). It argues that the church's living tradition should never "fossilize" (art 26) and that theologians are called to be "constructively critical" of movements in the church (art. 35). It acknowledges the importance of distinguishing different levels of teaching authority (art. 37). It underscores the critical importance of the *sensus fidelium* (especially art. 33–36) and mentions spiritual experience as an important source for theology (art. 88 and ff., especially 94). It explains that

> bishops and theologians have distinct callings, and must respect one another's particular competence, lest the *magisterium* reduces theology to a mere repetitive science or theologians presume to substitute the teaching office of the Church's pastors. (art. 37)

This acknowledgment of the creative role of theology suggests that bishops should not criticize the work of theologians who go beyond simply repeating the formulations of the *Catechism of the Catholic Church*.[42] However, as positive as the ITC's statement is, it rarely cites the work of any major contemporary theologians (e.g., Rahner on the self-communicating mystery of God, von Balthasar on the beauty of revelation, or Lonergan on theology as a framework for creative collaboration), and once again it makes no recommendations on how to protect the legitimate rights of theologians. Although the document states that all criticism is to be "constructive," there will surely be differences of opinion as to what constitutes constructive criticism. And while the unity of theology is understood as not requiring uniformity, the degree of legitimate diversity will continue to be debated. While it remains to be seen how much influence this study will have on how bishops and theologians interact, that it exists and is approved by the Vatican is encouraging.[43]

The 2018 document offers a theological commentary on the renewed emphasis that Pope Francis has given to the role of Synods in the life of the church. Theologians are to listen to the Word of God; understand faith in "sapiential, scientific and prophetic ways"; evaluate in the light of the Gospel the "signs of the times"; and, in the service of the Gospel, dialogue with society and cultures (par. 75). All the members of the church, anointed with the Holy Spirit, "do not err in faith, even when [they] cannot find words to explain the faith" (par. 56). For this reason, the "entire People of God" must be consulted because "what affects everyone should be discussed and approved by all" (par. 65). The document distinguishes between "decision-making," which a diocesan assembly of the faithful does, and "decision-taking," which is the responsibility of the pastor and the local bishop (par. 69). Finally, practices that lack a true spirit of synodality, namely, "the concentration of responsibility for mission in the ministry of Pastors; insufficient appreciation of the consecrated life and charismatic gifts; rarely making use of the specific and qualified contribution of the lay faithful, including women, in their areas of expertise"—all these harmful practices must be "quashed" (par. 105).

Taken together, these documents, one published with the approval of Pope Benedict and the other Pope Francis, are remarkable statements that advocate creative roles for theologians, an essential role for the laity in grounding church teaching, and a creative collaboration among theologians, bishops, and the People of God. What is needed, of course, is the consistent implementation of these practices throughout the church.

A second positive development is the recognition by some theologians that organizing public dissent is rarely helpful. In 2007, Daniel Finn, then president of the Catholic Theological Society of America (CTSA), devoted his presidential address to issues of power, and more specifically to how power plays out between theologians and bishops. He recommended that to foster dialogue it would be wise for the CTSA to stop making public statements defending themselves against ecclesiastical power. Not only were votes by the members of the organization on statements concerning controversial issues divisive, but also, in his opinion, they damaged their organization. One of the consequences, according to Finn, was that "conservative and liberal theologians in the United States largely attend their own meetings, read their own journals and talk mostly to one another." None of this, he continued, serves the church well. He did not hesitate to support individual theologians or even groups of theologians making public statements, nor did he disagree with the content of the organization's public statements. However, he did doubt their positive impact. In his judgment, the CTSA needed to do more to foster a dialogue that would bring into conversation and collaboration a wider variety of theologians.

Third, prominent and well-respected theologians have made strong public recommendations to improve how bishops deal with theologians. Shortly before he died, the then Cardinal Dulles wrote that bishops should do more to moderate charges and counter charges between theologians of different schools, avoid issuing too many statements that appear to carry with them an obligation of assent, consult with a wider variety of theologians before issuing any binding statement, anticipate objections and seek to address them before issuing a statement, and, finally, be more sensitive to multiple cultures in the world.[44]

In a similar vein, when German bishop Gerhard Müller was appointed the head of the Congregation for the Defense of the Faith (CDF) in 2012, Gerald O'Collins, a long-time professor at the Pontifical Gregorian University, called for similar reforms. He stressed the importance of respecting subsidiarity (i.e., allowing matters to first be addressed locally, and if unable to be resolved at that level, only then in Rome). He recommended that a more diverse and internationally representative group of theologians advise the Congregation for the Doctrine of the Faith. He emphasized especially that bishops should recognize "the right of the accused to be present from the outset, to meet their accusers, to be given the accusations in writing well beforehand, and to be represented by someone of their own choice,"[45] something that never happened in the Johnson case.

Conclusion

The relationship between bishops and theologians remains critically important for the church. There are many reasons to keep that relationship dynamic and positive. Progress has been made on these issues at Vatican II and since then, but there have also been some setbacks. In all such matters, we should exercise the virtue of hope. The future of Catholic higher education depends on dedicated faculty and fruitful tensions between theologians and bishops.

PART III

FACULTY AND THE UNIVERSITY MISSION

After looking at the complex relationship of the Catholic university with the Catholic Church, and more specifically of theologians with bishops, I address faculty issues in this section. Fifty years after the Association of American University Professors defined the meaning of academic freedom in 1915, Catholic universities began to think through what that academic freedom should mean for them. The Second Vatican Council had just ended. Catholic universities began to establish lay boards of trustees, increase faculty governance, and, for the first time, grant tenure. Before then, the religious orders ran the universities they founded, designed the curriculum, and hired and dismissed lay and religious faculty, sometimes at will. In the late 1960s and into the 1970s and 1980s, the members of the religious orders that had exercised near-total control over their universities had greatly diminished in number, either by leaving their orders or by retiring. A brand-new chapter in the history of Catholic higher education began to emerge, the shape of which is still uncertain.

The chapters in this part of the book attempt to understand how best to navigate the rough seas stirred up by controversies over academic freedom, hiring and forming faculty, achieving the best balance between teaching and research, and acquiring habits that form supportive and hospitable academic communities.

I pay particular attention to two of the most important and necessary characteristics of Catholic universities: liberal education in general and theology more specifically. Secular universities typically pay only perfunctory attention to the liberal arts and, as we have already seen, do not believe that theology is a legitimate academic discipline.

Taken together, all these challenges are every bit as formidable for all faculty at Catholic universities as are those faced by theologians and bishops who, following the extraordinary changes issued in by the Second Vatican Council, sometimes trip up as they learn in this new context to respect each other's roles and foster fruitful collaboration.

8

Academic Freedom and the Open Circle

Introduction

Academic freedom is, has been, and always will be a contested issue. Evangelical historian George Marsden asked a provocative question: "Are there historical forces operating that make it virtually inevitable that Catholic universities will follow the path taken by formerly Protestant universities in moving away from meaningful religious identities?" More specifically, he asked, "Will Notre Dame become, say, within two generations, another Duke or Syracuse?"[1]

There are some positive signs that Catholic universities will remain Catholic, due in part to the impact of St. John Paul II's 1990 apostolic exhortation on Catholic higher education, *Ex corde ecclesiae*.[2] As I explained in chapter 4, the secularization of Catholic higher education is not inevitable, nor is secularization all bad, depending on what you mean by it. There are, nonetheless, continuing serious threats. Academic freedom could be one of them. In this chapter, I will argue that depending on how we understand academic freedom, we will find that it is, as I understand it, an important part of the heritage of the American Catholic university that will help it be more, rather than less, Catholic. This happy outcome—a Catholic university with genuine academic freedom—can, I believe, enrich all American higher education.

Current State of Catholic Higher Education

I begin this chapter not with a discussion of the American Association of University Professors' (AAUP's) understanding of academic freedom and the Catholic university, but rather with a brief summary of three recent assessments of how Catholic colleges and universities seem to be doing with regard to their distinctive mission. I realize that it is dangerous to make generalizations about such a diverse group of institutions. Some struggle every year just to keep their doors open, while a few are now among the most sophisticated and respected in the world.

Despite their great diversity, they face similar challenges according to several recent assessments of their Catholicity. In 2012, the Association of Jesuit Colleges and Universities released a report produced by a task force assigned to

The Future of Catholic Higher Education. James L. Heft, S.M., Oxford University Press. © Oxford University Press 2021.
DOI: 10.1093/oso/9780197568880.003.0009

identify the distinctive characteristics of Jesuit higher education, along with the challenges that their institutions face.[3] Their list of distinctive characteristics is articulate and extensive. The second assessment is based on the conclusions of a discussion of the board of trustees of *Collegium*, founded and led by Tom Landy of Holy Cross College. Each summer, *Collegium* organizes a week-long gathering for scholars who are encouraged to examine their professional lives as vocations. They are also encouraged to find positions in higher education that support a religious vision of the academic life. In preparation for their twenty-fifth anniversary in 2017, the board members discussed how things had changed since the organization was founded (full disclosure, I was one of the founding board members). The conclusions of the Jesuit task force and the *Collegium* board members identified similar trends.

Both the Jesuits and the *Collegium* board are seriously concerned about sustaining a robust Catholic identity and single out various initiatives that support that effort, including Catholic studies programs, faculty retreats, some newly created endowed chairs of Catholic thought, and the appointment of mission officers. But their list of what has changed in Catholic higher education and the challenges they face is daunting: religious illiteracy among not only students but also younger faculty, the marginalization of the liberal arts by professional education, lay leaders who are not very knowledgeable about the Catholic intellectual tradition, the information revolution and scholarly specialization that make building community and integrating knowledge more difficult, and the tensions that arise from the promotion of vigorous debate on contested issues that make church officials anxious. The Jesuits, along with all the other religious orders who have founded Catholic colleges and universities, also worry about their decreasing membership.

With regard to academic freedom, the authors of the Jesuit task force stated that "there is, at times, mutual misunderstanding both from the bishops and the universities on what 'academic freedom' requires of Jesuit Catholic universities."[4] They stress that a Jesuit university cannot be considered excellent "unless it fulfills its mission to be an excellent university within the American academy, and therefore values highly academic freedom and peer review."[5] Whether this combination is possible—that of being a Catholic university and having genuine academic freedom—will become clearer later when I contrast the Jesuit understanding of academic freedom with how the AAUP defines it.

Besides these two assessments, Boston College and the Association of Catholic Colleges and Universities (ACCU) surveyed presidents of Catholic universities in 2013. Their survey revealed another troubling trend. One of the questions on the survey asked the presidents how they dealt with the "Catholic dimension" of their universities. Unfortunately, they never asked them what they understood by it. What they did ask, however, was the extent to which various campus constituents understood and promoted it. Nearly all the presidents were in agreement that not many of their faculty really helped students understand the "Catholic dimension." In fact, the presidents thought that the faculty contributed the least to carrying out this responsibility, a particularly sobering assessment, since faculty have tenure, remain in their positions longer than most administrators, shape the curriculum, and interact daily with students. In short, the presidents reported that faculty were at the bottom of their list when it came to promoting their institutions' Catholic dimension.[6] It would be interesting to know how presidents on the one hand and their faculty on the other understand academic freedom, and whether that contributes to the presidents' perception that faculty do not support the mission of the university.

In summary, all three assessments focused primarily on the problems. Academic freedom was mentioned several times. Must academic freedom be, in fact, a threat to Catholic identity? ⭐

The AAUP Understanding of Academic Freedom

It would be difficult to argue that academic freedom, as understood and defended by the AAUP, has played a major role in creating the many challenges these surveys have identified. After all, most Catholic universities never adopted policies of academic freedom and tenure until the 1960s, when the church as a whole took a more positive stance toward the modern world. Long before the 1960s, the dominance of science, technology, and the commercialization of American culture was well underway. However, during the 1950s and 1960s, the extensive professionalization of higher education had begun, various forms of faculty governance were established, and local chapters of the AAUP began to appear on Catholic campuses.[7] Putting our discussion of academic freedom into its historical context in the early twentieth century will help us understand better the choices we have today.

Between 1890 and 1915, several professors in well-publicized cases were dismissed or resigned from universities on account of their views on evolution, pacifism, and economics. Two of the most famous cases involved two economists, Richard T. Ely, at the University of Wisconsin-Madison, and Edward Ross, at Stanford University. In 1894, a committee was appointed to investigate Ely for discussing "dangerous" ideas in the classroom and disturbing students. The Board of Regents eventually exonerated Ely by stressing the importance of "sifting and winnowing" ideas to determine the truth. More colorful is the 1901 case of economist Edward Ross at Stanford. Stanford was founded by the railroad magnet Leland Stanford, whose widow, Jane, continued as a trustee to wield significant influence at the university. Ross advocated the monetization

⭐ This narrative raises questions of
advocacy & the objective purse
academics normally adopt

of silver and supported in 1896 the presidential candidacy of William Jennings Bryan (faculty who spoke in favor of the candidacy of William McKinley were not reprimanded). Jane Stanford wanted Ross dismissed. The president, David Starr Jordan, was able to protect Ross for a while. But then Ross went on to criticize the importation of Asian laborers to build railroads, hitting more closely to the source of Leland Stanford's wealth. By 1900, Ross was forced to resign from the faculty. His resignation triggered other resignations at Stanford, including that of philosopher Arthur Lovejoy, who became one of the principal architects of the AAUP's doctrine of academic freedom.

Religiously Affiliated Colleges

From the time of its foundation in 1915, the AAUP dedicated itself to defending the rights of individual professors against arbitrary actions of administrators, board members, politicians, and, in general, people with power but who were not part of the academy. Of the original thirteen professors who signed the 1915 statement on academic freedom, eight had studied in Germany and seven were social scientists. Focusing on the academic freedom of the professor, their 1915 Declaration of Principle declared that in all disciplines "the first condition of progress is complete and unlimited freedom to pursue inquiry and publish its results," adding that "such freedom is the breath in the nostrils of all scientific activity."[8] They acknowledged that the board of trustees of a "denominational college" had the right to govern according to its religious tradition, but they also made it clear that they had serious reservations about the academic quality of such institutions. They sharply distinguished authentic universities from sectarian colleges—evangelical and fundamentalist Protestant colleges—that were especially threatened by scientific theories of evolution and higher biblical criticism. At that time, the leaders of Catholic colleges and universities, almost all members of the religious orders that founded them, were preoccupied with meeting the needs of Catholic immigrants and raising the academic quality of their recently founded institutions. The AAUP confidently claimed that since religious colleges did not "advance knowledge through unrestricted research and unfettered discussion of impartial investigations," they therefore "should not be permitted to sail under false colors."[9]

Also at the beginning of the twentieth century, with the widespread influence of the movement of higher criticism of the Bible begun in Germany and the increasingly influential research of Darwin on evolution and various subsequent evolutionary theories (e.g., "survival of the fittest" and eugenics), a group of scholars at Princeton University published in the 1910s a multivolume series called *The Fundamentals*, hoping to safeguard conservative Protestant orthodoxy and the inerrancy of the Bible from theological liberalism and cultural modernism. The famous 1925 Scopes trial in Dayton, Tennessee, led more denominational colleges to require faculty to take "faith tests" and to stress the literal inspiration of the scriptures. By 1940, the AAUP addressed again the status of denominational colleges, recommending that such colleges should make clear to faculty the "limitation in academic freedom because of religious and other aims" at the time of their appointment. This recommendation became known as the "limitations clause," or the "lim clause."[10] And though in 1970 the AAUP thought that most religious schools no longer needed to state such limitations, by 1982 it changed its mind, stating that "a college or university is a marketplace of ideas, and it cannot fulfill its purpose . . . if it requires conformity with any orthodoxy of content or method."[11] This view was expressed once again in 1988 when an AAUP subcommittee submitted a report that concluded that the 1940 statement was essentially right on two points: "(1) the prerogative of institutions to require doctrinal fidelity; and (2) the necessary consequences of denying to institutions invoking this prerogative the moral right to proclaim themselves seats of higher learning."[12]

Is Theology an Academic Discipline?

Should Catholic universities agree with the AAUP that their institutions cannot be "seats of higher learning"? While the entire membership of the AAUP never endorsed the 1988 report, it raised questions about how we should think of Catholic universities and Catholic theology, especially since Catholicism requires "creedal orthodoxy."[13] More specifically, how should Catholics understand the work of their theologians? In 1990, the year that the Vatican published *Ex corde ecclesiae,* Fr. Avery Dulles, SJ, who subsequently was made a cardinal, explained that theologians do not merely repeat what is in the Bible and what the church teaches, but also ask about the intelligibility of those teachings by probing those sources in the light of questions posed by modern society. Using their own methodologies "competently," he explained, Catholic theologians are "free to reach whatever conclusions are indicated." He adds that "pope and bishops have no mandate to tell the theologian how to do theology, beyond the negative mandate of seeing to it that theology does not undermine the life of faith itself." Theology, therefore, possesses a certain freedom over against even the hierarchical *magisterium.* "Without that freedom it could not be theology, and hence it could not be of service to the church. The medieval axiom, *non ancilla nisi libera* ('of no help unless free'), holds for theology."[14]

If epistemologically the AAUP's understanding of academic freedom is overly restrictive, I believe that operationally it recommends some valuable practices.

It defends peer review, due process, and tenure. Had the Jesuit task force distinguished between these commonsense operational dimensions of the AAUP understanding of academic freedom and its epistemological constrictions, it would have made clearer how a Catholic university should understand academic freedom: namely, to welcome it operationally but expand it epistemologically. There need be no opposition between theology, for example, understood as an authentic, rigorous, and critical academic discipline on the one hand, and affirming on the other the importance of due process, peer review, and tenure. If the AAUP's operational and epistemological dimensions were separated from each other, debates about where to draw the line between the rights and the prerogatives of those who seek to emphasize an individual professor's rights and those who emphasize the distinctive mission of the institution would be a little easier to address.

My argument, then, is that peer review, due process, and tenure are important. In its 1940 *Statement of Principles on Academic Freedom and Tenure*, the AAUP drew attention to other commonsense practices that faculty, as professionals, should follow: they "should be at all times accurate, should exercise appropriate restraint, should show respect for the opinions of others, and should make every effort to indicate that they are not speaking for the Institution."[15] Furthermore, they should not introduce controversial issues extraneous to their courses. Catholic universities, in my opinion, should also embrace these guidelines.

The problem for Catholic universities, then, remains the narrow epistemology that restricts without good reason what counts as credible scholarship. That narrow epistemology imposes the scientific method on all disciplines. In 1915 the AAUP stated that in questions about the "spiritual life" and the "general meaning and ends of human existence, . . . the first condition of progress is complete and unlimited freedom to pursue inquiry and publish its results." Putting aside what "unlimited freedom" might mean, the statement describes such freedom as the basis of all scientific activity.[16] Such an assertion, however, does not really apply to scientists who know the limits of their methodologies. Rather, it represents scientism, a particular methodology that has morphed into a metaphysics. When properly employed, the scientific method has produced extraordinary results over the past two centuries. One needs only to think of the great advances in recent years in the fields of genetics, neuroscience, astronomy, and physics, advances that all religious people should celebrate. If, however, all the humanities to be considered genuinely academic need to use scientific methodology, then the, nature of research in the humanities is radically and arbitrarily limited.

Catholic colleges and universities should weigh carefully other cultural, methodological, and financial developments that have shaped the academy during the past century. By the end of World War II, the US government began to pour extraordinary amounts of money into universities to further the government's own research priorities. Needless to say, very little of this money was earmarked for research in the humanities, and certainly, given the separation of church and state, not a penny supported research in theology. Consider the following statistics:

In 2012 the National Endowment for the Humanities [NEH] received $146 million compared to the 30.9 billion for the National Institutes of Health and 7.033 billion for the National Science Foundation. The NEH figure represents 0.38% of the federal allotment to these three agencies and 0.1% of the total 2012 federal funding for research and development, including also such agencies as the Department of Defense.[17]

By contrast, Germany has supported research in the humanities at the level of roughly 9% between 2008 and 2012. Two consequences flow from this powerful trend in the United States: (1) most universities, especially research universities, have become commercial enterprises, pursuing scientific objectives determined by the government and private enterprise, powerful institutions that, ironically, are external to universities, creating what some have described as the "kept university,"[18] and (2) research judged to have commercial value gets nearly all the funding. In such an academic environment, scientific and professional education marginalizes the humanities and makes theology irrelevant.

As a consequence, faculty in Catholic universities who wish to pursue questions for which there are no immediate answers, to seek the truth of things simply for the purpose of knowing the truth, and to spend time reflecting on why there is anything rather than nothing will find little support from the federal government. With the exception of grants from the Templeton, Lilly, and Luce Foundations, faculty lack the funding to wrestle with the so-called big question, many of which are theological by their very nature. Instead, faculty have to do it on their own time, without external financial support.

This narrowing of epistemology is all the more dangerous for a Catholic university. The AAUP claims that it trusts only "complete and unlimited freedom" uncontrolled by the distortions that ideologies—orthodoxies external to the academy—make inevitable. As Alasdair MacIntyre and others have shown, all intellectual traditions are based on assumptions that cannot be proven, including the liberal tradition, which thinks that there are no such limits.[19] As Jaroslav Pelikan once pointedly stated, "With a naiveté matching that of many believers, the secularist critics of religious belief have sometimes proceeded as though assumptions *a priori* that cannot be proven were exclusively the property of believers, and therefore as if their [own] scholarship and their university were free of presuppositions."[20] In insisting on a narrow epistemology, one

Agreed

ironically limits freedom. The AAUP, which thinks of itself as a liberal organization, actually narrows the areas of inquiry it is willing to protect as authentically academic. It has arbitrarily excluded the excellent and influential work both on religious and nonreligious topics produced by scholars of many faith traditions and disciplines.

There is another way in which the AAUP understanding of academic freedom is too limited. In focusing on the rights of individual professors, the AAUP leaves out two other important forms of academic freedom: that of students and that of the institution itself. This chapter has focused so far on the academic freedom of professors. Can an argument be made for the academic freedom of the university as a whole, especially those with distinctive religious missions?

Corporate and Individual Academic Freedom

If, as I have argued, we understand academic freedom so that it embraces both the AAUP's recommended procedural dimensions and a broader epistemological framework, how would these adjustments change the picture, not just for the individual professor, but also for the institution as a whole? Catholic universities need to affirm their corporate freedom, that is, the institutional space necessary to explore as an academic community fundamental questions. The mission of a Catholic university emphasizes, therefore, both the rights of individual professors to academic freedom and the rights of the university to the freedom to pursue its mission. However diverse they are in other respects, Catholic universities must, as institutions, enjoy a freedom to be themselves, all the while respecting the rights of individual professors. Few observers of American higher education would disagree that the great diversity among its many institutions is one of its greatest virtues and distinctive strengths. Why should that diversity not be strengthened in an especially valuable way by intellectual distinctiveness that should characterize Catholic universities? How, then, should we describe the distinctive contribution of a Catholic university? Among the many possible institutional models for universities, which ones should Catholic universities embrace?

Three Models

I think that we can distinguish at least three different models that colleges and universities have taken in the United States. As mentioned briefly in the introduction to this book, we can think of the university as a marketplace of ideas (the AAUP version), a closed circle (a sectarian college that welcomes only faculty and students from the same faith community), and an open circle (a model that offers an educational institution the best chance to be both a university and Catholic).[21]

In its 1982 statement the AAUP used the economic metaphor of the university as a "marketplace of ideas."[22] The "marketplace" metaphor suggests that all ideas are examined and debated, and the institution takes no position itself. This model appeals to those Catholic universities that aspire to be respected like elite secular institutions. Such institutions believe that by taking no position, they are able to foster truly open debates. However, as mentioned earlier, it is hard, if not impossible, to think without presuppositions. As the philosopher Thomas Nagel puts it, a "position from nowhere" exists nowhere.[23] There is a real danger, to quote Alasdair MacIntyre once again, that the most prestigious Catholic universities will uncritically aspire to imitate their secular betters: "So we find Notre Dame glancing nervously at Duke, only to catch Duke in the act of glancing nervously at Princeton."[24]

A very different way of thinking about a university is as a closed circle. In this case, the leaders of these institutions require full agreement on all significant aspects "related to" the religious mission of their institution, allow on campus only speakers who represent their version of Catholic teaching, and locate their Catholicity primarily in moral teachings, fully reinforced by campus ministry and the theology department; no disagreement is permitted. Little publishing is done at these institutions, and fidelity to the Catholic tradition as interpreted by the *magisterium* represents the only reliable indicator of orthodoxy. Typically, the theologians of these institutions apply happily for the *mandatum* and advertise to their constituents that they have done so.

For those academics committed to the marketplace of ideas, the closed circle looks like a place that "subsidizes the promotion of opinions held by persons usually not of a scholar's calling."[25] And for those who prefer "closed circles," the marketplace of ideas looks like the institutional embodiment of a chaotic relativism.

The Open Circle

There is a third model for a Catholic university, what I call the "open circle." In this model, the faculty and student body need to be sufficiently distinctive to sustain a community with a common discourse but also open enough to examine a wide variety of ideas. Grammatically, the metaphor "open circle" is both a noun and an adjective. To be a circle, a Catholic university needs to foster and engage critically a particular tradition, the Catholic intellectual tradition. In other words, the circle ensures that there will be a community that shares enough in common to make vigorous and informed discussion possible. Without that circle, almost every discussion will be in search of first principles and often not arrive at compatible ones. The smaller a circle is, the more intimate the community, and the larger the circle, the more diverse it can be. A Catholic university in the modern world should want to be both distinctive and open.

To be open, the university also has to value the contribution of every member of the academic community—those who form part of the circle and those interacting with it—precisely to engage more comprehensively the great questions that humanity faces. The voices of scholars from other religious traditions who respect the Catholic tradition enrich the discussion. The Enlightenment, as Catholic philosopher Charles Taylor reminds us, defended human rights and freedom of conscience. Had not the Enlightenment broken away from the structures and claims of Christendom, Taylor believes, certain facets of the Christian life would not have been carried further than they were, or could have been, had they remained within Christendom.[26] After all, it was only in 1965 that the Catholic Church officially endorsed religious freedom, understood as the right not to be coerced in matters of religious belief. Scholars from other religious traditions keep the circle more honest and raise questions and contribute insights that, enclosed within themselves, Catholic scholars may be unlikely to do. In his encyclical Fides et ratio, Saint John Paul II called on Catholic scholars to include in their research the study of African and Asian philosophies. From this perspective, a Catholic university is neither secular nor sectarian. It is not secular because it affirms the importance of the religious realm as an area of scholarship. It is not sectarian because an integral part of being Catholic is seeking truth wherever it can be found, be it in the study of other religions or welcoming scholars from other religions as colleagues.

To sustain the "marketplace of ideas" model is to embrace modern secular culture. To keep a closed circle opposes modern culture. To create and maintain an open circle is more difficult than either embracing or rejecting modern culture. Given all the forces of modern culture and the current fragile state of Catholic universities that desire to remain Catholic, we might ask again whether these "open circle" Catholic universities will become, as George Marsden asked, what major Protestant universities found they had become a hundred years ago: institutions wedded to the dominant secular culture.

Keeping a Circle That Is Open

What might Catholic universities do to sustain their Catholic identity while they also welcome the participation of people of other faiths and even no faith? How should they deal with the powerful secular forces of academic culture, which is more secular than that of the general public? If this wider definition of academic freedom takes deeper root, what are its implications at Catholic universities for faculty, curriculum, and the kind of intellectual resource a Catholic university can be for the church and for the world?

A Catholic university should support a more robust atmosphere for research on religious and ethical topics than is possible at secular universities. Moreover, in an open circle, one that welcomes people of other faiths, and even of none, who wish to contribute to such an educational mission, paths to new research are opened up. Augustine enriched the Catholic tradition through what he learned from his teachers in the secular schools of rhetoric. Thomas Aquinas's extraordinary contribution to the intellectual life of the church drew deeply and critically on the writings of the pagan Aristotle, the Jew Moses Maimonides, and the Muslims Averroes and al Ghazali.[27] In an "open circle," Catholic scholars dedicated to deepening the Catholic intellectual tradition would not only study the texts of thinkers from other religious traditions but also welcome them to become members of their universities so that the dialogue might take place in "real time." Such diversity also aids learning, so it helps students as well.

Faculty and the Open Circle

It should be obvious that to thrive, this model of a Catholic university must hire faculty carefully. The "open circle" depends on the presence of Catholic intellectuals who welcome interdisciplinary and interreligious dialogue. An open circle is sustained in large part by hiring Catholic intellectuals, who are, unfortunately, fewer in number than Catholics with doctorates. I make frequent use of the phrase "Catholic intellectual tradition." In functional terms, what does that tradition look like in action? How do Catholic intellectuals think?

They approach their disciplines with certain presuppositions: that the more deeply they explore what it means to be human, the more inescapable are religious questions, and that the more deeply they plunge into any area of scholarship, the more likely they will find it necessary to make connections with other areas of knowledge. Catholic intellectuals realize that any intellectually vibrant religious tradition learns from and influences the larger culture in which it is located. The doctrines of creation and the incarnation remain for Catholic intellectuals the theological focal points for all these presuppositions.

One of the major challenges that Catholic higher education faces today is finding, hiring, and developing such intellectuals. If the faculty at a Catholic college gives priority only to hiring a diverse faculty, then they will have diversity within their faculty but eliminate diversity among universities. A genuine pluralism of higher education ceases to exist. Legal scholar John Noonan wrote that it is "unquestionable that corporate bodies have religious freedom protected by the First Amendment."[28] The AAUP does not deny that corporate bodies have this right, but they do doubt that religious universities with a distinctive, religiously grounded, intellectual tradition can call themselves true universities.

On a more personal note, I might add that while serving for eight years as provost of the University of Dayton, I interviewed hundreds of candidates for faculty positions. I never asked any of them if they were Catholic; I did not need to. By raising questions about their research interests, what they hoped to achieve in the classroom, what they thought was most important for students to learn, what career they would have chosen if not one in the academy, why they chose to be a professor, and other questions like these, I could usually tell whether they could flourish in and contribute to the distinctive mission of the university—especially in the case of senior hires. We all know faculty who, though they are members of other religions and may even be part of no religious tradition, still contribute to the research and conversations that are essential to the mission of a Catholic university. There are also scholars who are not believers, who might describe themselves as secular, and still contribute thoughtfully to the mission of the university. Scholars such as these keep the circle open.

Of course, after hiring faculty, it is just as important to offer them opportunities to become more familiar with the distinctive mission of the university through, for example, research support and faculty seminars. A Catholic university needs, then, to spend considerable time and money to support such intensive forms of faculty development, not for purposes of indoctrination, but rather to ensure religious literacy, to increase scholars' ability to see connections between disciplines, and to work at developing important links between liberal and professional education. I have devoted chapter 9 to the recruitment and formation of such faculty.

The Center of the Open Circle

A second way of sustaining this "open circle" model requires the creation of a core curriculum that embodies the distinctive characteristics of the Catholic intellectual tradition. Revising core curricula is a regular contact sport for faculty: turf fights erupt; religious zealots claim the high ground; and professional faculty rest secure, protected by their large numbers of majors, the wealth of their graduates, the university's development staff, and the many required courses accrediting agencies say are necessary for their accreditation. If the mission is not understood in compelling and distinctively intellectual ways, there is little hope that the development of a core curriculum will embody a sense of the Catholic intellectual tradition.

Research interests influence the courses that faculty prefer to teach. If the core curriculum and degree programs are structured to embody a distinctive mission, the university is more likely to hire faculty whose research supports these academic priorities. There is no need to think of such academic priorities narrowly. Pope St. John Paul II outlined a broad and rich research agenda in paragraph 32 of his 1990 apostolic exhortation, *Ex corde ecclesiae*, that includes the dignity of every person, the protection of the environment, international justice and structures for political stability, overcoming the huge gap between the rich and the poor, and the support of marriage and the family.[29] All of these priorities are grounded on Catholic philosophical and theological principles, but secular thinkers can also find them important. A sustained reflection on such issues exposes students to ways of thinking that are constructive and transcend the sterile culture wars that polarize Catholics in the United States. It would be a mistake to think that theology and philosophy alone carry the mission; they are the necessary but not sufficient, and even sometimes not the most effective, means of imparting a sense of the Catholic intellectual life. Mark Roche offers many excellent suggestions for creating a distinctive curriculum, most recently in his article "Principles and Strategies for Reforming the Core Curriculum at a Catholic College or University."[30] Building a faculty that can shape and support a distinctive core curriculum takes years. There is no quick fix in these matters.

The Catholic University and the Church

My third and final recommendation is that Catholic colleges and universities should not lose their living relationship with the global church. The Catholic Church, with its 1.2 billion members, is the largest multinational organization in the world. While we in the United States talk a great deal about the necessity of "diversity" among our faculty and students, that diversity hardly reflects the truly deep diversity of global Catholicism.

Bishops are important, but Catholicism is much more than the hierarchy. Fostering a living relationship between Catholic universities and the bishops needs to protect academic freedom as I have described it in this chapter. When is the last time you have heard a bishop publicly defend the academic freedom of a Catholic university? Happily, according to *Ex corde ecclesiae*, bishops have no direct authority over nonpontifically chartered Catholic universities. That means that in over 90% of the more than two hundred or so Catholic colleges and universities in the United States, bishops do not have the authority to hire or fire anyone. *Ex corde* affirms that Catholic universities enjoy both institutional autonomy and academic freedom, "so long as the rights of the individual person and of the community are preserved within the confines of the truth and the common good."[31] Catholics recognize that bishops officially have the responsibility to determine, in consultation with other bishops and ultimately with the entire church, what can be described as authentically Catholic. There have always been tensions around whether the judgment of an individual bishop and the process by which that judgment has been reached are fair. Catholic time stretches out at great length and, with eternal vigilance and the occasional martyr, learns to correct itself and to embrace, as it did under St. John Paul II and Pope Benedict and is doing now under Pope Francis, the global experience of Catholics.

It would be unwise for a Catholic university to unhitch its future from the life of the church. To paraphrase St. Peter, to whom should Catholic universities look? We need only to remember the two-thousand-year-old Christian intellectual tradition (actually four thousand years if we include, as we should, the Jewish tradition), the great theologians, philosophers, artists, scientists, musicians, saints, and sinners—all of whom need to be part of our conversation and research today.[32] Surely it would be a mistake to wed ourselves only to contemporary academic culture and trends, or to government and proprietary funding priorities. If Catholic higher education is to contribute to the pluralism of education in the United States, then let that contribution be in the form of a distinctive intellectual vision and carefully argued moral judgments. I for one am blessed to be a member of a religious tradition that opposes abortion and capital punishment and that grows increasingly doubtful that war can be a just response to political conflicts. I welcome Pope Francis's challenge to care for the gift of God's creation. These are teachings of the universal church that offer guidance not just for Catholics but for all of humanity. At the same time, I believe that the Catholic university can enrich the church itself through its practices of due process, open debate, studies of the natural world, participating in and influencing the incredible advances in the fields of genetics and neuroscience, and vibrant theological and philosophical debates.

Conclusion

Will Catholic colleges and universities go the way most Protestant universities have gone? I hope not. But to make it less likely that they will, they must exercise serious, sustained, and strategic planning. Academic freedom with a more capacious epistemology than that afforded by the AAUP will actually strengthen and contribute to the deepening of the mission of Catholic universities. Catholic universities also need to hire carefully, invest in extensive faculty development, create distinctive core curricula and signature degree programs, and retain a living link with the global church. If they are able to do that, they will foster a distinctive intellectual mission that will contribute to the common good and to the pluralism of higher education in the United States, and beyond.

9

Faculty Recruitment and Formation

Introduction

This chapter explores three related topics: understanding in an intellectual way the "mission" of a Catholic university, hiring faculty committed to that mission, and confronting the widespread view of Catholicism as anti-intellectual. Throughout this chapter I will mainly be drawing on my experience with the faculty at the University of Dayton from 1977 to 2006.

Given the great diversity of Catholic higher educational institutions, the University of Dayton cannot presume to be a template for faculty initiatives for all other Catholic colleges and universities. However, most Catholic colleges and universities have been affected by similar national trends. For example, from the latter part of the nineteenth century to the present, disciplines in the sciences have mushroomed and professional education has become part of university education, especially in Catholic universities, where for decades programs in law and education have enrolled a growing number of students. Today, even though the number of students majoring in the liberal arts has decreased dramatically since World War II (they were small to begin with), and more rapidly decreased at the beginning of this century, the number of students majoring in the professions, especially business, has soared. In the early decades of the twentieth century, preprofessional and technical majors accounted for less than 30% of undergraduate degrees; today, 60% of undergraduate degrees are in preprofessional and technical fields.[1]

The first half of Vatican's 1990 apostolic constitution on Catholic universities, *Ex corde ecclesiae*, presented an engaging and challenging vision of the mission and identity of Catholic university education. While not ignoring other academic disciplines, the document put particular emphasis on the importance of theology. We have already discussed in a previous chapter the expectation, inserted unilaterally by the Vatican in their final version of the document, that theologians request a *mandatum* from their local bishop. Virtually all Catholic universities in the United States require a course in theology. However, very few students major in theology, especially when compared to those who major in the professions. Business students often graduate with little or no exposure to Catholic social teaching. Some of these same students are much more likely several decades later to make substantial contributions to their alma mater, often

The Future of Catholic Higher Education. James L. Heft, S.M., Oxford University Press. © Oxford University Press 2021.
DOI: 10.1093/oso/9780197568880.003.0010

to the academic programs from which they graduated. Graduates who have majored in theology rarely become wealthy, at least if they work as religion teachers or theologians.

At many of our universities, more students show an interest in theology than choose it as their major. Their parents are understandably concerned that their sons and daughters find jobs that pay a decent wage. Of the few who do major in theology, they often double major, that is, major in a second degree that is a good "backup," one that provides more financial security than if they relied only on their degree in theology. The forces of the commercialization of the culture and of universities, both secular and religious, keep most students from majoring in the study of religion and theology.

The pervasive commercialization of higher education in the United States has hardly gone unnoticed. In recent years, many books have described a profound crisis in higher education, a lack of a moral center, a faculty reluctance to address the spiritual and religious needs of their students, exorbitant student debt, and courses that teach students to memorize more than to think. Nor does it help when new administrators spend a great deal of time to create strategic plans only to move on to another institution before their plans can be implemented.[2] While some of these books can be described as extended jeremiads, they all point to the absence of a coherent, intellectually rigorous, humanities-rich, and ethically astute vision of education.

I believe that Catholic colleges and universities willing to address this crisis have two advantages: (1) the immensely rich and many-faceted Catholic intellectual tradition and (2) faculty from all the disciplines who are able and willing to find in that tradition a religious, ethical, and intellectual resource. The Jesuit Howard Gray once remarked that good events on campus should be turned into programs and programs into structures.[3] The challenge, of course, is how to institutionalize such events and programs so that they become a regular part of a university's distinctive mission in ways that strengthen its moral center and deepen the intellectual engagement of both the students and faculty—but especially the faculty.

Academic leaders in Catholic higher education face three challenges in institutionalizing their Catholic identity: understanding Catholicism as an intellectual tradition, hiring and working with faculty to support that tradition, and shaping a curriculum that embodies that tradition.

Hiring for a Distinctive Intellectual Mission

It is important to realize at the outset how difficult it is to understand the mission of a Catholic university in intellectual terms understood by faculty in all the disciplines. Unfortunately, many academics assume that the mission of a religious university belongs only to campus ministry and the theology department. Faculty may reduce the mission to being fair and kind to students and being good colleagues—certainly desirable qualities, but not sufficient for an adequate embodiment of the mission. Few faculty understand Catholicism as an intellectual resource that could shape distinctive curricula and research. Intellectual distinctiveness contributes to research and teaching that can be every bit as demanding, and rigorous as the teaching and research that most faculty learned in their secular PhD programs.

Besides the difficulty of understanding the mission of the university in intellectual terms, the way in which faculty approach hiring often puts mission-related hiring either in second place or in competition with other priorities, often a preoccupation in recent years to create a more diverse faculty. These two issues—Catholic identity and diversity—are often thought to be in conflict. Some faculty believe, wrongly, that hiring for mission means hiring only Catholic faculty, regardless of competence. On the other end of the spectrum, some faculty avoid this conflict by interpreting Catholic as "catholic," that is, universal, a version of "all are welcome." With this interpretation, they recruit a diverse faculty regardless of whether they understand the distinctive mission of a Catholic university. One approach leads to a "closed circle," the other to a loss of distinctive mission. Neither approach achieves what faculties at Catholic universities should be.

Conversations about Catholic mission and faculty diversity should not be carried on as though they have nothing to do with each other or are easily compatible. If hiring for mission does not mean hiring only Catholic faculty, nor should it also mean giving top priority to hiring only minorities. It is appropriate, even necessary, for a Catholic university understood as an "open circle" to do both. If hiring is not done with a both/and balance, the consequence will be a serious loss of identity or a closed-circle form of Catholicism. What's more, as Mark Roche, one-time dean of the College of Arts and Letters at the University of Notre Dame, warns, "If hiring for diversity results in Catholic universities losing their religious identity, then American higher education as a whole will become less, not more, diverse."[4]

Another approach is needed, one that avoids the false dichotomy of hiring only Catholics regardless of intellectual accomplishments or hiring minorities regardless of their ability to contribute to the Catholic intellectual traditions. Search committees need to learn how to hire faculty who both enhance Catholic distinctiveness (rather than accept as adequate the categories, as they are typically understood, of inclusivity and egalitarianism) *and* enrich the diversity of the faculty. In other words, the faculty should understand that increasing diversity need not come at the expense of Catholic mission as long as the deeper, dynamic inclusivity of Catholic intellectual life is embraced—an inclusivity that understands that all faculty regardless of race, creed, or color can and ought to understand the university's distinctive intellectual commitments and, over time, in ways appropriate to their disciplines and academic rank, learn how to explore it in their research and teaching.

In intellectual terms, how might the Catholic tradition be described? First, as a tradition, Catholicism is best understood as an ongoing conversation, sometimes contentious, regularly multifaceted, global and culturally immensely diverse, celebrating and searching for what is good and true and beautiful wherever and from whomever they can be found. Catholicism poses a distinctive set of questions and affirms certain truths that stress the transcendent character of the human person created in the image and likeness of God (which are also fundamental teachings of Judaism and Islam). Catholicism emphasizes the importance of community, of liturgical and sacramental practices, the types of philosophy that are open to religious questions and theological traditions open to rational critique. Catholicism affirms the doctrine of creation and the sacramental character of all physical reality, and therefore fosters a nonmaterialist but fully empirical approach to the natural sciences. Finally, Catholicism has developed a sophisticated tradition of social ethics, especially valuable for professional education. One does not have to be Catholic or a Christian to appreciate or contribute to the development of these traditions. At the same time, for these conversations to be carried out well, some committed Catholic intellectuals are a necessary part of such an intellectual community.

When the intellectual mission of a Catholic university is understood in this way, it is possible for faculty from other faiths and even no faith to make valuable contributions to the university. So whether candidates for a faculty position are Catholic or not, persons of color or not, a man or a woman, they should be persons who as competent scholars can in their own way contribute to the distinctive intellectual mission of the institution.

Moreover, it could also be said that the distinctive mission of a Catholic university is actually both intellectual and religious for the simple reason that seeking the truth of things, be it in science or the humanities, is a religious act. Jesuit Michael Buckley has written:

> The fundamental proposition that grounds the Catholic university is that the academic and the religious are intrinsically related, that they form an inherent unity, that one is incomplete without the other. . . . Any academic movement toward meaning or coherence or truth, whether in the humanities, the sciences, or the professions, is inchoatively religious.[5]

At their best, faculty study and search for the good, the true and the beautiful. Some more than others will engage in that research and search by including in an explicit way intellectual themes related to Catholic intellectual traditions. Diversity among disciplines and topics within disciplines need to be respected and explored, but the most important goal is that all diversity, disciplinary and personal, enriches the mission of the university as a Catholic university. In other words, all diversity is within, enriches, and questions, but is not parallel or indifferent to, that mission.

Media and the Public Image of Catholicism

Media coverage of Catholicism often projects a negative image, and for quite understandable reasons. Most everyone knows what the church teaches on gay marriage, women priests, abortion, and birth control. Most people know about the sexual abuse scandals, the failures of bishops, and the censuring of theologians. Few faculty candidates know that in the United States the Catholic Church is the largest provider of kindergarten-through-twelfth-grade private education, higher education, and health care (one out of seven Americans receives their health care from Catholic hospitals), and the largest resettler of refugees (larger than the federal government). If you Google the phrase "world's biggest charitable organization," you will find that it is the Catholic Church.[6] Unfortunately, few faculty candidates know what the church teaches on immigration, support for universal health care coverage (even for undocumented immigrants), the dynamic relationship between faith and reason, evolution, and economics and the characteristics of a just society. As a result, if most scholars seeking an academic position know only what the media presents about the Catholic Church, they will likely not even apply for a position at a Catholic university, or even imagine that it would be possible as a faculty member to enjoy an open and robust intellectual life there.

Some Catholic universities founded by religious orders try to sidestep the negative media coverage of the Catholic Church by emphasizing the attractive qualities of their religious orders' traditions. Most religious orders, however, are not known for their intellectual achievements. Catholic universities should emphasize first the Catholic intellectual and spiritual traditions, and only then the particular traditions of their individual religious orders. They will also need to help rehabilitate the public perception of Catholicism. Sometimes, instead, they do not advertise their religious character. The posted faculty job descriptions omit any reference to the university being Catholic; this too is a mistake. There are many ways to draft job descriptions that include an understanding of Catholicism that would attract a candidate who might otherwise hesitate to apply: simply describe what Catholicism means, intellectually.

Hiring for Mission

If too many faculty in Catholic universities have difficulty understanding Catholicism as an intellectual tradition, pit hiring Catholics who can enrich that tradition against those who add intellectual and ethnic diversity to their ranks, and do little to overcome the perception that Catholicism is anti-intellectual and close-minded, what, then, can be done to turn these negatives into positives? For nearly thirty years I had the privilege of participating with and watching faculty work together to create and sustain a distinctive mission at the University of Dayton. One of the first things we did was find a way to approach "hiring for mission" that would not worry faculty interested in strengthening the academic reputation of the university. The particular approach we took may not work at every Catholic college or university. But any Catholic university unwilling to tackle the challenge of hiring for mission will doom itself to replicate what is already available in secular higher education and, through neglect, add to an already bland commercialized mediocrity.

While I am not sure who coined the phrase "hiring for mission," I discovered that faculty often misunderstand what it means. Their misunderstanding appears in the questions they ask: Is hiring for mission something other than hiring good researchers and teachers? How academic is the mission? Do Catholics have special academic qualities, or is hiring a Catholic mainly an effort to increase the number of Catholics on the faculty? Is a "critical mass" of Catholics the same thing as having a faculty that is 50% Catholic? Should we even be paying any attention to the percentage of Catholics on the faculty? Does "hiring for mission" apply only to hires in theology departments and campus ministry? Is it more relevant for certain parts of the university than others, for example, more in the humanities than in professional education? Does it mean hiring pious people who are academically mediocre? Are we to presume that Catholics enjoy an epistemological advantage or see things more deeply than those who are not Catholic? Isn't it illegal to ask candidates about their religious faith? Would it even be relevant to ask a candidate about his or her personal faith? Does hiring for mission exclude hiring Jews, Muslims, agnostics, and atheists? What does "being Catholic" mean, academically speaking? If it were possible to hire only Catholics, should that really be the goal? Is our current commitment to diversity and pluralism just an effort to make a virtue out of necessity, that is, applauding diversity because that's the gender and ethnic profile our faculty already has? Should our aim be to create the standard categories of diversity among faculty, or rather to create diversity between faculties at different institutions, for example, at a Catholic in contrast to a secular university? If all universities, Catholic and secular, set as their highest goal hiring a diverse faculty, then would not faculties at Catholic and secular universities end up looking the same? Is that desirable?

Such questions rise spontaneously when faculty discuss what hiring for mission means. At the University of Dayton, which has four professional schools (Engineering, Business, Law and Education and Allied Professions), we decided the best way for us to approach this issue was from the "bottom up." By "bottom up," I mean that we decided to begin to work directly with faculty and especially with department chairs and heads of search committees—that is, with those individuals at our institution who play key roles in the hiring process. We also included a dean in each of the groups. Finally, we thought that to address the many typical misunderstandings of what it means to hire for mission, it would be best to set aside a generous amount of time for confidential discussions in small groups.

Therefore, we organized off-campus overnight workshops, usually held at a state park an hour's drive from Dayton. We put together a folder of readings, none very long, which the participants received several weeks before the workshop. After a reception and dinner the first evening, we devoted the first session to a discussion of several readings that covered some of the historical background of Catholic higher education in the United States, described some of the current challenges it faces, and ended the evening with a social. The next morning, we held two sessions, one that focused on some of the obstacles and typical misunderstandings of what it meant to hire for mission, and a second that focused on a candid description of the strengths and weaknesses of the University of Dayton, especially in terms of what a distinctive intellectual culture at a Catholic and Marianist university would look like, whether it would be desirable, and what difference it might make. After lunch, we evaluated practical initiatives ("best practices") in hiring for mission and concluded the workshop with a brainstorming session by all the participants, who usually numbered no more than twenty. This last session was devoted solely to what the participants thought could and should be done at the university to hire more consistently and intelligently for mission. Their suggestions were written up and submitted to the university administration and distributed to academic departments. These workshops have been conducted annually since the 1980s. After three years of these workshops, the provost, seeing the positive reception of the faculty to these workshops, required attendance by all faculty who were leading searches in their departments. "Top-down" reinforcement, needless to say, supported our "bottom-up" approach, but only after the bottom-up initiative had created a positive buzz among the faculty.

One of the most important reasons these workshops went well was that they were led by respected lay faculty, opinion leaders whose teaching and research were highly regarded and who grasped well the university's mission. They introduced each session briefly, leaving well over an hour for discussion. They set an open and honest tone, which facilitated fruitful discussion. It was not uncommon for persons to say that they were not really looking forward to attending these workshops but admit afterward that they found them very helpful. Some of them had expected "lectures" on Catholic and Marianist identity rather than what they actually experienced: thoughtful and honest discussions of the complexities and importance of hiring for mission. Clarifications of what "hiring for mission" should mean not only alleviated their initial anxieties about the workshop but also turned them into advocates for the practice of approaching the hiring process with a clearer sense of what kind of faculty the university needed if it was going to offer a distinctively Catholic education.

The university also began to conduct a second-year tenure track faculty retreat in the spring, and a little later a special program for newly tenured faculty who by that time had settled sufficiently into their identities as faculty to understand more clearly the challenges and possibilities of embracing a distinctive mission at the university.

During the eight years I was privileged to serve as provost of this university, I chose to interview all finalists for faculty positions. Given that typically there were three finalists for each position, and that each year we usually had about thirty positions to fill, that meant at least ninety interviews that consumed most of my days throughout January and February. I found these interviews to be fascinating, revealing, and rewarding: fascinating because of the very different personalities and backgrounds of the candidates; revealing because I found various ways to get them to talk about why, in the first place, they wanted to be professors and what their goals as teachers and researchers might be at a Catholic university; and rewarding because I learned a great deal that I don't think I ever world have learned if I had limited my conversations to my departmental colleagues. I began to learn about the many different disciplines that made up the university. These interviews were well worth the time they required. It was also very encouraging for me when more and more search committees recommended candidates who were also my first choice.

Mission-Oriented Curricula and Faculty Research

Besides hiring for mission, how can a Catholic college or university help faculty already hired to understand and own that mission? First, it is important to show the relationship that their research might have to the mission. Research should engage faculty precisely where their deepest intellectual interests lie. One of the best ways for this to happen is to have a curriculum, and disciplinary programs within the curriculum, that express and explore that mission. For example, the core curriculum or the general education program needs to embody themes that reflect the mission. The University of Dayton's newly approved common academic program, building on the previous general education program dating from the 1980s, offers an integrated Humanities Commons (courses in philosophy, English, history, and theology) staffed by faculty who teach in a coordinated way what it means to be human. All four first-year courses in the Humanities Commons include perspectives of the Catholic intellectual tradition. This requirement was not approved without controversy, and the faculty development necessary to make it meaningful was considerable and ongoing. Upper-level courses in the new Common Academic Program include themes related to the Catholic intellectual tradition; the university has made grants available for pilot courses that allow faculty to take up these themes in new ways. This wholesale curricular revision has been accompanied by the development of degree programs, most often initiated by faculty, in areas related to the university's mission as Catholic and Marianist: for example, the creation of the first major in the United States in Human Rights Studies and interdisciplinary minors in Marianist Social Transformation (an emphasis on social justice and Catholic social teaching) and another in Sustainability, Energy and the Environment, which recently received national recognition. All of these curricular commitments have grown out of the faculty's research expertise and pedagogical commitments and their appreciation of the Catholic intellectual tradition.[7]

One of the first things I did as provost was to established a faculty-driven Forum on Catholic Intellectual Tradition Today. With a representative from each division of the university supported by an annual budget, these faculty-organized conferences invited speakers, funded research projects, and kept the conversations on Catholic intellectual traditions alive and visible not only on campus but also beyond it. Their efforts focused on faculty development in two ways—exploring models of excellent scholarship in the Catholic intellectual tradition in a wide variety of disciplines and inviting faculty to conversations that built and sustained unique intellectual communities. The faculty who ran the forum organized several university-wide faculty seminars (about twelve to eighteen participants, all with reduced teaching loads) on Catholic intellectual traditions. The seminars lasted a full academic year.

On the graduate level, where it is often hardest to establish a mission-related emphasis, the university has also created some important programs. For example, as mentioned earlier, in the early 1990s we established a PhD program in theology. We now have a highly respected group of theologians doing research and teaching in conversation with faculty in the humanities, the social sciences, and most recently the sciences, especially on the topic of the environment. The English department has hosted Christianity and literature conferences. Established in 1950, the University's Marian Library is recognized both nationally and internationally as a center for research, and the university's PhD program in theology offers a Marian concentration.

We have endowed a number of chairs in various parts of the university to which members of the faculty are appointed for four years. The faculty who compete for these positions are typically individuals who are highly respected teachers and researchers, and who have demonstrated an understanding of the university's mission. They "model" research related to Catholic intellectual traditions and organize programs related in creative and broad ways to the mission. The appointees have reduced teaching loads, secretarial help, and budgets that allow them the time and resources to organize workshops and national conferences and bring speakers to campus. They also initiate collaborative research among faculty.

There is a real advantage in appointing to these chairs tenured faculty who belong to established departments: they are able to make it clearer that departments have responsibility for the mission of the university. I do not favor presidential appointments to endowed chairs not located within departments, nor do I favor creating stand-alone mission-focused centers isolated from the rest of the faculty. Administrative arrangements that drive the mission in and through the faculty increase faculty responsibility for the mission.[8] They are, I believe, the best way to institutionalize the mission in the university—through the faculty.

Dayton has also distinguished itself in how it has organized an annual cross-disciplinary faculty seminar. Ten to twelve faculty, especially young tenured faculty who give signs of intellectual leadership, are invited to participate in a seminar that is held weekly for four months. Besides the reduced course load, participants receive stipends to do summer research aimed at creating a new course, writing a publishable article, or championing a proposal for curricular innovation. While such faculty seminars are expensive, they have proven well worth the investment.[9]

Over the years, this multifaceted approach to orienting faculty research to mission-related topics has created a distinctive culture. When we started to encourage this sort of mission-related research in the mid-1980s, we faced a good deal of hesitation and suspicion from some of the faculty. However, probably because we went about this effort in a way that put serious intellectual work front and center, an excellent group of scholars gravitated around these initiatives. A good number of the faculty now takes for granted that doing this sort of research not only is legitimate but also enriches their understanding of their own discipline. A vibrant intellectual community conducting such research makes it easier to understand why hiring for mission makes sense. These initiatives require serious money. As George Marsden once rightly observed about the building of an excellent Catholic university, "No such program to move in a direction counter to major historical trends is going to be accomplished with pocket change left over from normal university activities."[10] On the other hand, many effective strategies for developing an intellectual community are not expensive. For example, purchasing a book or buying dinner for a reading group that meets several times over a semester or over the summer costs relatively little and forms interdisciplinary communities.

Giving such importance to the Catholic intellectual tradition throughout the university counters the overall secularization of higher education. Enlightened leaders of Catholic universities who embrace a religiously based intellectual culture should never be embarrassed. Some academic leaders of secular universities are uneasy when they learn that institutions were founded decades earlier with a definite religious mission. As Andrew Delbanco explains:

> If you were to remind just about any major university president today that his or her own institution arose from this or that religious denomination, you'd likely get the response of the proverbial Victorian lady who, upon hearing of Darwin's claim that men descend from apes, replied that she hoped it wasn't so—but if it were, that it not become widely known.[11]

Finally, one of the most important outcomes of all these research, curricular, and structural innovations is friendship among faculty. In exiting their disciplinary silos, faculty have met and built relationships with faculty in other parts of the university—relationships that have grown into new research projects, team teaching, curricular adjustments, conversation partners, good friendships, and a large community of shared academic interests. In the opening chapter of this book, I pointed out that one of the characteristics of Catholicism is its communitarian ethic. These efforts in faculty development have helped build a distinctive academic community.

The Catholic University's Relationship to the Catholic Church

The intellectual traditions of the Catholic Church preceded by a thousand years the first universities in the West to which the church itself gave birth. Catholic colleges and universities enjoy an advantage over almost all higher educational institutions in the United States if they do not sever their relationship with the church and its two thousand years of history. The issue, however, is how that relationship should be structured and carried on. We have discussed aspects of that relationship in Part II of this book. What I would like to do here is explore the importance of how faculty understand Catholicism.

It is fairly common in academic circles to distinguish between Catholicism with a big "C" and a small "c." Both are important. The academic culture we live in, however, leads some faculty and administrators to emphasize only the small "c." They focus on ideas and teachings that most faculty find unobjectionable, that are more likely to be embraced by more liberal individuals, that are "inclusive," that affirm a both/and approach, and that celebrate the importance of reason and a natural law tradition that stress a common humanity and human rights. More recently, papal leadership on protecting the environment has received a warm reception. In doing so, faculty sometimes avoid less attractive dimensions of Catholicism, such as the claims the hierarchy makes for their binding teaching authority, their reliance on dogmas, and their insistence on moral teachings that condemn abortion and gay marriage. For liberal-leaning people, Jesus becomes more of a moral example than also the Son of God. They prefer to speak of "values" rather than "truths," of perspectives rather than dogmas. Catholics might speak of the "people of God" more than the "body of Christ," and the Eucharist as a celebration more than as a sacrifice. This tendency is widespread in the Catholic academy.

On the other hand, I understand why people want to promote the more inclusive dimensions of Catholicism. Universities are not parishes; they welcome a much more diverse membership than a parish does. Nevertheless, the big "C" remains important. Without it, the small "c" will soon morph into Christian values, and if we are not careful, it will soon become a secular humanism, and eventually all that is truly distinctive of Catholicism will disappear. Catholic universities need to be not just generically Christian but also explicitly Catholic, with all that includes, such as a commitment to ecumenism, interreligious dialogue, and social justice. As I explained in chapter 6 on the *mandatum*, it is perfectly legitimate to question official church teachings. In fact, a Catholic may disagree with some noninfallible teachings for good reasons and remain a Catholic in good standing. Why not all noninfallible teachings? Because there are some infallibly true teachings that have never needed to be infallibly defined since they have always been acknowledged by believers—teachings such as "repent and believe in the Gospel," or the great commandment of love.

(The paradox is that a good argument can be made that Catholic universities will be even more inclusive if they affirm big "C" teachings. For example, universal human rights rest on the dogmatic foundation that every person, regardless of gender, race, or sexual orientation, is created in the divine image. A belief in the reality of things both visible and invisible gives faculty much more to think about than just what can be empirically verified. A sense of interconnectedness of all humanity animates Catholic social teaching and is lived out in the global membership of the Catholic Church.

That some nondogmatic teachings will be pushed by some Catholics as though they were dogmatic, and that some members of the hierarchy discourage critical thinking and worry that a legitimate diversity of views among Catholics borders on heresy—none of these exaggerations gives Catholic universities reason to de-emphasize what is authentically Catholic, or to play Catholicism's little "c" against its big "C."

Bridging Liberal and Professional Education

Ideally speaking, professional schools form a bridge between the liberal arts and the world of work. When the relationship works well, the liberal arts help students in professional schools learn to speak and write, while the professions teach students skills that prepare them to function well in the marketplace. In reality, however, some faculty in professional schools erect walls between them- selves and their colleagues in the arts and sciences, while some faculty in the arts and sciences see faculty in the professional schools not as scholars but as trainers. Faculty in the liberal arts dislike how their professional colleagues welcome their accrediting agencies that advocate for them, setting curricular requirements, the number of courses a professor is to teach, and the salary they should be given. What outside agency advocates for the liberal arts? While this division between liberal and professional faculty may be overdrawn, there is some truth to it. Bridges between these two groups can be built when faculty in the humanities find ways to articulate the mission in language that makes sense to faculty in the professions. Faculty in professional schools need to show faculty in the humani- ties, especially theologians and philosophers, the special relevance that Catholic social teachings have for professional education. Interdisciplinary conversations on the Catholic intellectual tradition has much to offer both the humanities and professional education and builds a common language that can be used by fac- ulty in both divisions.

With the leadership of the provosts, the deans, and several faculty, especially those occupying endowed chairs at the University of Dayton, the institutional- ization of the unique Catholic mission of the university has continued and ex- panded. Bridges are being built between the liberal arts and the professional schools. Faculty and administrators who supported these initiatives also helped shape a 2006 university-wide conversation that resulted in the *Habits of Inquiry and Reflection: A Report on Education in the Catholic and Marianist Traditions at the University of Dayton.*[12] *Habits of Inquiry and Reflection* outlined a set of learning outcomes that have been used to design requirements for all under- graduate students called the Common Academic Program (CAP).[13] The CAP was launched in the fall of 2013. Endowed chairs in the humanities and in social justice have continued to foster interdisciplinary conversations to bridge liberal and professional education in Dayton's School of Business and to incorporate the Catholic intellectual and social tradition in its undergraduate curriculum. These conversations have resulted in a comprehensive set of recommendations to the provost and the deans of the College of Arts and Sciences and the School of Business Administration. The design and implementation of the CAP courses have helped the university leadership become even more aware of the extent to which the institutionalization of the Catholic vision of higher education needs constantly to be expanded and engage even more faculty.

Conclusion

I have briefly described several challenges to institutionalizing the mission: understanding the Catholic mission intellectually, finding ways to balance mission and diversity in hiring practices, addressing directly the misconception that Catholicism is anti-intellectual, and building bridges between faculty in the humanities and the professions. These challenges are formidable. But they can be met by a more deliberate process for hiring faculty, by creative approaches to faculty research and curricular designs, and by establishing degree programs that are rooted in Catholic social teaching. This work is never done. And what has been done at the University of Dayton needs constant improvement. But the programs, workshops, interdisciplinary conversations, and mission-centered intellectual initiatives have helped form a faculty that embraces a distinctive Catholic intellectual tradition.

10
Teaching and Research

Introduction

Before finishing my doctorate in medieval history, I led retreats for high school students for two years and taught high school for three. I also wrote a few articles during that time, mainly about the youth work that I was doing. I found that it took me a good bit of time to write an article, even for the local newspaper or a Catholic magazine. Once I began teaching at the University of Dayton, the task of writing changed—not only because, like my dissertation, it required extensive research and footnotes, but also because of the demands of teaching and preparing classes. As a recently ordained priest, I also found myself called upon to engage in quite a few pastoral duties. I had a hard time finding a balance with all these new responsibilities.

Gradually, over a period of several years, I learned gradually how to handle these simultaneous involvements, but did not realize then the extent to which that balance was influenced by being at a Catholic university. In retrospect, the emphasis on the integration of knowledge, on a close relationship with students, most of whom were residential, began to align. And gradually, the ways in which faith and reason became more than a slogan helped me bring different responsibilities into a more productive balance.

In this chapter, I want to focus on finding a balance among several responsibilities, in particular between teaching and research, and how at a Catholic university these activities weave together. Since teaching and research take many forms and can be done in different ways, I will look at what some scholars and academic leaders have said about them. I believe that faculty at Catholic universities have some advantages in finding the needed balance in their professional lives. I begin, however, with a description of some of the ways the general public misunderstands the work of professors.

Popular Misunderstandings

Let me begin with a question that young faculty often ask: Is it realistic to give equal attention to both teaching and research? Isn't it often rather a matter of teaching versus research—if I concentrate on doing the best possible job in the

The Future of Catholic Higher Education. James L. Heft, S.M., Oxford University Press. © Oxford University Press 2021.
DOI: 10.1093/oso/9780197568880.003.0011

classroom, then I have to cut back on the time I devote to research? How do I find the balance?

The general public, and some politicians in particular, do not hesitate to say what they think the balance should be. It should be no problem at all. Just teach! One typical misunderstanding appeared in an article in *The Chronicle of Higher Education*, which reported that "governors, legislators, and state auditors across the country are moving to determine how much time faculty members spend working with undergraduate students."[1] Though almost never having been teachers themselves, lawmakers in several states, the article reports, presume to lay out expectations, even draft laws, governing the time that professors should give to teaching and research. Another *Chronicle* article in that same issue described how one state initiated a year-long project "to identify what state and institutional policies could best make teaching—rather than scholarship—more central to academic life."[2] As one old priest friend of mine commented when he read the same article, "Those lawmakers seem to have forgotten that teaching without research is like going to confession without having sinned: you really don't have anything interesting to say!" Lawmakers such as those quoted in the article skipped research but didn't hesitate to legislate formal load policies (the number of students in a class and the number of classes) and annual performance plans. They even wanted to mete out punishments for faculty whose teaching they deemed subpar.

Books by authors who criticize the failures of higher education have incited distrust in the public and emboldened lawmakers to intervene. For example, Charles Sykes argues in *Profscam* (the title certainly waves a red flag) that universities ignore teaching responsibilities and promote the production of arcane and trivial research. He concludes that there is little good teaching because universities fail to reward it.[3] Targeting elite universities, William Deresiewicz criticizes how students become robots, are not taught to think and write, and are subjected to curricula that do not help them understand how to live a meaningful life.[4] With such sweeping indictments from some in both the political and academic worlds, it is not surprising that the general public lacks a grasp of what the real issues are. Indeed, even in the pages of the *Chronicle*, the proposed solutions sometimes pit teaching against research. One gets the impression that for many outside the academy and even some within it, the only real responsibility for the professor is teaching. Henry Rosovsky, for many years the dean of the Faculty of Arts and Sciences at Harvard University, tells the story of a professor who testified before a state committee in Sacramento, California. The chair of the committee asked the professor: "How many hours do you spend teaching, doctor?" "Eight hours," the professor replied. The chair replied, "That is excellent. I have always been a strong supporter of the eight-hour day."[5]

Even inside the academy, some faculty view the relationship between teaching and research as a zero-sum game, where "more of one means less of the other, or better research leads to worse teaching."[6] Even faculty at some liberal arts colleges where research is not strongly emphasized still express the view that the time they devote to teaching is taken away from research. Rosovsky admits that this perception exists even at Harvard, because of the "behavior of a few university professors [who confirm] the negative stereotypes: casually prepared lectures, office hours skipped, students snubbed, all in the name of some great god called research." This can even happen, he continues, "without the excuse of research. . . . Temptations in the forms of leaves, consulting contracts, conference invitations, and similar activities are greater."[7] I guess "stars" can act like that!

If there are serious problems at research and state universities, and even at liberal arts colleges, is the situation any different at Catholic universities?

Refining the Argument: Comprehensive Universities

Whatever the public may think about the proper relationship between teaching and research, and whatever stereotypes the misbehavior of some professors may generate, I believe that Catholic universities can and should stress both good teaching and quality research, even though the amount of time faculty may give to each may vary from time to time and depend on the types of courses (undergraduate and graduate) they teach.

An extensive study, "Colleges That Emphasize Research and Teaching: Can You Have Your Cake and Eat It Too?," found that very few institutions do both well.[8] Institutions that emphasize teaching and giving real attention to students do not rate high on research, and those that emphasize research rate low on teaching. The only exception seems to be selective liberal arts colleges that maintain a significant emphasis on both.

The authors of the "Cake" study argue that faculty at almost any institution, if they choose, "can interact more with undergraduates, involve more undergraduates in their research, teach more interdisciplinary courses, or give more written evaluations of their undergraduates' work." What really makes this possible, the authors conclude, are "institutional will, policy and tradition."

Most Catholic universities in the United States are neither research universities nor liberal arts colleges. As we continue through this chapter, it is important to keep in mind that Catholic universities not only tend to be smaller than most secular universities and give priority to undergraduate education but also have the advantage of a distinctive intellectual tradition. We will return to these important advantages and how they affect teaching and research.

Two Arguments for Both Teaching and Research?

Let us now take a closer look at ways that some academic leaders look at the relationship between teaching and research. What constitutes good teaching? What constitutes good research—research that includes different fields of knowledge and is rigorous enough to be acknowledged by academic peers? More specifically, what can be done to support faculty at Catholic universities to become good teachers and competent researchers? Let us consider first what some prominent academicians have argued about both teaching and research being important.

In 1927, the great mathematician and philosopher Alfred North Whitehead addressed the topic of teaching and research in a speech given to the American Association of the Collegiate Schools of Business, arguing that both were possible and both necessary. He describes how the interaction between a teacher who does research and eager students creates the best pedagogical environment for learning. Whitehead puts great emphasis on teachers being imaginative:

> Do you want your teachers to be imaginative? Then encourage them to do re-search. Do you want your researchers to be imaginative? Then bring them into intellectual sympathy with the young at the most eager, imaginative period of life, when intellects are just entering upon their mature discipline. Make your researchers explain themselves to active minds, plastic and with the world be-fore them; make your young students crown their period of intellectual ac-quisition by some contact with minds gifted with experience of intellectual adventure. Education is discipline for the adventure of life; research is intel-lectual adventure; and the universities should be homes of adventure shared in common by young and old.[9]

Not all students, of course, are models of eagerness for learning, whose open minds readily absorb everything their teachers say. And, for that matter, not all students meet teachers who exude intellectual adventure. Nevertheless, Whitehead stresses, rightly it seems to me, that meaningful research enlivens dedicated faculty, particularly when they share it imaginatively with their students.

In an address given at the annual meeting of the American Association of Colleges, Leon Botstein, the president of Bard College, unequivocally states that any professor not involved in research should not darken the classroom:

> No one not engaged in his or her field or areas of interest should be teaching on any level in a university. Minimally, faculty members must make

active contact regarding their interests with some community of peers—not students—outside the boundaries of the institution in which they work. This criterion, valid for all colleges and universities, constitutes the fundamental difference between high school and college teaching. It has nothing to do with the notion of "public or perish"; rather, it reflects an essential dimension of university teaching: the love of subject and sustained inquiry. If one is not engaged in research, if one does not do what one asks students to do—collect and interpret data, experiment, and write or perform—as a matter of pride and affectionate interest, then one should not teach in programs of liberal learning, either in general education or in a specialized field. Assigning papers is ethically suspect if the faculty member also does not grapple with the act of writing and being reviewed critically by others.[10]

Though Botstein makes a trenchant case for research, he does not explain more concretely how the relationship between research and teaching works. How, for example, does a professor sustain a research agenda in her specialty while she teaches only introductory or general education courses? How should a professor go about communicating effectively to his sophomore students, most of whom are not majoring in his discipline, the most recent relevant scholarship that pertains to the subject he is required to teach? The answers to such questions are most likely ideographic and difficult to address if one stays at the level at which Whitehead and Botstein speak. While teaching and research are both essential, how do they mutually enrich each other given the great diversity of subjects taught at a university and the very different personalities of faculty, even faculty in the same academic department? So what does good teaching look like?

What Constitutes Good Teaching?

Is it possible to standardize good teaching? Professional journals suggest many ways to evaluate teaching, but few measure its effectiveness for student learning. The ratings that students give to teachers have some reliability, but the act of teaching itself is sufficiently personal that no widely accepted generalizations exist about what constitutes good teaching. Rosovsky warns that students' evaluations have inherent limitations:

> Students can tell us whether or not they like a teacher, whether or not the material in the course is interesting, whether or not the lectures are clear, stimulating and perhaps amusing. To some degree, these are measures of popularity and may have little to do with the essence of teaching: to cause someone to understand a subject.[11]

Peer evaluations can compensate for the limitations of student evaluations. Those who defend peer review insist that teaching should be subject to the same rigorous evaluation that a scholar's published works receive. In their view, peer evaluation is the best way to do this. Whether a teacher is tenured or not also affects evaluation. For the untenured, Rosovsky continues, peer review can "lead to a command performance that bears little relation to what happens in the classroom on a daily basis. Unannounced visits, in many places, are viewed as breeches of etiquette."[12] We are faced, then, with a difficult challenge: how best to evaluate teaching.

One way to understand what good teachers look like in action is to read what authors have written about teachers that have made a difference in their lives. Consider the following four descriptions of good teaching. At the age of sixteen, C. S. Lewis met his most influential teacher, William T. Kirkpatrick. Lewis loved how Kirkpatrick challenged his already acute logical mind. Good ole' Kirk, as Lewis liked to call him, believed that students were to use language for one purpose only: to communicate and discover truth. "The most casual remark," Lewis recalled, "was taken as a summons to disputation." To a "torrent of verbiage," Kirkpatrick would yell, "Stop!" He did this not from impatience, but because it was leading nowhere. More sensible observations, Lewis explained, might be interrupted by "Excuse!" ushering in some parenthetical comment. Full approval would be encouraged by the acknowledgment "I hear you"—but usually followed by a refutation: "Had I read this? Had I studied that? Had I any statistical data? And so to the almost inevitable conclusion: do you not see then that you had no right." Unlike most students today, Lewis thrived on such sharp dialectics and withering cross-examinations. They were for him the red meat and dark beer of learning.[13]

But as we have already seen, for Alfred North Whitehead, it was not logic, but imagination that characterized great teaching. He believed that since the invention of the printing press, universities had no justification for existence unless they preserved "the connection between knowledge and the zest of life, by uniting the young and the old in the imaginative consideration of learning."[14]

Rather than focus on logic or imagination, the Jewish philosopher Martin Buber identified the capacity for "dialogue" as the most important skill of the great teacher:

Teaching itself does not educate; it is the teacher that educates. A good teacher educates when silent as well as when speaking, during recess, during an occasional conversation, and through his own behavior, provided he really exists and is really present. He is an educator by touch. [Education] is based upon the encouragement of contact between teacher and students—upon the principle of dialogue; dialogue of questions from both sides, and answers from both sides, dialogue of joint observation of a certain reality in nature, or in art, or in society, dialogue of joint penetration into one of the problems of life, dialogue of true fellowship, in which the breaks in conversation are no less of a dialogue than speech itself.[15]

Buber believes that the practice of dialogue requires full attention, real presence, and sharing moments of speech and silence. He does not reduce good teaching to a skill or technique; it is the capacity for encounter or a personal relationship between the student and the teacher. As we have seen in an earlier chapter, John Henry Newman's commitment to the moral formation of students, both intellectually and personally, or what we might call the education of the "whole person," is what he believed education at its most profound was about: *Cor ad cor loquitur*, when heart speaks to heart, Newman's motto and his description of education as transformation.

Besides logic, imagination, and dialogue, consider still another description of effective teaching. A. Bartlett Giamatti, when he was president of Yale University, compared good teaching to the art of acting: "Teaching is an instinctual art, mindful of potential, craving of realizations, a pausing, seamless process, where one rehearses constantly while acting." In Giamatti's description, good teachers are always on alert, picking up signals from their audience. I can identify with this description. I performed in theater for twenty years and have found that experience useful in the classroom as well as in the pulpit. Of course, I am not thinking of acting as making something up. Rather, a background in acting increases one's ability to communicate in ways that enliven the audience. The skilled actor, Giamatti explains, "sits as a spectator at a play one directs, engages every part in order to keep the choices open and the shape alive for the student, so that the student may enter in, and begin to do what the teacher has done: make choices."[16]

What, then, best describes effective teaching? Is it Lewis's rigorous logic, Whitehead's imaginative exchange between teachers and students, Buber's dialogue, or Giamatti's art of acting? Of course, these approaches are not mutually exclusive, nor can they be used the same way in teaching every subject. Some teachers are introverts, others extroverts. What makes teaching even more complex is that students also have different learning styles. It is difficult, I believe, to identify a single way of teaching as the best, despite the attempts by accrediting agencies to quantify learning objectives and list pedagogical outcomes. Good teaching is simply not quantifiable or its impact predictable. However, at least this much can be said: good teachers know and love their subject matter, relate well (if not necessarily affectionately) to their students, and are organized in their presentations and fair in grading.

What Constitutes Good Research?

At research universities faculty are expected to publish their research in prestigious (peer-reviewed) journals and their books in top university presses. That is their most important responsibility. Not surprisingly, Harvard's Rosovsky defends this practice. He argues that it protects against professional burnout and gives a more secure protection than the "Mr. Chip's solution," that is, the excitement one feels each year standing before a new generation of students. Good faculty don't just read a bunch of books without producing one themselves: "a research-oriented faculty is less likely to be the home of intellectual deadwood. Active, lively, thoroughly current minds that enjoy debate and controversy make better teachers," he believes.[17] He claims that these professors are best positioned to generate the most intellectual excitement and learning in students. The work of great researchers is public in ways that teaching is not. Published research can be tested by peers. Rosovsky represents the consensus of most research universities: the most valuable scholarly record—indeed, really the only one—is the published one.

Rosovsky speaks for research universities. There are many different types of universities in the United States, and a more capacious view of what faculty in diverse institutions should do is needed. Fifty years after Alfred North Whitehead lauded the role of imagination in teaching, Ernest Boyer wrote in a widely acclaimed book, *College*, that "scholarship is not an esoteric appendage; it is at the heart of what the profession is all about."[18] Like other authors we have already cited, Boyer believes that all scholars need to remain students throughout their careers. If the phrase "lifelong learner" does not characterize every teacher, their students will be short-changed. But unlike Rosovsky, Boyer championed a more comprehensive description of scholarship and a more inclusive understanding of the types of activity that give evidence of it. He recommended thinking of scholarship in four ways: discovery, integration, application, and teaching. We develop knowledge, he explained, in at least four ways: research, synthesis, practice, and teaching. Boyer and others[19] base their argument for a more inclusive understanding of scholarship that takes into consideration the different talents of professors and the diversity of the disciplines in which they work.

For example, the type of scholarship that scientists do is unlike the scholarship of humanists. Scientists typically search for new knowledge, while humanists pass on and interpret afresh received knowledge that has stood the test of time. J. R. R. Tolkien, the author of *The Hobbit* and *The Lord of the Rings* and professor of philology at Oxford for many years, wrote to his grandson in 1966 explaining that he had always been "skeptical about 'research' of any kind as part of the occupation or training of younger people in the language-literature schools." In Tolkien's opinion, humanists who were then increasingly emphasizing research as creating new knowledge were desiring "to climb on the great band-wagon of Science (or at least onto a little trailer in tow)." As far as he was concerned, humanists, in contrast to scientists, had "such a lot to learn first."[20]

Jacob Neusner, also a humanist and an internationally known scholar of Judaism, and coauthor Noam Neusner make the same point more forcefully than Tolkien: "The creation of new knowledge is less important than the recapitulation of received knowledge. Most professors most of the time in most universities know little about what it means to create new knowledge." The Neusners cite studies that revealed that nearly two-thirds of professors have published almost nothing, and those who publish books usually publish only one, a version of their doctoral dissertation. The reality, they conclude, is that most university professors do not do what they are expected to do. They argue, therefore, that the expectations of professors need to be altered radically so that what most professors really want to do, and often do well, is properly valued and evaluated: "Most professors should teach more than they now do; but they should study more than they now do in order to teach what they themselves have made their own."[21]

Expanding on more forms of research, other authors have urged that greater attention be given to more than only published forms of scholarship, for example, the casebook studies that law professors create, the construction of syllabi, and unpublished lectures. The arts present special challenges, in that many faculty do not have any idea how to evaluate a musical performance and works of art. Nor, according to Boyer, should highly regarded textbooks be dismissed out of hand. The time that individuals and faculty committees put into creating new syllabi, new courses, clusters of courses, and designs for general education programs can be a reliable indicator of intellectual depth and productivity. And what about innovations in engineering projects and the writing of research grants? Or creative writing, novels, writing plays, and producing them? The wide variety of these activities and the criteria to evaluate such diverse forms of scholarship elude most faculty at most universities. Even faculty from different parts of the university who serve on a university-wide promotions and tenure committee struggle to evaluate the great diversity of scholarship of their peers. It is much easier to count the number of publications and how often they have been cited. But that alone is unlikely to indicate the quality of the scholarship.

Balance and the Catholic Intellectual Tradition

Granting that there are significant differences between the types of research done in the sciences and the humanities, and in the professions and the arts, how can Catholic universities address ways to balance teaching and research? An essential claim that Catholic universities make, and at least should make, is their commitment to the integration of knowledge and the ever-present intimate relationship that faith and reason are expected to have for the university community.

Although the difficulty of integration of knowledge should not be underestimated, Catholic universities have as a part of their very mission a commitment to work at the integration of knowledge. Again, Catholic universities are typically smaller than most secular universities.[22] Those that are smaller (e.g., 90% enroll fewer than ten thousand students) have smaller departments. Smaller departments require faculty to teach a wider range of subjects within their disciplines. Because of this, most faculty in smaller universities don't become hyperspecialized and are more comfortable with covering several areas within their discipline. They do not find interdisciplinary collaboration as difficult as specialists often do. Specialization plays an important role in large research universities. But Catholic universities, due to their typically smaller size, create a more hospitable environment for the integration of knowledge.

One creative example of integrating knowledge is featured in a recent *University of Dayton Magazine*. Glenna Jennings, an acclaimed associate professor in the Department of Art and Design, writes about the way in which the university makes it possible for her to move around the strict guidelines drawn for academic disciplines:

> While most artists can't claim to be social scientists, we are often effective instigators. I love and rely on academia, but I don't do so well with rules. I battle with the role and category of photographer as often as I grapple with disciplinary silos. I am not a photojournalist, nor am I a traditional documentary photographer.[23]

Jennings explains that at Dayton she can work beyond a single discipline, making it possible to be both an "artist and an advocate for social change." But that is not all. She has also found there a group of other faculty from other disciplines as well as others in the local community who have become for her "doers and thinkers that I love and admire." I am sure that many other Catholic colleges and universities could give examples of similar forms of integration made possible by the size and mission of their university.

Before Vatican II, Catholic colleges and universities integrated knowledge quite successfully in one important part of the curriculum. They did this through a large number of required theology and especially philosophy courses, all built upon the thought of St. Thomas Aquinas (1225–1274). Today, these requirements have been reduced to one or two courses. In the opinion of historian James Turner, Catholic education "has pretty well given up on any serious attempt to demonstrate and exemplify the unity of knowledge."[24] Turner criticizes this lack of will on the part of faculty. Not only should faculty at Catholic universities not give up on integrating knowledge, but also they should draw upon the distinctive intellectual resources of Catholicism. Turner realizes that to integrate knowledge in a serious way requires that faculty work out of a common intellectual tradition: "For only within an ongoing framework of shared questions and axioms, rooted in shared texts, can inquirers find common ground even for coherent disagreement, much less mutual engagement."[25] Not every professor in a Catholic university needs to be fluent in that tradition, but there needs to be a significant number of professors, those to whom I refer as the circle part of the open circle, to engage others on the faculty from within that tradition. Otherwise, the burden falls upon theologians and philosophers to bring everything together, an impossible task for them unless faculty in other disciplines share the commitment to integrate knowledge.

In a previous chapter I described the positive outcomes of interdisciplinary seminars for faculty at the University of Dayton. Efforts on secular campuses often emphasize the importance of interdisciplinary study and teaching. It takes time for professors to stop teaching their peers and instead start learning from them. That is a breakthrough moment. What is even more impressive, however, is when faculty together try to understand what none of them knows much about. When scholars persevere in their efforts to understand how the Catholic intellectual tradition can enrich their research and teaching, their arrival at new ways of imagining the integration of knowledge is rewarded.

Also, consider that foundational principle of Catholicism—that faith and reason should guide the work of faculty in a Catholic university. Let's assume again that the circle is open and that not all the faculty are Catholics. Affirming that faith and reason enrich each other means that it should not be assumed that people who are religious are, by that fact alone, anti-intellectual, any more than it means that very bright people are likely to be atheists. Critical thinking and convictions of faith can benefit each other. What the faith and reason combination opposes are fideism and rationalism, the former being blind faith and the latter being that the rational alone is real. Catholics distinguish among rationalism, irrationalism, and trans-rationalism. To be irrational violates reason. To be trans-rational respects reason but realizes that there is more to reality than simply the rational. To be rational is to acknowledge the existence of the trans-rational. These distinctions open up more ways to understand reality and offer more ways to imagine how knowledge might be integrated.

Affirming the complementarity of faith and reason makes conversations between scientists and theologians fruitful. Catholicism respects the work of an evolutionary biologist as long as the scientist is not a rationalist. Catholicism affirms theories of evolution that are not reductionist—and thus important interdisciplinary conversations are possible. Catholicism teaches the dignity of every person created in God's image. This opens the way for a finance professor at a Catholic university to ask her students about the impact of economic theory on the poor, because the poor are as important as they are. A neuroscience professor who accepts Christian anthropology is not likely to equate the human mind with the human brain.[26] The arts—visual, paint and sculpture, music and drama—are very important in Catholicism. Faculty in these disciplines can put together courses on aesthetics rooted in the theological principle of sacramentality, so central to the Catholic intellectual tradition. It is tragic when they are put on the budgetary chopping blocks in times of financial stress.

When most of the students at Catholic universities are residential, there is also a greater opportunity to form "the whole person." Depending on how students live—in residence halls on campus or in apartments near campus—the possibility of faculty interacting with them beyond the classroom is greater. The interaction between students and faculty and other adult mentors (campus ministers or student development personnel) is also greater than at large nonresidential universities. Faculty at Catholic universities should foster the opportunities for dialogue between students and teachers recommended by Martin Buber. At some of our universities, faculty live in residence halls. John Henry Newman located the moral formation of students in the interaction between students and their tutors who lived with them in colleges. These types of interaction already take place at a number of Catholic universities. The connection between learning and friendship, and trust and insight, plays out more often in such settings than in large lecture halls at universities where students don't live.

Conclusion

The relationship between teaching and research at Catholic universities draws upon rich educational presuppositions: that faith and reason are complementary, that interdisciplinary teaching enriches both faculty and students, and that the education of the whole person—body, intellect, and soul—is important. Some teachers will excel in their imaginative pedagogy, others in their critical reasoning, and still others in their sheer enthusiasm for their subject. Although scientists and humanists approach research differently, they will learn to appreciate what each other does and work to integrate what they know. Catholic universities offer unique opportunities for exploring the relationship between teaching and research. They have an advantage over large secular universities in imparting not just information but also, more importantly, a formation in how to integrate knowledge and live meaningful lives.

Learning as a young faculty member at a Catholic university how to balance various responsibilities, integrate knowledge, and make a real difference in the lives of students was, I believe, more possible for me than it would have been had I started out my academic career at a large secular university. At a Catholic university that draws deeply on its distinctive intellectual tradition, beginning teachers should be able to find an institutional setting that helps them not only balance teaching and research but also seek wisdom and form a truly distinctive learning community.

11

Humility and Courage

Introduction

In 1996, Charles Taylor, a world-famous Catholic philosopher, gave an extraordinary lecture at the University of Dayton. Because I believed that what he said needed to be heard by more people than those who were able to hear it, I decided to find a way to publish it. With his agreement, I invited four scholars, two Catholics and two Protestants, to comment on the lecture. Taylor then wrote a response to their critiques. His lecture and their conversation were published in 1999 as a book, *A Catholic Modernity?*[1]

Being Fair: An Even-Handed Analysis of Modernity

The main ideas of Taylor's lecture can be summarized as follows. On the one hand, modernity has brought us good things, such as the defense of human rights, the affirmation of ordinary life, a deeper sense of philanthropy (by which Taylor means, literally, the love of other people, especially those suffering from poverty and disease), an emphasis on individual freedom, a great capacity for inwardness, and an ethic of authenticity. Many of these good things, Taylor believes, would not have come about had not Christendom—that is, the coercive arm of the state acting in support of the church—collapsed in Europe after the Reformation.

> The notion is that modern culture, in breaking with the structures and beliefs of Christendom, also carried certain facets of Christian life further than they ever were taken or could have been taken within Christendom. In relation to the earlier forms of Christian culture, we have to face the humbling realization that the breakout was a necessary condition of the development.[2]

On the other hand, modernity has also brought with it some bad things, such as a suffocating secular humanism (which he calls "exclusive humanism," since it excludes the transcendent dimension), an individualism that fragments any strong sense of community, and an inability to articulate fundamental goods that would enable us to live moral lives. According to William Shea, one of Taylor's

The Future of Catholic Higher Education. James L. Heft, S.M., Oxford University Press. © Oxford University Press 2021. DOI: 10.1093/oso/9780197568880.003.0012

interlocutors, Taylor allows Catholics to engage modernity constructively, seeing both its positive and negative dimensions.

Finally, Taylor makes it clear that he is not interested in promoting a "modern Catholicism," which "sees itself as having freed itself from the crudities of the past and as having, at last, got it right," any more than he is interested in a "Catholic modernism," which embraces the central tenets of the Enlightenment and loses the transcendent dimensions of life. Rather, what he proposes is a "Catholic modernity," one in which Catholics participate fully in modern Western culture and do so in a way that's appreciative of its achievements but still critical of its shortcomings. Thus, for Taylor, modern humanism is not open enough to sustain people in the difficult task of discernment. In the end, he affirms the importance of Christian spirituality, which he grounds on unconditional love, that is, love not based on what an individual has made of him- or herself, but rather on what one most profoundly is: a being made in the image and likeness of God. He explains: "Our being in the image of God is also our standing among others in the stream of love, which is that facet of God's life we try to grasp, very inadequately, in speaking of the Trinity."[3]

I believe Taylor's lecture is significant for at least two reasons. First, he has accepted the starting point of modernity, the importance of the experience of the individual person, without embracing individualism or subjectivism—no small achievement. Several times Taylor emphasizes the importance of being in community as a necessary condition to be oneself. Just as importantly, he describes the search within oneself—what in his 1989 *Sources of the Self* he calls "inwardness"—a search that must open outward. The type of inwardness that Taylor proposes remains "open to what is beyond, if not discontinuous with, the self."[4]

Second, his appraisal of modernity flows from his sense of what it means to be Catholic. He is able to affirm a number of developments in modern Western culture as very important but still only partial achievements—developments such as an insistence on human rights, the desire for authenticity, and the affirmation of ordinary life. Before Vatican II, official statements of the church about society were largely negative. But even with the more positive approach to society found in the documents of Vatican II, Taylor is not fully at ease with the modern age. Our society today, he writes, lacks a sense of the transcendent; it needs to be opened up. A Christian vision of life does precisely that, as does the vision of a Catholic university as an "open circle." Taylor's diagnosis of our secular age is, in my opinion, nuanced, critical, and gracious.

In Taylor we find the reflections of a mature scholar whose previous philosophical works have explored at much greater length his analysis of modernity in the West. In his *Sources of the Self*, he explores the historical, philosophical, cultural, and artistic streams that come together to form Western modernity. In the last chapter of that major work, he makes explicit his theism and asks whether a naturalism that ignores spirituality can provide us with the vision and hope we need:

> Is the naturalist affirmation conditional on a vision of human nature in the fullness of its health and strength? Does it move us to extend help to the irremediably broken, such as the mentally handicapped, those dying without dignity, fetuses with genetic defects? Perhaps one might judge that it doesn't and that this is a point in favour of naturalism; perhaps effort shouldn't be wasted on these unpromising cases. But the careers of Mother Teresa or Jean Vanier seem to point to a different pattern, emerging from a Christian spirituality.[5]

Without a religious dimension or radical hope in history, the naturalist, concludes Taylor, performs a "spiritual lobotomy" on our age. In *Sources* Taylor is trying to "bring air back into the half-collapsed lungs of the spirit."[6] In doing so, Taylor makes a major contribution to modern philosophy. Richard Rorty, who regularly disagrees with Taylor, nonetheless numbers him "among the dozen most important philosophers writing today, anywhere in the world."[7]

The Virtue of Intellectual Humility

Anyone who reads the much shorter book *A Catholic Modernity?* will be struck by the way Taylor interacts with his commentators. It is his method of sympathetic retrieval and open conversation with the reader that offers a valuable example of how scholars ought to discuss serious and complex issues. He has a knack for finding a middle ground between extremes, a point of tension that goes beyond making compromises with each extreme. In his book on authenticity, for example, Taylor sees both good and bad in the three trends of modernity that he identifies: authenticity, individualism, and instrumental reason. He shows how each has both destructive and creative possibilities. Obviously, he doesn't side with those who simply reject or affirm modern culture. And he does this analysis in the spirit of dialogue exemplified in the following paragraphs:

> What I am suggesting is a position distinct from both boosters and knockers of contemporary culture. Unlike the boosters, I do not believe that everything is as it should be in this culture. Here I tend to agree with the knockers. But unlike them, I think that authenticity should be taken seriously as a moral ideal. I differ also from the various middle positions, which hold that there are some good things in this culture (like greater freedom for the individual), but that these come at the expense of certain dangers (like a weakening of the sense of

citizenship), so that one's best policy is to find the ideal point of trade-off between advantages and costs.

The picture that I am offering is rather that of an ideal that has been degraded but that is very worthwhile in itself, and indeed, I would like to say, unrepudiable by moderns. So, what we need is neither root-and-branch condemnations nor uncritical praise; and not a carefully balanced trade-off. What we need is a work of retrieval, through which this ideal can help us restore our practice.

To go along with this, you have to believe three things, all controversial: (1) that authenticity is a valid idea; (2) that you can argue in reason about ideals and about the conformity of practices to these ideals; and (3) that these arguments can make a difference.[8]

Taylor's manner of reasoning and conversing with the reader exemplifies an unusual degree of openness. For example, at one point in his Catholic modernity lecture, after reviewing the positions of secular humanists, neo-Nietzscheans, and those who recognize transcendence, he states that "no position can be set aside as simply devoid of insight."[9] At the end of his lecture, he calls his readers to a "difficult discernment"—that of distinguishing in modern culture what furthers the gospel and what closes off the transcendent. He speaks of the danger that "we will not be sufficiently bewildered, that we think we have it all figured out from the start and know what to affirm and what to deny." Despite continuing bewilderment, he encourages us to find our voice from within the achievements of modernity, "measure the humbling degree to which some of the most impressive extensions of a gospel ethic depended on a breakaway from Christendom, and from within these gains try to make clearer to ourselves and others the tremendous dangers that arise in them."[10]

Three of the four discussants who responded to Taylor's Marianist lecture compliment him on his capacity for careful sympathetic retrieval. William Shea applauds Taylor's ability to enter a conversation without taking it over and believes Taylor's way of speaking about human dignity, religion, and freedom creates a mediating path: "neither surrender nor rejection, neither 'booster' nor 'knocker,' but participant, voice, critical engager, respecter of the rights of each person and each religious tradition, and one who admits (sometimes cautiously) that there is truth to be found in them."[11] George Marsden admires Taylor's "balance," which synthesizes "the best achievements of modernity with authentically Christian traditions."[12] Jean Bethke Elsthain notices Taylor's "principle of charitable interpretation" and how he models what he calls for: "charity and clarity in interpretation, a recognition of a human fellowship that honors particular cultures and countries but urges us to cross borders as peaceful pilgrims, the possibility of authentic dialogue by contrast to the clamor of those who demand that we interrogate the past relentlessly."[13]

As formidable a philosopher as he is, Taylor remains open to, even welcomes, criticism. Rosemary Haughton, another respondent to Taylor, questions whether he was wise in his lecture to use the word "transcendence" to describe what must be rediscovered today. She thinks the word suggests ideas that should be avoided, not least of which is the individualistic dualism that allows spirituality to escape the messiness of material existence and interdependence. Taylor takes her point, admitting that her criticism reawakened in him a sense of doubt and uncertainty:

> [She] has captured it so clearly: the words just aren't adequate for what has to be said. You struggle, then put down one term, then erase it impatiently, and try another, and another. And then sometimes you end up using the first one, re-inscribing it with a sense of defeat on the grounds that it's not as catastrophically misleading as its rivals.
>
> Reading her, I feel this again about "transcendent." How could I ever have used such an abstract and evasive term, one so redolent of the flat and content-free modes of spirituality we can get maneuvered into in the attempt to accommodate both modern reason and the promptings of the heart? I remember erasing it with particular gusto. Why ever did I reinstate it? What pressures led in the end to its grudging rehabilitation?[14]

Taylor then explains that he kept the word to open up breathing space against the suffocating secular humanism of today and to be inclusive enough to allow people other than Christians—for example, Buddhists—to enter the conversation. Still, he admits, that the word presents its own problems.

Numerous other examples of Taylor's humility could be given. I limit myself to just one more. In the introduction to Taylor's *Philosophy in an Age of Pluralism*, Isaiah Berlin admits how much he admires Taylor's work, even though he cannot believe, as Taylor does, that human beings and the universe have a basic purpose:

> Let me repeat that Charles Taylor is a noble, gifted and deeply interesting thinker, every one of whose works has stimulated and excited me, as it has many other readers. His unique position among social and political philosophers is due as much to his humanity as his empathy with differences of groups, individuals, societies and nations, which prevent him displaying any degree of dogmatism or narrow insistence on some cut and dried schema in which along salvation is believed to lie, which, whatever one may think of his central beliefs, cannot fail to broaden the outlook of anyone who reads his works or listens to his lectures or, indeed, talks to him.[15]

What is it, it might be asked, about Taylor's way of thinking that others so admire? I believe it is Taylor's gift for sympathetic but principled retrieval, his ability to see truth in a position that he does not fully accept. Taylor exemplifies an intellectual humility often missing in the writings of other academics. Too many academics are prone to be condescending, even "pretentious," a bad habit that Fr. Brian Daley laments has "always ranked among the worst vices of the academy."[16]

Another reason for humility is the realization that our knowledge of things is inescapably limited, but despite that not simply reducible to assertions totally shaped by one's gender, race, or class, as some forms of postmodernism claim.[17] If that were the case, our "knowledge" is nothing more than subjective impressions—distortions rather than disclosures. It its most radical forms, postmodernism leads to a sort of tribalism, "to a lack of genuine engagement and a hardening of the lines that divide human beings from one another, and finally to the argument that diversity is an end in itself rather than a means to a larger end that is connected to the pursuit of the truth of matters."[18] The alternative to relativism need not be a naïve objectivism, because all knowledge is to some degree perspectival. John Dunne, a Holy Cross priest at the University of Notre Dame, recommends that when we think about our relationships with others, we should seek understanding rather than certainty.

Admitting that we never grasp the truth fully does not make attaining something of the truth impossible. What is needed is a more humble approach and a more circumspect practice of science. In the words of folklorist Henry Glassie:

> Science is made better, not worse, by the disciplined incorporation of the scholar's subjective existence. Hidden, it perverts, exposed it can be controlled for. Science is improved, not lost, when scholars recognize understanding not predictability to be relevant for human study. If the oxymoron be not too thick-witted, modern social science begins when things are discovered to be finally unknowable. Unreplicatable procedures and unprovable theories can still be judged on coherence, elegance and usefulness. When scientists decide not to solve little puzzles but to front genuine problems, they can continue to approach and present their interests with rigor and clear minds.[19]

For all these reasons then—to enlarge the way we reason and broaden the scope of research, to suggest ways to go beyond the false epistemological alternatives of subjectivism or objectivism, to affirm the importance of exploring the religious dimensions of human experience and the reality of God—and to do all this with an awareness of the complexity of reality and subsequent need for intellectual humility make it clearer that the virtue of humility, especially for academics, allows us to discern the truth of things more reliably than if we presume to understand reality fully.

In a superb short book, *Exiles from Eden*, Mark Schwehn talks about how a scholar he admires is humble.[20] To illustrate the importance of intellectual charity, he cites with approval the way in which philosopher Jeffrey Stout, a non-theist, approaches the thinking of other authors, especially those with whom he disagrees. Stout explains that he was able to say more clearly what he wanted to say only by carefully reading and engaging other philosophers.[21] For example, in writing about Richard Rorty, Stout avoids criticizing Rorty's "pithy statements," which could easily be dismissed, and concentrates instead on Rorty's more discursive explanations. Stout explains: "I remain inclined toward a charitable reading of Rorty's writings on justice and truth. I therefore find it frustrating when Rorty relies excessively on pithy little formulae." Instead of cherry-picking Rorty's short phrases for criticism, Stout chooses the best formulations of an author's thought to criticize. Schwehn concludes that "Stout's charity is everywhere tempered by justice." That is to say, Stout "neither overlooks nor excuses culpable errors."[22]

Christians should not assume that intellectual humility and charity can be practiced only by theists. Whether Christian or not, academics can benefit by emulating the practices of scholars like Taylor and Stout. Catholic and other scholars who remain open to the transcendent and welcome scholars of other religions to their universities, create learning institutions that I have described in this book as "open circles." Additionally, scholars who participate in an intellectual tradition, such as Catholicism, that affirms the doctrine of analogy (that what we don't know of God is always more than what we know), that finds useful the *via negativa* (that it is better at times to say God is "not" than what one thinks God "is"), and that talks about God by resorting often to metaphors and parables (instead of presuming that one can adequately define God with only rational tools) have ample reason to practice intellectual humility.

The pathways to intellectual humility are many, if not often trod. St. Teresa of Avila wrote somewhere that the humility is simply the truth. But as a friend of mine, a veteran of Alcoholics Anonymous, likes to say: the truth will make you free, but first it will make you miserable. Less grim, Flannery O'Connor once quipped: the truth will make you free, but first it will make you odd. I know that for myself, and not a few of my friends, the speediest path to humility is the one on which you are humiliated. I am not sure how Charlies Taylor has acquired the virtue of humility, but I am grateful that he has.

The Virtue of Courage

Taylor's way of thinking models for scholars the benefits of practicing humility in the search for truth. Affirming that we can come to know something of the truth, but not all of it, requires not just humility; it also requires courage. Thinking in different ways often meets resistance. Scholars are likely to criticize people who think differently. Suggesting a middle way draws fire from both sides. In the midst of tense conversations, courage is needed to forge a fair and just way forward without veering to the left or the right. It is the form that all virtues take at their testing point, and the academy tests us at many points.

But when does being even-handed actually show a lack of courage? George Marsden worries that too many Christian scholars engage in self-censorship. Taking up a theme he has developed extensively elsewhere,[23] he explains how the secular academy requires that Christian scholars privatize their faith, thereby preventing their faith from having any effect on their scholarly work. The two domains, faith and learning, must be kept separate in the modern academy, especially when faith is understood as the fallback position of the unlearned. As much as Marsden admires Taylor, he chides him for engaging in self-censorship in his book *Sources*. Marsden thinks that *Sources* could have been "a considerably more *Christian* tour de force had he [Taylor] spelled out his position and argued for its superiority." In fact, Marsden recommends that the Catholic modernity lecture would have been an appropriate conclusion to *Sources*, making it a "more complete, well-rounded and effective book."[24] Marsden reminds Taylor that another major Catholic philosopher, Alasdair MacIntyre, has been explicit about being a Catholic and still is, despite that public confession of faith, a formidable and highly influential scholar. Marsden, an evangelical Christian, recommends that Taylor be more open and forthright about his Catholic faith.

How does Taylor respond to Marsden's criticism? He admits that he and others do more self-censoring than they should.[25] In our very secular universities, there are certain advantages, not very admirable ones to be sure, in not being explicit about one's religious faith, such as reputation, tenure, and promotion. But underneath such dissimulations, Taylor sees a "remarkable fact," one that I mention in the first chapter of this book: namely, that "academic culture in the Western world breathes an atmosphere of unbelief."[26] He explains that this fact is remarkable since this feature fairly describes the academic subculture rather than the larger society in which it exists. He adds that the deeply secular academic culture exists throughout the Western world. What is more, the absence of faith not only influences the answers we give but also even determines the questions we ask. Taylor illustrates this by describing the situation of a typical undergraduate who

> might have a strong faith or be looking for ways of clarifying it through courses
> in history, politics, philosophy or whatever. But in face of what is actually being
> discussed, it is often unclear how this relates to the student's agenda and even
> less clear how the things that are personally important could impinge on the

discussion that is going on. There just seems to be no relevant place to make the kind of remarks that this student would like to make.[27]

In effect, the academic agenda has been preshaped in such a way that fundamental moral issues are rarely addressed. Instead, we concentrate on ethics, continues Taylor, on questions of what we should do. But as important as those questions are, we need to concentrate even more on what it is good to be and what we should love—issues that he says just "fall off the agenda" of most modern moral philosophy. After all, it is not just a question of what is the right thing to do; it is also, he stresses, a question of whether people, once they recognize what the right thing is, can then actually bring themselves to do it. In view of this analysis, Taylor concludes that the fundamental obstacles to belief in Western modernity are "primarily moral and spiritual, rather than epistemic."[28] It is not so much a matter of getting the right answer, then, as it is of making worthwhile commitments and learning to love.

Taylor is painfully aware that such statements oversimplify reality and easily confuse people. Nevertheless, in the face of the exclusive humanism that strongly circulates through the secular academy, he recommends that the most important thing that Christian academics can do is to "open up the agenda," and indeed change it, so that issues related to Christian faith might contribute to shaping both questions and answers. At the core of the Christian faith are neither ideas nor philosophies, but the story of one person's life and death, commitment and sacrifice. Christianity's teachings are communicated more through parables, signs, and sacramental rites than proofs, theories, belief systems, or memorized doctrines. At the core of Christianity is another way of understanding truth, a way that the secular academy, populated by scholars practicing disciplines that are not open to the transcendent, finds difficult to grasp.

Part of our difficulty might be explained by Taylor's remark that we live in a "postrevolutionary climate." He explains that people who lead successful revolutions win great victories over the previous establishment: "a postrevolutionary climate is extremely sensitive to anything that smacks of the *ancien régime* and sees backsliding even in relatively innocent concessions to generalized human preferences."[29] Catholic higher education underwent a sort of revolution in the late 1960s and early 1970s with the adoption of lay boards of trustees, policies of academic freedom modeled on those of the American Association of University Professors, and practices of greater shared governance. Some Catholic colleges, threatened with the loss of government money on account of the Blaine Amendment, downplayed in court the religious mission of their institutions.[30]

These changes have been described both positively and negatively, and to be sure, both positive and negative things have happened. A lengthy book by

✓

✱

* Perhaps a return to christianity as community (present at baptisms, weddings, funerals) would fare better than propositions

James Burtchaell, CSC, *The Dying of the Light*, describes the history of American church-related colleges and universities, including three Catholic ones, as a general caving in to strong cultural forces of secularism.[31] Burtchaell makes some excellent points, arguing that the Christian academy should keep a living link to its faith tradition, strengthen the liberal arts, and avoid neutering theology by turning it into religious studies. However, his overall assessment strikes me as dour, and his tone sharp and often condescending. By contrast, mainly positives assessments may be found in Ursuline Sr. Alice Gallin's *Negotiating Identity*, which covers the recent history of Catholic colleges and universities, or in David O'Brien's *From the Heart of the American Church: Catholic Higher Education and American Culture*, which emphasizes the benefits that Catholic colleges and universities enjoy by being part of American higher education.[32]

Finding ways in a time of "culture wars" to foster the interaction of the Catholic tradition and modernity requires both skill and courage. At the end of his comments on Taylor's lecture on Catholicism and modernity, William Shea states that the mediation of Catholicism and culture that Taylor advocates should be carried on in a special way in Catholic colleges and universities. The roots of the modern Catholic university, writes Shea, are to be found both in modernity and in Catholicism, or in the dialogue between Athens and Jerusalem, as I put it in chapter 1 on "Jesus and the University." These two sets of roots, the Christian gospel and the Enlightenment's secularized reason, have undoubtedly created tensions for each other. Keeping these roots in a positive and mutually critical conversation is not for the faint-hearted. Shea believes that St. John Paul II's call for the church to enter a "fertile dialogue with people of every culture"[33] invites Catholic universities to play a special role in mediating between Catholicism and modernity. He asks to what extent and in what ways a Catholic university locates itself in the "heart of the Church" and Catholicism in the "heart of the university"?[34]

For a Catholic university to be open to secular reason means welcoming secular scholars as members of an "open circle," where they can, through humble and courageous conversation, find aspects of the truth wherever those aspects are to be found. Catholic scholars learn from modernity as well as from the church. That means that bishops also need to learn. Shea writes, for example, that scholars at Catholic universities can "question the Church's more than occasional introversion, its intellectual and spiritual mediocrity, its lack of interest in public discourse and process, and its inertial classicism by simply doing their job as a home of researchers and teachers and as a support and platform for Catholic intellectuals."[35]

At the same time, I will also add, as I did in the last chapter, that here are things that Catholic academics can learn from bishops and the global reality of the Catholic Church. First is the vision that *Ex corde* calls Catholic educators

to work harder at the integration of knowledge, to explore the ethical and religious dimensions inherent in their disciplines, and to create a community of
scholars in which the religious and intellectual identity of the institution plays
a substantial role. Shea says something quite similar when he suggests that
Catholic colleges and universities can play a special role in American higher education: "[They] can engage the culture in ways impossible for the large research
universities (as their way is impossible for us) and display the harmony between
religious commitment and democracy, between faith and reason, between low
social status and the highest social and political ideals, between individual intellectual responsibility and communitarian practice and learning."[36] Without
using the image of the open circle, Shea believes that Catholic universities oc-
cupy a unique niche, both faithful and open, that should ensure their future.

Conclusion

If *Ex corde* offers us a challenging vision for Catholic higher education, Charles
Taylor offers us an example of how a Catholic scholar might work to bridge the vision of *Ex corde* and the culture of modernity. I stressed his humility and charity
in the way he interacts with other scholars. He also calls for courage and for less
self-censoring to open up breathing space in the overly secular atmosphere of
the university. When scholars at Catholic universities become better known for
their humility and courage, the distinctive character and unique contribution of
Catholic higher education will be that much more evident.

12
Liberal Education

Introduction

The college of arts and sciences forms the heart of a Catholic college or university. At most Catholic colleges and universities, it encompasses three broad categories of intellectual inquiry: the humanities, the social sciences, and the natural sciences. All three categories are important for liberal education. The humanities typically include art, literature, history, languages, theology, and philosophy and explore themes most explicitly related to the Catholic intellectual, empirical, spiritual, and aesthetic inquiry and practice.

After discussing the role of liberal education in the medieval universities and tracking its development through the Renaissance, I will offer several descriptions of the purpose of liberal education, discuss some of the efforts that universities have made to include it in their core curricula, and finally look at ways in which liberal education can assume a particularly rich form when pursued in the context of the Catholic intellectual tradition.

Historical Background

Some historical background will allow us to see more clearly why today a college of arts and sciences plays such a central, but not exclusive, role in transmitting liberal education. Historian John O'Malley, SJ, distinguishes two major traditions in education in the West: the scientific and professional tradition on the one hand, and the humanistic tradition on the other.[1] Scientific and professional education began when universities were founded in thirteenth-century Europe. They typically included faculties of law, medicine, theology, and arts. The first three were clearly professional. As strange as it might seem today, the liberal arts prepared students for the study of one of the professions, which allowed them to serve as midlevel civil servants in emerging governments. Most students who attended these universities did so not just to be educated in the liberal arts, but to develop professional skills that would help them find gainful employment at a time when their careers and vocational paths were becoming less fixed.

The humanistic tradition emerged in the fifteenth and sixteenth centuries, partly in reaction to the university's emphasis on skill training more than moral

The Future of Catholic Higher Education. James L. Heft, S.M., Oxford University Press. © Oxford University Press 2021. DOI: 10.1093/oso/9780197568880.003.0013

formation. Humanists emphasized the study of the classics, Roman and Greek authors, and the practice of rhetoric, the effective use of language. According to O'Malley, this educational tradition emphasized the *studia humanitatis*, that is, "the subjects that are about our human strivings, failings, passions, and ideals—about wonder, as expressed especially in poetry, drama, oratory, and history."[2] These educators were concerned about the religious and moral formation of their students. In the words of the poet Petrarch (1304–1374):

> It is one thing to know, another to love, one thing to understand, another to will. Aristotle teaches us what virtue is—I do not deny it—but his lesson lacks the words that sting, that set afire, and that urge toward love of virtue and hatred of vice.[3]

These two traditions have continued side by side ever since, often in tension but sometimes complementing each other. Today, the most striking difference between the two can be seen in two very different educational institutions: the research university and the liberal arts college. What are now called comprehensive universities try to be both a university and a college at the same time—not an easy combination to keep in balance. Some authors have referred to comprehensive universities as "ugly ducklings." Ugly or not, in our highly commercialized culture, most universities put their greatest resources in professional education.

In the eighteenth century, most of what became universities in the United States started out as grade schools and boarding schools and only gradually evolved into colleges and then universities. Consequently, in the United States, the American college, according to Andrew Delbanco, has always taken a different path than the European universities, which presupposed that students knew what they wanted to study before matriculating.[4]

Over the last one hundred years, the number of college students in the United States has increased exponentially; most students are drawn to the professions. The majority of these students now attend community colleges, state universities, and for-profit institutions. The current emphasis on STEM (science, technology, engineering, and mathematics) programs prepares students for certain professions and receives government support. STEM programs have prestige. The liberal arts, unfortunately, do not. The small number of liberal arts colleges, many of them highly selective, continue to offer a traditional liberal education, but in most other institutions the odds are stacked against a robust and widespread commitment to the liberal arts. Given their distinctive mission, Catholic colleges and universities—most of them neither liberal arts nor research institutions but rather "ugly ducklings"—should retain, but often have not, a strong commitment to liberal education.

Purpose of Liberal Education

What are the aims of a liberal education? There are many descriptions, some drawing upon John Henry Newman's now-classic description found in his nineteenth century book *Idea of the University*. Newman there describes such learning as a "knowledge which stands on its own pretensions, which is independent of sequel, expects no complement, refuses to be informed (as it is called) by any end, or absorbed into any art, in order duly to present itself to our contemplation."[5] More plainspoken and down-to-earth descriptions of a liberal education also exist. For example, at around that same time, in the middle of the nineteenth century, a young student at a Methodist school in Virginia had just listened to a bracing sermon that forced him to think about the purpose of his life. That night he wrote in his journal a quite simple description of liberal education: "Oh that the Lord would show me how to think and how to choose."[6]

In 1861, William Johnson Cory, a master at Eton, an excellent boarding school in England, told a group of young men that their education would broaden their sensibilities and deepen their understanding. The students were not yet in college, but Cory's vision of education would also benefit today's college students:

> You are not engaged so much in acquiring knowledge as in making mental efforts under criticism. A certain amount of knowledge you can indeed with average faculties acquire so as to retain; nor need you regret the hours you have spent on much that is forgotten, for the shadow of lost knowledge at least protects you from many illusions.
>
> But you go to a great school, not for knowledge so much as for arts and habits; for the habit of attention, for the art of expression, for the art of assuming at a moment's notice a new intellectual posture, for the art of entering quickly into another person's thoughts, for the habit of submitting to censure and refutation, for the art of indicating assent or dissent in graduated terms, for the habit of regarding minute points of accuracy, for the habit of working out what is possible in a given time, for taste, for discrimination, for mental courage and mental soberness.[7]

Cory sums up his vision of education by telling the students that they "go to a great school for self-knowledge." Published just a decade after the appearance of Newman's work, Cory's speech echoes many of Newman's almost lyrical descriptions of the fruits of a liberal education. It is possible that Cory may have read Newman's *Idea*.

More recently, Terrance Sandalow, once the dean of the School of Law at the University of Michigan, wrote of the importance of moral formation, which has typically been a part of the Catholic vision of education:

Universities . . . play an important role in the moral development of students when they assist the latter in developing the capacity to think clearly, to identify and articulate premises, and to develop arguments that flow in an orderly fashion from those premises. Enhancing the ability of students to read, similarly, contributes significantly to their capacity for informed moral judgment.[8]

A university education, he continues, liberates a person from certain habits that prevent moral judgment—habits such as "self-interest, provincialism of time and place, overdependence on familiar categories of thought, sentimentality, and an inability to tolerate uncertainty."[9]

Moral education is not the primary focus of professional schools. Michelle Alexander taught law at Ohio State University but moved to a religious setting, Union Theological Seminary in New York City, so that she could shift her focus "from questions of law to questions of justice," a shift of focus that one would hope would not require a shift of institutions. But, she explains, "in my experience, in policy roundtables, in legal conferences, even in law-school classrooms, it's relatively rare to have deep, searching dialogues about the meaning of justice."[10] Faculty in professional schools find it difficult, if they are interested, to address these bigger questions.

Martha Nussbaum of the University of Chicago, who like Alexander is also not publicly associated with any religious tradition, recently published a short book on the importance of liberal education entitled *Not for Profit: Why Democracy Needs the Humanities.*[11] She identifies several radical changes that now threaten democracy as never before: entire countries dedicated to making a great national profit, and in the process discarding the skills needed to protect democracy. Rather than graduating students who can think, read, write, appreciate, and make a good argument, universities in these countries are now graduating "useful machines." Students with only technical educations have trouble understanding people who are unlike themselves and often have difficulty understanding the sufferings of the less fortunate.[12] To avoid this cultural and political catastrophe, she calls for true citizens who can think critically about both tradition and authority, who recognize the dignity and human rights of their fellow citizens, not reducing them to mere means to get what they want, who understand the human journey in all its complexity, who are able to judge critically political leaders, and who can think about the common good, including the global common good.[13]

Since Nussbaum wants to protect democracy, she writes for a broader and mostly secular audience and devotes little time to how religious traditions might strengthen her case. She does, however, recommend the study of world religions that introduce children and college students to the traditions and festivals of other religions.[14] The study of religion requires attentiveness to texts, a sense of history, an appreciation of art, and a realization that the deeper things in life resist neat conceptualizations: "For this reason, I have argued that all colleges and universities should follow the lead of America's Catholic colleges and universities, which require at least two semesters of philosophy, in addition to whatever theology or religious courses are required."[15]

A Catholic Vision of Liberal Education

Several Catholic authors have also weighed in on the importance of a liberal education. At the beginning of this chapter, I referred to an essay on the aims of liberal education by historian John O'Malley. In that same essay, he describes those aims, slightly edited by me, in five points: (1) "The Fly in the Bottle," a metaphor that suggests that liberal education frees students from remaining in their own "bubble" and opens them to a wider world with fewer prejudices; (2) "Heritage and Perspective," which develops through the study of history students who know better who they are and rescues them from "cultural amnesia"; (3) "We Are Not Born for Ourselves Alone," which conveys the moral imperative of service to others; (4) "*Eloquentia perfecta*," which educates students to speak well and to present their ideas persuasively and effectively; and (5) "The Spirit of Finesse," which is exercised by a person who respects the complexity of life and exercises prudence and good judgment, without becoming a bore or a klutz.[16]

A second author, Louis Dupré, whose wonderful graduate course on Soren Kierkegaard I had the privilege of taking in the summer of 1968 at Georgetown University, years later published an article in the *Christian Century* entitled "On Being a Christian Teacher of the Humanities."[17] Dupré singles out three essential characteristics of liberal education. First, it conveys historical and aesthetic education, refines style and taste, and exposes students to the works of poets and writers and artists of the past.[18] Second, liberal education fosters critical thinking, deepens a person's capacity to question, and teaches the learner that the quest for a fuller understanding of life and its meaning is never-ending. The study of the sciences forms an essential part of growing in intellectual maturity, as philosophy does, which must be "complemented by the light of the spirit." Finally, liberal education enhances a moral formation, teaches norms for conduct, and reins in the rugged individualism of modern culture. Dupré laments the unwillingness of modern universities to take on this responsibility: "sociology is a legitimate, serious science, but it is no substitute for ethics."[19] He stresses that in a Catholic university moral education must be complemented by the study of theology, the development of an interior life and a contemplative attitude, and the habit of welcoming times of silence. Without creating a certain interior "emptiness," the necessary predisposition for liberal learning is absent.[20] Without reverence, people become sociopaths; for them, nothing is sacred. Reverence, explains Dupré, fosters gratitude and respect, attitudes that are by nature essentially religious.

Finally, Mark Roche, the third Catholic thinker, published an important book in 2010, *Why Choose the Liberal Arts?* A professor of German and philosophy and dean of Notre Dame's College of Arts and Letters from 1997 to 2008, Roche brings not only a professor's sensibility to the topic but also an awareness that he gained as an educational leader who frequently met skeptical parents worried that if their children majored in the humanities, they would be unable to get a good job when they graduated. As dean at a Catholic university, he learned how to describe the value of a liberal education and to explain the practicality of a liberal arts education without undercutting its intrinsic value.[21]

Roche distinguishes three goals of liberal education: first, learning "for its own sake" and the capacity to simply enjoy the life of the mind as it explores the great questions of civilization; second, teaching intellectual virtues needed for success once students graduate; and third, forming character and creating a sense of vocation. The idea of a vocation presupposes someone who calls and someone else who hears and responds to that call; people who believe in calls know the importance of developing an interior life and learning how to listen. Roche's point is similar to the one Dupré makes in stressing the importance of developing the capacity for silence. People who believe that God speaks to the hearts of individuals also believe that God is alive and active, not just in some generic way, but in a way that communicates with and even calls individuals personally in the here and now. Few authors who write about moral formation include this theological dimension, which introduces the transcendent as an essential dimension of liberal education. In this way, a Christian understanding of the liberal arts goes beyond secular versions of them.

In the light of the transcendent, therefore, liberal education is not about deciding who we want to be, but rather discovering whom we have been called to be. Calls in this sense are invitations, neither coercion by the caller nor blind obedience by the called. Rather, those who accept their call find a power and freedom that guide them on a deep personal level. Roche puts it this way:

> [Catholicism] ... brings to the liberal arts ideal a strong existential component. At a Catholic university students pursue theology not as the disinterested science of religious phenomena but as faith seeking understanding. They study history and the classics in order to learn not simply *about* the past, but also *from* the past. Students employ the quantitative tools of the social sciences not simply as a formal exercise with mathematical models but in order to develop sophisticated responses to pressing and complex social issues.[22]

In other words, in the Catholic tradition, the liberal arts inhabit a transcendent framework. The Catholic framework assumes that everyone, whether they realize it or not, is called by God to use his or her talents to benefit others. Liberal education is less a process of self-realization or even self-building (*Bildung*) than it is a gradual discovery of what individuals are called to do with the gifts God has given them.

The liberal arts teach students how to think clearly, do logical analysis, sift through and evaluate the persuasiveness of an argument, and evaluate the information that is accessible through multiple news sources, including the internet. Today this might be called "critical thinking." It is not enough to be only a critical thinker; otherwise, persons would never get married or trust other people. When advocates of critical thinking claim that it is the only way to think, they are not thinking critically. Absolutizing critical thinking leaves out a moral framework. As Hugh Heclo notes, "The whole business of teaching critical thinking really has nothing to say about what one should do with this ability. It may just as easily make a person a better scoundrel as a better citizen."[23] In a Catholic perspective, critical thinking is a tool that helps people search for the truth, a truth that ultimately is found in a person, Jesus, a commitment to whom leads to true freedom: "the truth will make you free" (John 8:32). At a Catholic university, therefore, the liberal arts necessarily include both moral and theological dimensions.

What's the Problem Then?

These descriptions of the aims of liberal education, by both secular and religious authors, make a case for liberal education that everyone, one might think, would find not just attractive but even compelling. In an age when social media has dramatically shortened people's ability to speak and write clearly, you would think people would be able to see more than ever before the value of speaking words "that set afire, and that urge toward love of virtue and hatred of violence." In an age when the attention span of students has dramatically shortened and their prose greetings have become "how r u?," who would not see the importance of an education that develops the "habit of attention" and the "art of expression"? In an age when more and more young people are enveloped in a social media bubble, who would not value the ability to enter into "another person's thought"? In an age when we are inundated with information of widely varying degrees of truth, and some without any truth at all, who would not treasure a "capacity to think critically" and "to identify and articulate premises" and an education that fosters an interior life and a sense of vocation? And in an age of political polarization, when the practices of democracy and civic engagement have withered, who

In an age when... [handwritten marginal note]

would not seek an education that strengthens democracy and forms students in the art of understanding others so that together they can work together for the common good?

But alas, as most academics know, most parents do not find liberal education attractive or compelling enough to encourage their daughters and sons to major in the liberal arts. The reasons are not hard to find. In an article in the *Wall Street Journal*, "Liberal Arts Colleges, in Fight for Survival, Focus on Job Skills," one former college president put the challenge bluntly: "People just can't afford to be educated; they almost have to be trained." Between 2012 and 2014, the numbers of degrees in the humanities dropped by 9% according to the American Academy of Arts and Sciences. Among all bachelor's degrees, only 6% are in the humanities, the lowest percentage since records began to be kept in 1948. Instead, business degrees tally 20% of all bachelor's degrees awarded; degrees in health care, homeland security, and parks and recreation jumped in 2015 to 17% when just ten years earlier that figure was 9%.[24]

In the first chapter of her book, Martha Nussbaum describes some of the major threats to liberal education, including a report from a 2005 faculty retreat at the University of Chicago where professors complained how wealthy parents wanted their children to develop skills that result in financial success and a 2006 White House document that reduced education to expanding the national economy. She was especially disappointed in a conversation she had with the head of a search committee looking for a new dean of education. She told the person in charge of the search that the humanities and arts were very important for educators. The head of the search committee responded that no one else she had consulted ever suggested that these subjects were important.[25] Dennis O'Brien, a former college president, put it simply: the liberal arts lack prestige, and prestige is the name of the game.[26]

The shrinking support of public higher education by state and federal agencies adds cost for students and makes majors that promise jobs upon graduation more popular. Not long ago, the University of Louisiana, for example, dropped its philosophy major and Michigan State abandoned its majors in classics and American studies. In response to this crisis, one liberal arts college in Maine guarantees graduates will get jobs or they can return to the college and take more courses free of charge. All this has occurred despite the fact that many recent studies document that over time, liberal arts majors actually move up in management positions in corporations faster than those with business degrees, and often make more money.[27] But the problem for faculty in the liberal arts is exacerbated by the fact that even though teaching humanities courses like English and history actually makes money for the university (humanities classes are less expensive to teach than science classes, especially those that require lab work), that money is not redistributed to the humanities faculty who teach those courses. In the category of "no good deed goes unrewarded," external funding for professors in the humanities receives next to no government support, whereas the sciences do.

Does a Required Core Curriculum Address the Problem?

One way to address the weakening of the liberal arts is to establish a core curriculum that includes a substantial number of required courses in the humanities. In response to the rise of the research universities in the late nineteenth and early twentieth centuries, some universities established general education programs. To create such programs, faculty committees at various universities across the country began discussions to determine, not without considerable disagreement, what all their students should know when they graduate from college. In an age when liberal education lacks funding and prestige (two things that usually go together), it lands early on the curricular chopping block. Consider these examples.

Prestigious secular universities often do not offer the best curricular practices for Catholic universities. At Harvard, for example, the faculty recently tried to revise their core curriculum. The faculty committee in charge of proposing a revision to the entire faculty recommended that a course about religions be included. Some faculty vociferously opposed its inclusion because they believed that instead of serious study, such a course would foster superstition. In a 2013 report, "Mapping the Future," another committee of Harvard's humanities faculty referred to religion eight times in their report, almost always in a negative way: as fundamentalists who opposed higher biblical criticism, as a source of "ideological or religious pre-judgment," and for right-wing Christians who learn "from the pulpit in their houses of worship" how to oppose the left-leaning ethos of the academy.[28]

Identifying required courses is not the only way to revise the curriculum. Another approach concentrates not on courses but on how students should learn. It emphasizes process rather than content. At Duke, a committee, chaired by a philosophy professor, was charged to rethink the core curriculum of the College of Arts and Sciences and was instructed to clarify and simplify the logic of the curriculum and encourage more creativity. The committee wanted to give students more choices and permit them, up to four days after the final grade is posted, to choose a "credit/no credit option." To encourage further exploration, sophomores, before declaring a major, were required to finish one course in writing, one in a second language, and one in quantitative inquiry. All students were to be required to take six courses around a theme other than their major and would need to complete a mentored research project. Some faculty believed requiring only one course in a different language was "ludicrous." Others found the proposed new curriculum hard to understand. Faculty who opposed the proposal feared that students would misuse their curricular freedom to ignore the liberal arts. After five years (!) of discussion, the faculty tabled the proposal with the hope that in time, a stronger consensus could emerge regarding the way forward.[29] While the Harvard faculty refused even the comparative study of religion, the faculty at Duke never even brought up the topic of religion.

For Catholic colleges and universities, the debate is different and more is at stake. The University of Notre Dame offers a more immediately relevant example of the debate about a core curriculum. Notre Dame conducts a review of the core curriculum every ten years. In the most recent review, the most intense debates took place over how many theology courses should be required. Theologian Cyril O'Regan wrote an impassioned defense of the two-course theology requirement, without which he warned that Notre Dame would follow the path that the major Protestant universities traveled one hundred years ago—the path to secularization. Others, including Mark Roche, argued that students could learn about the riches of the Catholic intellectual tradition not just in theology or philosophy courses, but also through literature and art. Notre Dame ended up keeping the theology requirement, but a group of Notre Dame undergraduates asked why nearly two-thirds of their theology courses were taught not by tenured or tenure-track faculty but by graduate assistants or adjunct faculty. One of the ironies in higher education is that nearly every department that teaches undergraduates wants to keep and even expand their portion of the core curriculum, but few of their faculty want to teach introductory courses.[30]

But even if faculty at Catholic universities could agree on a core curriculum that incorporates a sufficient number of courses in the liberal arts, including philosophy and theology, they still face a skeptical external audience, including parents who worry about job prospects for their sons and daughters. Secular Stanley Fish, an acerbic former dean and professor of literature, urges administrators and faculty who want to strengthen liberal education in public institutions to mount an aggressive defense of the humanities, one that calls out and shames governors, like the 2013 governor of North Carolina, Pat McCrory, who told an interviewer that the amount of state support should be based not on the number of "butts in seats, but how many of those butts can get jobs."[31] Public shaming may work in the world of secular education and politics, but the question for Catholic universities is not about lobbying politicians, but how to strengthen the distinctive role that the liberal arts should have in their universities.

Catholic Universities and Liberal Education

Catholic colleges and universities have an even greater reason to commit themselves to a strong liberal arts education: it is through the liberal arts that many of the core insights of the Catholic intellectual, artistic, and spiritual traditions are most explicitly explored. I say "most explicitly" because all the disciplines, including those in the professional schools, can be taught liberally—that is, with attention to ethical questions such as justice and the common good. But given the secularization of the larger culture, the creation of an interior spirit responsive to ethical questions, to say nothing of responsiveness to the gospel of Jesus, is more important than ever. Catholic philosopher Charles Taylor identifies some positive characteristics of contemporary Western culture, such as its emphasis on authenticity, philanthropy, and human rights, but nonetheless criticizes the way today's "exclusive humanism" has performed a "spiritual lobotomy" on a mostly unsuspecting population.[32]

Exclusive humanism closes the transcendent window as though there were nothing beyond; as though it weren't a crying need of the human heart to open the window, gaze, and then go through it; as though feeling this need were the result of a mistake, an erroneous worldview, bad conditioning, or, worse, some pathology. With two radically different perspectives on the human condition, who is right?[33]

As a consequence of the culture of exclusive humanism, Catholic universities need to place special emphasis on the theological and spiritual roots of its vision of liberal education, to distinguish Christian humanism from its secular form. Separated from theological foundations, Catholic social teaching can appear to be a liberal secular response to poverty, immigration, and the distribution of wealth. Grounded in a theological vision, Catholic social teaching flows directly from the dignity of every person created in the image and likeness of God, and the bond we have with others, especially the most vulnerable and less fortunate. A university theologically grounded in this way is required to keep its circle open.

To avoid vagueness about what Catholic intellectual traditions are, their theological foundations need to be made explicit. These foundations are the doctrines of Creation, Incarnation, and the Trinity. Creation affirms that all that God created is good, that we have a responsibility for creation since we are tenants and not landlords. The Incarnation personalizes God in human terms and reminds us that every human being is an "*alter Christus*." Finally, the doctrine of the Trinity reminds us that the Godhead is a community of persons and that a commitment to building community and the common good is rooted in the very nature of God.[34]

A second emphasis, often missing in these discussions, is the importance of the spiritual life, especially as it is nourished liturgically. Liturgy is both ritual and word, the spiritual and the physical. It embodies drama and proclamation. And for Christians, the word is the Word, a theological claim that makes language at its root sacred. Louis Dupré writes, "Continuing the Hebrew tradition

[Christianity] interprets, preserves, and transmits God's revealing events through sacred language. But while Judaism coded its memory in the *Book*, for Christians the Word became a physical, personal presence."[35] A word that is spoken seeks a listener who can hear. In this age of excessive individualism, of young people hermetically sealed in their own social media world, the importance of the relational and community dimensions of liturgy and the sacraments should be obvious.

A defense of foreign language requirements as part of liberal education is not rooted first within the reality of globalization, which requires understanding people of other languages and cultures, but rather, within a Catholic vision, in the central importance of the global ramifications of the Word made Flesh. Catholic beliefs and practices ground a university education in a common search for the truth and a dedication to the common good. Scholarship inspired by Catholicism bears on real-life issues, not just for the benefit of that very small percentage of humanity fortunate enough to be professors or university students, but for everyone, and especially the poor.

Moreover, because reason and faith are ever intertwined in Catholic tradition, every part of a Catholic school's curriculum should be influenced in various ways by philosophical, ethical, and theological perspectives; such universities are not sectarian—they are Catholic. It is possible, of course, for faculty who are not Christian, or even not personally religious, to understand how they too share attitudes that Christians claim are important in their teaching and research. An agnostic science teacher who seeks the truth of nature and who respects, even reverences, what she studies is performing, at least from a Christian point of view, a religious act. In professional education, such as medicine, the Christian vision of the human person will influence the care for the sick, the poor, and especially the dying. In the study of history, the presence, forms, and vitality of various religions will be studied as an integral part of the human story. The teaching of philosophy will not ignore the vital relationship that has existed for centuries between philosophy and theology (even if much of modern philosophy weakens that relationship). In other words, at a Catholic university, Catholic intellectual traditions will affect all aspects of the curriculum, and even determine some of the majors that the university chooses to offer.

Conclusion

The liberal arts remain important today, especially when so many students find it difficult to express themselves, think clearly, read a book, and escape the social media bubble. To repeat what William John Cory told his Eton students in 1861: "You go to a great school, not for knowledge so much as for arts and habits; for the habit of attention, for the art of expression . . . for the art of entering into another person's thoughts." Philosopher Charles Taylor warns that today's pervasive secularism smothers the transcendent. It is therefore all the more important for Catholic universities to "open up" the intellectual atmosphere. A theological sensibility opens up the liberal arts to the transcendent, helping students to become not just refined, but holy. It follows, then, that a key advantage that Catholic universities have to keep the transcendent dimension alive is theology. We turn to theology and its role in a Catholic university in our next chapter.

13

Theology in the Catholic University

Introduction

It is possible to imagine a Catholic university without professional schools, but not one without the sciences, social sciences, the humanities, and, in particular, a department of theology. Throughout these chapters, I have emphasized the importance of the faculty. In this chapter, I will try to describe the role of Catholic theologians in a Catholic university and spell out some of the challenges they face in trying to carry out that role.

Given the power of contemporary academic culture, it will be helpful at the outset to have an understanding of some of the most important characteristics of Catholic theology. I will then step back and describe the rapid historical changes with regard to the teaching of religion and theology that took place in the United States after World War II in both the Catholic and secular universities. I then describe some of the challenges that Catholic theologians face because of the expectations for Catholic theologians spelled out in the 1990 apostolic exhortation on Catholic higher education, *Ex corde ecclesiae*. By the chapter's end, it should be obvious that much needs to be done if education at a Catholic university can claim to be both distinctive and excellent, and that theology plays a very important role in all of that.

The Nature of Catholic Theology

Excellent authors have written books about the nature and purpose of Catholic theology. Karl Rahner, Avery Dulles, Joseph Ratzinger, Elizabeth Johnson, Hans Urs von Balthasar, Rosemary Haughton, Thomas Rausch, and Gustavo Gutierrez, to name only a few, have written significant explanations of the unique character of Catholic theology.[1] While it does not make sense for me to try to summarize their important contributions, I would like to emphasize four characteristics of Catholic theology that, in my opinion, are most relevant today: Catholic theology should be both critical and catechetic, appropriately apologetic, and integrative, and influence the entire mission of a Catholic university.

First, Catholic theology is both critical and catechetic. Unfortunately, some theologians feel they have to make it clear that they are not catechists. Perhaps

The Future of Catholic Higher Education. James L. Heft, S.M., Oxford University Press. © Oxford University Press 2021.
DOI: 10.1093/oso/9780197568880.003.0014

they are overly sensitive to the doubts their critics have about theology as a legitimate academic discipline. In some ways, as Charles Taylor explains, they may be living in a "postrevolutionary climate," wanting to protect what they consider the recent liberation of theology from apologetics and ecclesiastical control (e.g., the *mandatum*). Inhabiting such a climate, some theologians tend to distinguish too sharply between, on the one hand, what they do, and on the other, what bishops and catechists do. They see as their opponents overcontrolling bishops. They also worry about condescending colleagues. They react to any threat to their hard-won new freedom, which looks to them like backsliding.[2] I shall argue, however, that teaching theology can be very sophisticated, even when teaching religiously illiterate undergraduates. Theologians, I hope to make clear, should not fear those who think that passing on the Catholic faith ends critical thinking.

Second, certainly rational arguments in favor of the faith, or apologetics, play an important role, even though they have their limits. Anglican philosopher Austin Farrer wrote that "though argument does not create conviction, the lack of it destroys." Why? Farrer continues, "What no one shows the ability to defend is quickly abandoned."[3] A popular saying encourages believers to "preach the Gospel at all times, and if necessary, use words." That might provide the witness part of teaching, but by itself that is not sufficient. Words are important. In fact, Christianity is the religion of the Word. The author of the first letter of Peter reminds us, "Should anyone ask you the reason for this hope of yours, be ever ready to reply but speak gently and respectfully."[4] Theologians shepherd the use of language about God. I will also say something later about the relationship between teaching and witnessing.

Third, theology, as Catholics understand it, is integrative. Theology draws upon both faith and reason; it rejects both fideism (faith without reason) and rationalism (reason without faith). And because faith requires reasoning, theologians think about everything that can be thought about—science, the cosmos, the social sciences, and the professions—in a word, about everything. Academic disciplines narrow the objects of their study and employ methodologies that ensure rigor and precision; there are some great benefits in this. However, it doesn't work well for theology, at least in the same way. The academic discipline of Christian theology studies not only what God has revealed in Jesus Christ but also what God has revealed in the Book of Nature—that is, how revelation is related to all of creation, and how all of creation sheds light on divine revelation. Though there are specialties in theology, as a discipline its scope is universal and includes care for everyone. To paraphrase the beginning of Vatican II's document, *Gaudium et spes*, the Christian theologians pay attention to the "joys and hopes, the grief and anguish" of everyone, not just Christians, and not just the well-to-do.[5]

Paragraph 32 of *Ex corde* describes the broad scope of what theologians should be writing about and teaching, studies that include all the disciplines, and concentrates on issues such as the dignity of human life, justice for everyone, family life, the protection of the environment, and the search for peace and political stability. At a Catholic university, theologians bear a special responsibility for the integration of knowledge. The exponential growth in knowledge makes its integration almost impossible; I doubt that even the most gifted theologians would be able to produce an encyclopedia that explains the proper relationship of theology to all the academic disciplines. However, as we shall see, it is important that they facilitate conversations with their colleagues in other departments.

Fourth and finally, what role ought theology play within the Catholic university? Surely it is not sufficient to limit the role of theology to offering required courses for undergraduates. A theological vision needs to influence the entire mission of the university. Some authors (Theodore Hesburgh, to name one) have claimed that a Catholic university must first be a university and then Catholic. I realize that in framing the matter in this way, he wants to stress the importance of academic quality. But expressing the concern in this way suggests that the noun is the university, with Catholic being only an adjective.[6] David Burrell prefers a different way of asking what the mission of a Catholic university is: we can ask what makes a university Catholic, or we can ask what makes for a Catholic university. Asked in the second form, we realize that a Catholic university is more than just a generic university with a few religious elements added, such as a theology requirement and campus ministry programs. Certainly, Catholic universities need to continue to increase their academic quality. But if that quality is not in some sense influenced, and even inspired, by a Catholic vision of the mission, we run the risk of thinking, as one university president once said to me, that "the university is part of the meat; the Catholic part is just the flavoring."

At a meeting of the International Federation of Catholic Universities held in Rome in 2009, I was asked to speak at a plenary session on a vision of a Catholic university.[7] One of my respondents, a professor from the University of Louvain, thought that my vision was sectarian. Perhaps he thought that the Catholic vision I supported did not respect the autonomy of the disciplines. Or perhaps he thought that theologians didn't need to be in conversation with their colleagues in other disciplines. In fact, my own approach for years at the University of Dayton fostered conversations among faculty that fully respected the integrity of their different disciplines but also did not shy away from asking fundamental questions about how the nature of the human person, the common good, the limits of science, and the importance of justice might affect the assumptions and syllabi of their disciplines.[8] David Burrell made much the same point when he wrote that "so long as the quest for Catholic identity can be pursued in a sufficiently inclusive manner, calling upon all who see their life as a gift, their work as *why the weakest academic discipline now?*

a call rather than a career," many members of the faculty will be quite willing to join the conversation.[9]

The Role of Catholic Theologians according to *Ex corde ecclesiae*

Along with the four important characteristics of Catholic theology, we also need to look at the role that the 1990 apostolic exhortation *Ex corde* assigns to theology. It asserts that theologians fill *the* most important role in a Catholic university, not only in shaping its mission, but also in providing for all the other disciplines what they themselves cannot provide from within their own methodologies:

> Theology plays a particularly important role in the search for a synthesis of knowledge as well as in the dialogue between faith and reason. It serves all other disciplines in their search for meaning, not only by helping them to investigate how their discoveries will affect individuals and society but also by bringing a perspective and an orientation not contained within their own methodologies. . . . Because of its specific importance among the academic disciplines, every Catholic university should have a faculty, or at least a chair, of theology. (par. 19)

How can such a bold and sweeping claim be understood, much less defended? Given the explosion of knowledge and the high degree of specialization within and between the disciplines, how can anyone think that all this knowledge might actually be synthesized? And does not the expectation that theologians will offer perspectives that other academics lack border on hubris?

The charge of "hubris" would be right on the mark if it weren't for a sentence that I left out of the *Ex corde* quotation: "In turn, interaction with these other disciplines and their discoveries enriches theology, offering it a better understanding of the world today, and making theological research more relevant to current needs." Thus, theologians need to learn from their colleagues in other disciplines. Theologians, therefore, have to meet two demanding expectations: they are to offer to their colleagues perspectives that they are unable to derive from within their own disciplines, and they are to learn from them about their disciplines. Instead of the charge of hubris, it might be more accurate to suggest that *Ex corde* expects extraordinary things from Catholic theologians.

How can theologians presume to shape the academic offerings of an entire Catholic university? Given the subspecialties in the discipline of theology and their high degree of specialization, it is difficult even for Catholic theologians to understand what some of their colleagues in their own department are doing. Given all this specialization, is it realistic to expect them to understand as well other academic disciplines and their subspecialties? We might also have difficulty imagining professors in the sciences, business, and engineering, to name only a few disciplines, welcoming the reflections of theologians on their research and subject matter. Is theology commonly perceived, even within the Catholic academy, as a rigorous and critically important discipline? With theology as it has traditionally been understood—as faith seeking understanding—wouldn't academics who start with faith lead other academics to doubt that theologians can be objective and critical in their work as theologians?

Let's add some other traditional expectations of theologians that would in all likelihood reduce their credibility: for example, the expectation that theologians sustain a spiritual life as a precondition for doing theology. Does a spiritual life, we might ask, have anything to do with the intellectual quality of their academic work? And what about the expectation that theologians should not only teach ideas but also move students to a deeper faith? Should theologians evangelize, or should they fear that if they do, their peers in other parts of the university will think that they are not able to be critical, and that they should be in a parish rather than in a university? Isn't the widespread opposition to indoctrination, sometimes well justified, one of the very reasons that only the "academic study" of religions is now more widely accepted in the secular university? Are there significant differences between the academic study of religion and theological studies?

Add to these challenges the expectation that theologians should also address multiple audiences, from religiously illiterate undergraduates to doctoral students, from other academics to administrators, and from bishops to the general public.[10] Of course, theologians are not the only academics who have multiple audiences. Think of scientists, who have difficulty persuading the general public on evolution and global warming, or political scientists, whose thought seems to have no effect on dysfunctional government. But the case for theologians is especially complicated. They must address not only their peers, other theologians, but also, according to *Ex corde*, all their academic colleagues in the rest of the university. But even more is expected. Theologians should also be able to speak to the whole church, which includes not just bishops and religious leaders but also lay Catholics, including, I would presume, religiously illiterate undergraduates. Besides speaking to the general public, non-Catholics, nonbelievers, and indeed, all of humanity, they are expected to publish articles in refereed journals. Is it realistic to expect some theologians to be skilled in addressing their academic peers, religious leaders, and the laity? Isn't it an achievement to be able to address even one audience effectively?

Stepping back from this litany of expectations for theologians, I would like to offer a historical perspective that may help us think through how at least some of these challenges might be addressed.

After World War II: Transformations in the Teaching of Catholic Theology

If we begin to examine the extensive changes in the teaching of Catholic theology in our universities over the past seventy years, we also begin to understand why theologians face so many challenges today. Since World War II, religious studies departments began to be established at secular universities, and since the 1950s, teaching "religion" in Catholic universities has changed dramatically.

Let us begin with the changes that have taken place in the teaching of theology and religion since World War II in two Catholic institutions: the seminary and the university. It is difficult to overstate the extraordinary changes in Catholic universities that have taken place since World War II. Founded in 1946, the Catholic Theological Society of America numbered just over a hundred men. A group photo of the founding members shows that they were all priests (all were wearing Roman collars), and nearly all taught in seminaries. Until the 1950s, many of them had earned their doctorates in Europe, since few American Catholic colleges and universities (the Catholic University of America was an exception) offered doctoral programs in theology. Still in the early 1960s, nuns and priests at these colleges and universities dominated the faculties of theology. For example, at the University of Dayton, the first lay professor of theology was hired in 1964. All the other theologians were Marianist priests.

Until then, the teaching and studying of theology, except in women's colleges, was a completely male enterprise. Anticipating almost by a decade Pope Pius XII's call in 1951 for the professional education of sisters engaged in teaching, Holy Cross Sr. Madaleva Wolff realized that sisters needed college degrees and, since some of them were expected to teach religion, would especially benefit from the study of theology. In 1943, Sr. Madaleva contacted Notre Dame, Saint Louis, Marquette, Loyola, DePaul, and the Catholic University of America to see if they would admit women to the full-time study of theology, especially at the graduate level. All these universities refused. Undeterred, she proceeded to found at St. Mary's College in Indiana the first graduate program in theology for women. As hard as it might be for us to imagine today, Sr. Madaleva's School of Sacred Theology was, in the late 1940s, the only place in the world where laypersons and religious, both male and female, could study theology full time at the graduate level.

Much has changed since then. By 2018, the Catholic Theological Society of America claimed over 1,300 members. The majority are still men, but an increasing number of women and minorities are now full-fledged members. Few of them teach in seminaries. Most have PhDs, academic doctoral degrees rather than ecclesiastical degrees (the STD, Doctorate in Sacred Theology, or the STL, Licentiate in Sacred Theology, the latter being roughly an advanced master's degree in the US system). A number of these theologians received their PhDs from prestigious secular universities, such as Yale, Chicago, and Harvard. Except for biblical scholars, many of these theologians work only in the English language, and except for historians, they write mainly about contemporary issues. Their inability to read texts in other languages from other periods of history limits their catholicity.

A second dramatic change since World War II affected the content of the courses. Before World War II, only seminarians were taught theology; they studied mainly summaries of the thought of St. Thomas Aquinas. At that time, in Catholic colleges and universities, lay students did not study theology; rather, they were taught "religion," and that in a form that stressed personal piety and morality. It was only in their required philosophy courses that they were taught how to remain Catholic once they graduated. These philosophy courses were mainly apologetic, designed to help them defend their faith in the marketplace. Only in the 1940s did Jesuit John Courtney Murray and others start a discussion on whether lay students should be introduced to and study theology. They understood, however, that the theology lay students studied should not be like the theology taught in seminaries. According to one of the leaders of this movement, lay students needed to be introduced to "a new and concrete expression of integral Catholic educational life and an indispensable aid to the apostolate of Catholic Action."[11] In the 1950s, Fr. John Montgomery Cooper of the Catholic University of America and others pioneered the movement to offer a more suitable form of theology for lay students.

From a historical perspective, then, after World War II, far-reaching changes transformed what lay students studied. Put simply, for the first time in history, lay students, who never had the opportunity before, began studying theology. What started out as men teaching theology only to men preparing for the priesthood has become men and women teaching different types of theology to lay students preparing for life in the world. Former archbishop of Canterbury Rowan Williams, following British lay theologian Donald Nicholl, remarked that for centuries, theology was done in the absence of women and children.[12] For the most part, teaching and learning continue in this way in Catholic seminaries that do not allow women to matriculate and/or teach. But in our Catholic colleges and universities today, many women do teach theology, sometimes bringing their own children to class. Married lay theologians, unlike priests and religious, have family obligations. What is clearly new, however, is that students with no interest in the priesthood can now imagine themselves becoming theologians, and some male lay students, excited about theology, can think about becoming priests.

Religious Studies and/or Theology?

Things changed not only on Catholic campuses. After World War II, scholars on secular campuses began thinking about including the study of religion for a variety of reasons. Religious literacy in a pluralistic democratic society seemed important. The "Red Scare" of the 1920s and 1930s morphed into the fear of godless communism in the 1950s. Traumatized by the war, and especially the Shoah—the execution of six million Jews—scholars and political leaders began to speak of the "Judeo Christian" tradition and developed courses that would help preserve democratic traditions. During the presidency of Dwight Eisenhower, the US Mint began to print "In God We Trust" on coins, replacing the motto *E pluribus unum.*

Aided by a 1963 Supreme Court ruling that sharply distinguished between "teaching about religion" and "teaching of religion," a legal opening was created that helped faculty at state universities establish religious studies departments. In the United States, given the strictly interpreted doctrine separating church and state and the growing secularism of the culture, especially the academic culture, faculty at secular campuses made it as clear as they could that they taught "about religion," not "for religion." They defined what they were doing in sharp contrast to what was already in existence at some major formerly Protestant universities: They were scholars, not professors of divinity teaching future ministers. Training for the ministry was done in "schools of divinity," where the academic standards and research expectations for faculty were different (i.e., "lower") than in the rest of the university. Education for the ministry was more practically than academically oriented. Today, it is still assumed, in my opinion incorrectly, that courses of a more practical orientation must be, for that reason alone, less academic.

Since the 1960s, scholars teaching in secular universities have distinguished between the academic study of religion on the one hand and theology on the other in somewhat different ways. However, the generally held view today might be expressed as follows: (1) the academic study of religion examines many religious traditions, while theology studies only one; (2) the academic study of religion presupposes no personal faith commitment on the part of the professor, while theology does; (3) the academic study of religion belongs in a secular university setting, while theology belongs in seminaries and divinity schools; and

(4) the academic study of religion may count as part of general education, while theology is appropriate only for committed members of the church or synagogue, or the relevant believing community.[13]

I think that Catholic thinkers should challenge these sharp distinctions between the academic study of religion and theology. The two approaches should actually complement each other. First, theologians at Catholic universities, depending on their resources and numbers, should study other religions, all the while giving a special place to the study of Catholicism, in the words of Cardinal Kasper, as "superior but not supercessionist."[14] Second, while doing theology presupposes a commitment of faith, that commitment need not render the critical study of that or any other religious tradition invariably prejudiced.[15] Third, a theology department in a Catholic university can combine critical and descriptive study of religious traditions characteristic of religious studies departments, even while it carries out the task of criticism from within a committed stance. Fourth, theology can and should form an integral part of the general education program and core curriculum at a Catholic university, rather than be isolated from the rest of the academy, demoted in academic status, and sent away from the university and located in a divinity school or seminary.

All four of my assertions are, of course, debatable and require more clarification and defense than I provide here. My point is only this: there are good reasons that Catholic theologians should benefit from many of the approaches to the study of religion as it is done in some secular universities. Theology and religious studies need not be mutually exclusive. "Theology," understood as I understand it, should be able to learn much from religious studies. That said, theologians do not hesitate to go beyond just the historical and comparative study of religions; they also explore its existential dimensions, which remains the heart of every living religious tradition: are these teachings true, and if so, what difference do they make, and in light of them, what should I do?

While departments of religious studies were being established and gaining support in secular universities, Catholic theologians had differences of opinion in the 1960s about how best to name their own departments. Once called "religion" departments, some theologians wanted to make clear that they were no longer teaching just "religion" or doing apologetics. They recommended the name of the department be changed to "theological studies," or simply the "department of theology." But other faculty, influenced perhaps by the perceptions of faculty in secular universities and concerned about their academic credibility, endorsed greater "inclusivity": they named their departments "religious studies departments," which is the name many departments have today in Catholic universities. Notre Dame theologian Lawrence Cunningham strongly opposed substituting "religious studies" for "theology" in Catholic universities: "Religious Studies as an encompassing field may well be appropriate for a secular school, but theology is a discipline, and its absence from the curriculum of a religious school is, in my estimation, an abdication of responsibility."[16] In my opinion, Cunningham is right: a Catholic university cannot be Catholic without theology. At the same time, however, I believe that research carried out in religious studies programs at secular universities often embodies a wide range of valuable humanistic learning that should be of interest to theologians at Catholic universities, unless, of course, the methodologies of religious studies are understood to disqualify theology as an authentic academic discipline. For this reason, theologians at Catholic universities should welcome theologians of other religions as well as professors of religious studies, creating space for the "open circle" in which they can all learn from each other.[17]

Internal Debates: Theology in the Catholic Academy

The relative merits of the academic study of religion, with its critical and comparative components, continue to be debated among theologians at Catholic colleges and universities. There are, however, some immediate and existential questions that Catholic theologians also face when they enter the undergraduate classroom today. Most theologians agree that the vast majority of their undergraduate students are religiously illiterate, including those who have been "raised" Catholic. How can students, some ask, be expected to study theology critically if, to begin with, they don't know any theology? And if even most Catholic students are religiously illiterate, what about the increasing number of students who have had no contact at all with Catholicism, students from other religions, and students who are secular and have never thought about religion? Except for those recently founded Catholic colleges that put their Catholicity and theology front and center, colleges like Ave Maria, Thomas Aquinas, and Christendom, most Catholic colleges and universities admit a wide variety of students, some of whom in increasing numbers describe themselves as "spiritual but not religious." Depending on one's perspective, such differences among student populations either dilute a college's Catholic identity or expose many religiously illiterate students to what they have never encountered before. Major Catholic universities could learn some things from these smaller Catholic colleges about integrating curricular and cocurricular elements, just as these smaller colleges might learn from major Catholic universities a more capacious view of Catholicism. Living as we do in an age of considerable polarization, we need to build bridges of understanding in the church, as well as between our educational institutions.

In the spirit of "meeting them where they are," some theologians realize that they must first create a theological baseline for nearly all of the students. In other words, they need to teach enough theology that students can think critically about the subject. For other theologians, teaching the "basics" lowers their academic standing and turns them into catechists, not critically thinking theologians. They seem not to realize that passing on the faith at whatever level has to be done intelligently, be open to questions, and be capable of sophisticated explanations that students need if they are to acquire a basic understanding of Catholicism.

Still, several questions need to be asked. Even with the lack of religious literacy, I have already suggested that teaching religion can be both critical and appreciative. In the article "Why Study God?" John Cavadini describes how faithful and critical thinking require each other. He believes that the very teaching of theology, even at a basic level, can be—indeed, needs to be—sophisticated and critical. He argues that university theologians are both to teach and think critically about all that they teach:

> The goal [of a university theology course] is to provide students with the as-tonishing awareness that faith—yes, the very familiar and "simple" faith of their family and friends—can speak just as articulately and sophisticatedly as the other sciences and arts; that it can withstand questioning and sophisti-cated critique; that it can be self-critical; that it has had expression in the many genres represented from Gregory's life of Benedict to Thomas's *summae*, from Hildegard's visions to Dante's *Commedia* and everything in between; that faith can still be itself and speak in a variety of cultural voices; that it is embraced by sophisticated liberals as well as sophisticated conservatives.[18]

Creating an "astonishing awareness" in students includes being witnesses to the faith, not as one does in a parish and while participating devoutly in the Eucharist, but as professors in love with their subject, God. Taking their cue from *Ex corde*, theologians "evangelize" in a different way, realizing that teaching theology inescapably involves not just teaching students but also witnessing.[19] Theologians love their discipline and are happy to encourage students to do like-wise, critically. But at this point, some academics worry that teaching religion becomes a form of "indoctrination." In chapter 6 on the *mandatum*, I explain how theologians who teach religion (and not just about religion) practice a form of advocacy that should not be confused with indoctrination or any other form of academic irresponsibility.

Sometimes theologians, alas, are squeamish about being witnesses. They would hesitate to agree with Newman when he wrote that faith is upheld "not by books, not by argument, nor by temporal power, but by the personal influence of such men as . . . are at once the teachers and patterns of it." I think that Newman is right about what brings people to believe: they believe people who are believable. Still, professors are believable not just because they witness, but also because they are competent. Such professor become "patterns" of what they teach are more often believed than those who are not. Pope Paul VI once remarked that people listen more willingly to witnesses than to teachers, and if they listen to teachers, it is because they are witnesses. What is most needed are theologians who are witnesses.[20]

Suggesting that witness makes teachers credible leads to the question of whether teachers and students need to be concerned not only about teaching theology but also about their spiritual formation. When only priests taught theology to seminarians, it could be assumed that both teachers and students dedicated themselves to continual spiritual formation. Jean Leclercq captured this intimate relationship between theological studies and spiritual growth in the title of his classic study of monastic culture, *The Love of Learning and the Desire for God.*[21] Of course, combining learning and love of God does not automatically confer on the believer an epistemological privilege. What I am suggesting is that including a concern for spiritual formation makes theology more than an exclusively intellectual exercise. It also helps students deal with some of their most basic questions. It is appropriate, I believe, that the study of theology coupled with a concern for spiritual formation offers a more holistic experience.

Today the vast majority of theologians are laypersons who may not have a spiritual formation analogous to what religious and priests did before them. Older clerical theologians who are members of religious orders often underestimate how little spiritual formation many of their lay colleagues have had. A young lay Catholic theologian observed that "older theologians who have fought courageously for academic excellence and freedom may not fully appreciate their own spiritual formation and the way it forged strong ecclesial identification and responsibility." This young theologian was less worried about the *mandatum* than he was about theology's "increasing captivity to the mores of the academy and its concurrent ecclesial deracination."[22] Without serious spiritual formation, secular approaches to teaching religion are likely to replace an integrated sense of what the teaching of theology requires. The author of the article argues that theological education should include spiritual formation.

Theology and Academic Legitimacy

I have already briefly mentioned the problem that the modern academy has with the academic legitimacy of theology. It gives the greatest value to scientific and analytic forms of thinking. Secular universities prohibit theology, seeing it, as one Catholic observer put it, as "part of the maintenance machinery of a sectarian subculture."[23] They quarantine schools of divinity at a safe distance from the university. Even at Catholic universities, some faculty, during slugfests over the content of the core curriculum for undergraduates, maneuver to create more space for their own disciplines by making expendable required theology and philosophy courses. I explain in the previous chapter on liberal education how some faculty at the University of Notre Dame questioned whether the Catholic tradition was best studied only in theology courses. Various Catholic studies programs have in fact shown how courses in more disciplines than only theology and philosophy can pass on a sense of the Catholic tradition quite effectively. It is sobering to ask, if the theology and philosophy courses are not well taught, how many students would, by their own volition, choose to take them?

The humanities in general, at least in the view of empiricists, lack rigor and authentic academic status. In many universities, schools of education rank in academic status even below the humanities. A similar sort of prejudice can be found even within some theology departments where theologians give more academic credibility to certain specialties within the department than to others. They assume that the brightest students, those who really think, let us say, philosophically, should study dogmatic or systematic theology. For those students not drawn to such higher levels of thinking, the study of scripture or the history of theology is deemed more appropriate. Students who study ethics want to have an immediate impact by addressing particular moral problems more than they want to rethink the very assumptions of morality in the way that systematic theologians are expected to do.

At the bottom of the intellectual talent pool, according to this prejudice, are students who study pastoral theology. "People-people," are not, it is assumed, critical thinkers. They are counseled to settle for master's degrees or for a doctor of ministry degree. They work in parish programs and teach catechism, help people through rough patches in their lives, and lead Bible study groups. Such ministries, some academics mistakenly think, do not take a lot of intelligence, just a caring heart. I realize that my description of this sort of academic snobbery borders on caricature. However, too many theologians do not give sufficient attention to the pastoral consequences of theology and to the spiritual formation that constitute all the subcategories of theology. To be a good pastoral theologian, it is necessary to not only have a grasp of systematic, biblical, and historical theology but also be able to communicate with people in need. Nor should it be forgotten that Karl Rahner thought of himself as a pastoral theologian, though communicating his thoughts clearly to the laity was not his greatest strength.[24]

Overwhelming Challenges?

I have described a variety of challenges that face Catholic theologians today: the perceived tension between being a theologian and being a catechist, how to teach the basics of Catholicism to the religiously illiterate, whether to be attentive to the spiritual formation of their students as well as to their own, how to deal with the pervasive reduction of useful knowledge to empirically verifiable forms, how to avoid the condescension that marginalizes the importance of pastoral theology, and finally how to address the extraordinary number of audiences theologians are expected to be able to address. I do not believe that I have exaggerated the complexities that Catholic theologians face as teachers, researchers, believers, and members of the academy. The challenges I have described are daunting.

Can theologians, even in a large Catholic university, teach required undergraduate courses and also teach graduate courses, write for their peers, communicate with the larger public, and, beyond all this, play a key role in conversations on their campus with scholars in other disciplines? How do theologians sustain a conversation with other faculty in other departments and still find the time to teach and do original research?

Sociologist Christian Smith and theologian John Cavadini, both at the University of Notre Dame, doubt that it is possible for any one theologian to meet all these expectations. Their university recently committed itself to three major goals: to offer an excellent undergraduate liberal arts education, to become a major research university, and to sustain for the whole university a rich Catholic environment and education. Smith and Cavadini believe that this mission requires three different types of faculty. To achieve the first goal, the university needs outstanding classroom teachers well read in a variety of fields. To achieve the second goal, the university needs to hire specialists recognized nationally as authorities in their field, academic "stars" who win research grants and publish groundbreaking papers and books. To achieve the third goal, they continue, the university needs to hire faculty in a variety of disciplines who have interests in philosophy and Catholic theology. To do all three, they believe, is nearly impossible: "There are not enough people in the world with all those diverse qualifications for the three types of faculty success."[25] What, then, do they recommend that their university should do? They recommend that they should give priority to undergraduate education grounded in the Catholic tradition.

Trying to integrate even undergraduate education, however, is not that easy. Has there ever been since the thirteenth century any Catholic university whose academic offerings were all integrated? Are we proposing once again an unrealizable expectation, not just for our own secular age, but also one that was not realized even in the Middle Ages? Historian John O'Malley asked whether the medieval universities had integrated professional schools and the arts. To be sure, the judgments of theologians carried a lot more weight in the church then than they do today. Some theological faculties (especially at the University of Paris) exercised an important *magisterium* to which bishops paid close attention, and whose judgment they even feared.[26] Acknowledging the major differences between medieval and contemporary universities, O'Malley concludes that "there are even grounds for asserting that in their core values, medieval universities more closely resemble the contemporary secular university than they do today's Catholic model."[27]

I am reminded of St. Peter Canisius, who, three hundred years later, in 1550, sent a letter to Ignatius Loyola in Rome complaining about his duties as the president of the University of Ingolstadt, which later became the University of Munich:

> Governing this place is bringing me a good deal of trouble and precious little so far in the way of obvious results. The rector's [read "president's"] principal duties are to enroll new students, to force debtors to pay their bills, to listen to the complaints which men and women citizens of the town bring against the young men, to arrest, reprimand and jail the students who get drunk and roam around the streets at night, and finally to preside at official festivities and at academic functions connected with the conferral of degrees. . . . They say, and it's true, that the lawyers run the place.[28]

Not unlike the presidents of many universities today, including Catholic universities, keeping the peace and dealing with town and gown tensions and problems with student and faculty behavior absorb as much if not even more energy than that needed to pay attention to the university's core mission. Rather than a preoccupation with the integration of knowledge and the central role they should play at Catholic universities, some theologians are more likely to complain about their teaching loads, about the financial support that goes to information technology and athletics, about the bishops, about how few students major in theology, about the lack of support for research, and about the amount of time they have to spend on university committees. They are not wrong. Reality on the ground is messy and difficult.

Conclusion: Success or Fidelity

Have I, and indeed *Ex corde* itself, idealized what a Catholic university should be, and what Catholic theologians should be able to do? Are scholars like Smith and Cavadini correct in believing that it is impossible to recruit three very different kinds of faculty to fulfill Notre Dame's triple mission? Have they themselves adopted, without realizing it, ideal models of specialization not necessarily best for Catholic universities, but typical of prestigious liberal arts colleges and research universities?

It might be a relief to realize that there has never been a "golden age" when Catholic colleges and universities embodied Newman's idea of one. All that said, certain lessons from the past should be obvious: our future requires us never to substitute religious studies for theology, believe that being faithful requires being servile or dumb, or think that holiness and being smart are somehow the same or incompatible.

Even though not many of our institutions have been able to meet the expectations that John Henry Newman described in his *The Idea of a University* and that the Vatican's *Ex corde* has placed upon them, they must continue to try to meet those expectations. Without educational leaders that understand the distinctive intellectual tradition of Catholicism—department chairs, deans and provosts, and presidents—faculty will be tempted to adopt models from the secular academy. It not only "takes a village," but it also takes all the members of the university to work together to begin to realize the educational and professional ideals that Catholic universities should pursue. It is a great undertaking, but very difficult to achieve. More important than achieving a goal is having one worth dedicating one's life to. As Mother Teresa once remarked, it is not success we are called to but fidelity.

PART IV

COCURRICULAR AND CURRICULAR DIMENSIONS

Any university that commits itself to the moral formation of its students needs to pay attention not just to what students should think, but also to how they live and act. In chapter 3, I mentioned several leaders of major research universities who believe that their institutions bore no responsibility for the moral formation of their students. By contrast, I have emphasized the responsibility that Catholic universities have for the formation of the "whole person," which includes not only the intellectual life of students but also their way of understanding themselves in their relationships with others and with God.

In these two chapters, that moral formation is addressed in two ways. The first chapter highlights the benefits that accrue from cooperation between faculty and campus ministers. I offer suggestions to strengthen their relationship without confusing their distinct roles. The second chapter describes how faculty at some Catholic universities have organized courses that teach about Catholicism through multiple academic disciplines. Some of these programs have structured ways for students to live their faith while they study it.

A Catholic university is not a Catholic parish. A parish is where Catholics, and those who want to become Catholics, are spiritually nourished and strengthened. As an open circle, a Catholic university welcomes faculty and students, not just those who are Catholic, to a learning community in which Catholicism, religion, and ethics are a central part of their education. At a Catholic university, moral and intellectual formation are not separated. Both are important and are integrated. The traditional pairing of "faith and morals" indicates that the Christian life is not just about what people believe but also how they act.

A Catholic university is, therefore, more than a parish: it is a learning community that fosters the moral life through the love of learning. In a Catholic university, you can study economic theory, jurisprudence, neuroscience, physics, theater, French, German, chemical engineering, philosophy, theology, languages, and computer science, among other subjects. You can study all these subjects as a believer in a diverse community that seeks wisdom.

14

Campus Ministry and Academics

Introduction

No single group on campus—not administrators, development officers, student development staff, campus ministry, athletics, and or even faculty—can alone address adequately the mission of a Catholic university.[1] How to facilitate cooperation among members of a community who have different talents is not simple; every basketball coach knows this. Although I have been deeply involved as a faculty member and administrator in Catholic higher education for nearly thirty years and played a lot of basketball, I have also been involved regularly, at least in some minor way, in the work of campus ministry—celebrating mass, preaching, hearing confessions, helping on retreats, and offering spiritual direction. It is the relationship of academics and campus ministry that I treat in this chapter. I ask forgiveness in advance if any of my generalizations do not sufficiently account for the many variations this relationship takes at today's Catholic colleges and universities.

This chapter proceeds in three steps. First, I set a context for our topic. That context includes three descriptions: a brief history of Catholic higher education, the establishment of the first campus ministries, and the new sociological context that has shaped college-aged students. Second, I will offer a general description of academics and campus ministers, the different cultures they inhabit, and how well those cultures facilitate collaboration. Third and finally, in light of these first two sections, I will offer some recommendations on how to improve collaboration between faculty and campus ministers.

A Brief History of Catholic Colleges and Universities

The first Catholic universities in Europe were founded in the twelfth and thirteenth centuries; in the United States, most were founded in the nineteenth and the first half of the twentieth centuries. In the nineteenth century, Catholics lived in a largely hostile Protestant culture, and then, especially in the twentieth, in an increasingly secular culture. From their founding most Protestant colleges were attentive to the religious formation of their students, but by the early twentieth century they began to dissociate themselves from their founding denominations

The Future of Catholic Higher Education. James L. Heft, S.M., Oxford University Press. © Oxford University Press 2021. DOI: 10.1093/oso/9780197568880.003.0015

and soon became secular.[2] Catholic colleges and universities have stayed in relationship with the Catholic Church and continue to commit themselves to the religious formation of their students; however, since Vatican II a variety of forces—ecclesial, political, and cultural—have presented a number of new challenges that have reshaped both the academic and religious characteristics of these institutions.

The turmoil over the Vietnam War only added to the cultural upheaval of the 1960s. At the same time, membership of the religious orders that founded the vast majority of Catholic colleges and universities went into a free fall. The tightly orchestrated set of required courses in Thomistic philosophy and theology disintegrated and mostly disappeared. Laypersons with graduate degrees, often doctorates from secular universities, were appointed to faculty positions that religious had once held. Instead of Thomistic thought, laypeople taught courses in modern philosophies, some of which were not that friendly to religious belief. In some important ways, the overall academic quality of these institutions rose. Theology courses replaced religion courses, which helped students study their faith more than just defend it. Some departments taught courses in "religious studies," which covered historical and descriptive dimensions of religions rather than treating exclusively Catholic theological perspectives. Some observers described the dissolution of the Thomistic synthesis as a severe blow to the intellectual basis for a clear Catholic mission and identity;[3] others welcomed the new diversity and lay leadership.[4] Credible cases can be made for both assessments.

Over the last fifty years, many Catholic colleges and universities have established lay boards of trustees who often were more skilled about finances and organization than the religious who founded them were. These boards, however, have struggled to acquire clarity about the Catholic, intellectual, and pastoral mission of their institutions. Controversies over faculty governance and academic freedom flared up and continue to raise difficult questions about the relationship between individual and institutional priorities, whether and how many courses in philosophy and theology should be required, and the proper relationship the institution should have with its local bishop.

Catholic colleges and universities are themselves very diverse. Today, only a few of the more than two hundred Catholic colleges and universities are well endowed; some annually face issues of economic solvency. Perhaps a quarter of them have won recognition for academic quality in the annual academic sweepstakes run by *US News & World Report*, while many others remain academically undistinguished, at least if judged by numerical standards of faculty-student ratio, library facilities, endowment, and selectivity—that is, the number of students who apply but are rejected. Some of these institutions are located in major metropolitan areas and serve many students who are not Catholic, while others are in smaller cities and serve predominantly Catholic student populations. Some universities in large cities enroll more than twenty thousand full-time students, while others enroll fewer than one thousand. While at some institutions most of the students live on campus, at others mainly commuters are enrolled, many of whom are not of the traditional college age. And since the 1960s, some lay Catholics concerned about the weakening of Catholic identity at Catholic universities have founded small colleges that present a very clear version of Catholic identity.

These differences among Catholic colleges and universities affect how campus ministry functions. In our largest universities, where specialization tends to dominate, close collaboration between faculty and campus ministry is typically minimal. In smaller schools, especially those that have a largely residential student population, extensive collaboration is more likely. At some schools, the charism of the founding order provides a focus, sometimes even more than does the Catholic tradition, while at others, the religious charism has become so generalized as to give little distinctive direction to the academic life of the institution. At some schools, faculty share a concern for Catholic intellectual life, while at others only a handful of faculty are concerned; some of them have established Catholic studies programs, which I will discuss in the next chapter. Given this great diversity among even Catholic institutions, it becomes difficult to make unqualified generalizations—difficult, but not impossible. Therefore, I will make some generalizations after I describe the history and current characteristics of campus ministries on Catholic college and university campuses.

A Brief History of Campus Ministry

Until Vatican II, the leaders of Catholic colleges and universities understood their primary mission as preparing mostly immigrant Catholics to enter professional life without losing their Catholic faith. Catholic campus ministries on secular campuses have typically been called Newman Clubs, after St. John Henry Newman, who for several years played that role at Oxford. The first organization for Catholic students at a secular university, the University of Wisconsin, founded in 1883, was called the Melvin Club, named after the faculty member who founded it. Then in 1893 at the University of Pennsylvania, a graduate of the University of Wisconsin, Timothy Harrington, founded a Catholic student organization and named it the Newman Club, a name that since then is commonly used for most Catholic campus ministries at secular universities. At secular universities, Newman Clubs could not be established on the campus and sometimes were met with hostility and distrust until after World War II. At first, Jesuits and leaders of other Catholic universities opposed these campus ministry programs at secular universities; they wanted Catholics to attend only Catholic universities.

Campus ministry on Catholic campuses, it is safe to assume, experienced no hostility from the rest of the university, though students might have been less than enthusiastic about some of the pre-1960 chapel and course requirements. Until the late 1950s and early 1960s, campus ministries at Catholic institutions were staffed exclusively by members of their founding religious orders. Before 1960, courses in religion were taught, again almost exclusively, by religious and priests. Colleges and universities required as many as six to eight courses in Thomistic philosophy and theology, required mass attendance on Sundays and holy days of obligation, strongly encouraged joining male and female sodalities, and required to obey curfews—all these courses and practices aimed to give Catholic students their religious formation. The pervasive presence of religious and priests as faculty and campus ministers gave visible proof of their university's Catholic identity. They drew the contours of the Catholic subculture clearly and sometimes narrowly.

It was not until the early 1980s that the US bishops thought it important to issue a statement in support of Catholic campus ministry programs. In 1985 they published a pastoral letter, *Empowered by the Spirit: Campus Ministry Faces the Future*, in which they described "healthy new developments" (par. 6) and many recent dramatic changes in Catholic universities that had ushered in a new and creative period in Catholic campus ministries: better relationships with the academic community (par. 7), ecumenical and interfaith developments (par. 8), and "a remarkable diversity of legitimate styles and approaches" to campus ministry (par. 9).

The 1990 apostolic constitution *Ex corde ecclesiae* devoted five paragraphs (par. 38 to 42) to "Pastoral Ministry" that emphasized the integration of "faith with life" through the celebration of the liturgy and the sacraments. It stressed the importance of both teaching and practice, not just for students but for the faculty as well, all of whom should "become more aware of their responsibility toward those who are suffering physically or spiritually" and "be particularly attentive to the poorest and to those who suffer economic, social, cultural or religious injustice" (par. 40).

A more extensive but still positive analysis was done in the fall of 2018 when the American bishops' Secretariat of Catholic Education published a quantitative report. It concentrated on campus ministers: who they are, where they are, and how they were prepared for their ministries. Of the nearly 3,000 four-year colleges and universities, only one in four has a Catholic campus ministry. Among community colleges, less than 2% has any form of Catholic campus ministry. The number of campuses that host Catholic campus ministries has decreased from 1,100 campuses in 2008 to 816 in 2018.[5]

In the fall of 2019, a qualitative report was published that gave voice to many campus ministers who described what they loved about their work, what they needed for support, and the importance of collaboration and consultation among staffs. Among the challenges were two approaches to ministering to students that are sometimes in tension with each other: one with mainly degree-educated staff who emphasize evangelization, service, social justice, and ecumenical and interfaith work with not only students but also faculty and staff, and the other missionary-trained young adults (FOCUS missionaries) who favor one-on-one meetings ("discipling") with undergraduate students to help them form a personal relationship with Jesus. Most FOCUS missionaries are on secular campuses, a few on Catholic campuses, and none on Jesuit campuses. Respondents to the survey also expressed their love for the faith and the students they serve but expressed concern about "clericalism," bishops assigning priests without consultation to lead campus ministries, and lay staff with few rights, long hours, too much paperwork, and low pay. A symposium held at the University of Notre Dame on the quantitative report recommended a revision and updating of national standards for campus ministers, a redesign of the certification process for campus ministers, and diversity training for greater intercultural competence.[6]

Both of these studies, the quantitative and the qualitative, are sophisticated and informative. They concentrate on Catholic campus ministry programs wherever they are, on both secular and Catholic campuses. These reports should be read by all Catholic campus ministers. My own remarks and recommendations will be limited mainly to campus ministries on Catholic campuses.[7]

The New Sociological Context

The third and final background comment is sociological in nature. Until the end of World War II, it was not unusual for young men and women to make life decisions at the end of high school. Before the early 1960s, it was common for young men and women to decide to enter religious life or the seminary and, while in college, or shortly thereafter, to marry. By the year 2000, men delayed marriage until they were twenty-seven (in 1950 they married at age twenty-two) and women till they were twenty-five (in 1950 they married at age twenty). The GI Bill made it possible for thousands of students to enroll in both Catholic and secular universities. In the 1960s there was a very large increase in the number of young men who enrolled in college to avoid the Vietnam War. The percentage of women attending college dramatically increased as well, and then minorities began to join them, along with nontraditional students.

One consequence of more people going to college was that their adolescence was prolonged and life decisions delayed. Sociologists of the 1950s and 1960s wrote frequently about a new demographic, "teenagers" or "adolescents," a stage created by America's commitment to mass education, the legal condemnation of child labor, urbanization and suburbanization, and the creation of a consumer and entertainment culture. But in the last few decades sociologists have identified still another stage of development located between adolescence and full-fledged adulthood: "emerging adulthood." Many students now extend their education to include graduate studies, which keeps them in school until their mid- to late twenties, and often in debt for many more years.

These and other changes have led sociologists to conclude that "transition to adulthood today is more complex, disjointed, and confusing than it was in past decades."[8] According to sociologist Jeffrey Arnett, the period of "emerging adulthood" is one of (1) intense identity exploration; (2) instability; (3) a focus on self; (4) a feeling of being in limbo, in transition, in between; and (5) a sense of greater possibilities, opportunities, and unparalleled hope.[9]

If a hundred years ago Freud thought that by age seven personalities were pretty well formed, most psychologists and sociologists today track continuous development, sometimes significant change for persons even in their thirties and forties. And most recently, life cycle and generational studies have discovered continuous change in persons throughout their lives. Gender roles have also changed, with many more women moving on to professional positions, demanding changes in the way that they are treated, and still meeting with continued resistance from the dominantly male corporate world and the church. The divorce rate among Catholics parallels that of the general population.

Historian and theologian William Portier of the University of Dayton has argued that over the past five decades our liberal democratic and consumerist culture has contributed more to the dissolution of the Catholic subculture than did either Vatican II or the turmoil of the Vietnam era.[10] While the loss of those strong Catholic neighborhoods of belief and practice is not all bad (after all, much racism, sexism, and nationalism—as distinguished from patriotism—existed within these Catholic enclaves of the 1950s[11]), the absence of this religiously rich subculture has meant that most Catholics today are more deeply influenced by the larger culture, which in many ways is indifferent, if not hostile to Catholicism, than they are by their Catholic culture.[12]

If Portier and these sociologists are correct, the implications for campus ministry—indeed, for the entire Catholic university community—should be obvious: young people take longer to find themselves, need more mentoring than before, and benefit greatly by learning skills for discernment and making life choices. In other words, Catholic colleges and universities today face the challenge of creating a Catholic culture that teaches these skills by drawing on the great Christian tradition, including the teachings of Vatican II (e.g., religious freedom, ecumenism, interreligious dialogue, lay leadership, and the renewal of liturgical life) without weakening the long-standing core beliefs and distinctive religious practices of Catholicism.

In summary, these three background considerations provide an important context for discussing our topic: the great historical changes in Catholic higher education and campus ministry since the late nineteenth century, the especially dramatic changes since the end of the Second Vatican Council in 1965, and finally the cultural changes that have delayed the arrival of adulthood and made the passing on of a robust sense of Catholicism a longer and more difficult process than it has been in the past. How have these developments affected the culture of faculty and campus ministry in Catholic colleges and universities and their capacity to collaborate?

Two Different Cultures: Academics and Campus Ministers

The word "academics" as used today can mean two quite different things. When people say that a question is only "academic," they usually mean that it is unimportant, even irrelevant, and deserves no answer. Or the word can mean, and this is the sense of the word I am using in this chapter, the important work that professors do: teach, research, and serve. All these activities, done well, are hardly irrelevant. All faculty members teach, some do research and publish, and many do various forms of service, especially on university committees.

How do faculty approach their work? Despite the great diversity among Catholic colleges and universities, the following generalizations may be made: faculty want their students to learn what they have to teach. They also push students to question their assumptions, to take seriously points of view to which they have not yet been exposed, to improve their ability to read and write, and, if it is a theology course, to raise critical questions about the nature and benefits of religious belief. Some professors believe that questioning can lead students to a deeper understanding and commitment to their faith; others fear that it will weaken their faith, which is already under attack.[13] In professional schools some professors emphasize skills and material and professional success, while others teach the sciences.

But it should be asked, how many faculty, whatever their discipline, concentrate on teaching the "whole person"? It is difficult to exaggerate the difficulty many faculty have in stepping outside the boundaries in which they have been socialized as doctoral students and in professional associations. Joseph Appleyard describes some of the barriers that block faculty from attending to the development of the "whole person":

the professional pressures on faculty and the *de facto* reward system they operate in, the scant knowledge many administrators and faculty have of theology and spirituality, the persuasion of students and their families that professional or pre-professional preparation is the main function of undergraduate education, and lure of online education and other technological solutions, and of course a lack of resources everywhere for implementing even effective programs.[14]

Some faculty fear a loss of status in the eyes of their colleagues. Junior faculty often lack models of senior faculty who have bridged disciplines and discuss the ethical and religious dimensions that are an inherent part of their own disciplines. Some faculty think that they are not competent to address moral and religious issues. Some faculty lack a commitment to integrate knowledge and fear that doing interdisciplinary work could cost them tenure or the disapproval of purists in their academic departments. To be clear, I am not suggesting that every faculty member, or even most faculty members, should try to "import" into their courses moral and religious perspectives; in fact, the very word "import" should be a dead giveaway that the ethical and religious dimensions inherent in nearly every discipline are there but unrecognized. They don't have to be "imported" since they are already there.

In too many instances, faculty lack the knowledge to see these dimensions; an ability to see them, however, can be developed through additional research and collaboration with other faculty who have taken up this challenge. At the same time, courses in political science, English, or biology can communicate profound ethical and religious insights. Every one of these subjects, when taught by faculty who grasp the many different issues their subjects actually include, will necessarily, at some point, deal with religious and ethical issues. Courses like these meet a profound need today: they help integrate knowledge.

As mentioned at the beginning of this chapter, the likelihood of faculty collaborating with campus ministers often depends on the size of the university and its mission. Larger and better-endowed Catholic universities publicize their academic achievements. They want to be recognized by prestigious universities as academically excellent. It is not unusual that at such universities little collaboration exists between the faculty and campus ministry. They do not disrespect what campus ministers do; they are simply happy to hand off to them the responsibility for the moral and religious formation of their students. They are focused on building the academic prestige of their institution. Again, of course, at smaller institutions, where the faculty are less specialized and work more closely with the students, collaboration with campus ministers is easier. An exception to this difference between big and small institutions can be found when faculty at highly ranked Catholic universities, even with large enrollments, have a strong sense of the mission and embrace the basic principles of Catholic intellectual life. Students at these institutions are more likely to see the necessary relationship between academic and religious formation.[15]

Both faculty and, especially, theologians and campus ministers face the increasing religious illiteracy of students. One of the most sobering chapters in Christian Smith's extensive study of the religious lives of American youths, *Soul Searching*, is devoted to Catholic teenagers. Their lack of religious literacy is stunning—lower than the teenagers surveyed from *any* other religious group.[16] Conscientious faculty and campus ministers struggle to find the best ways to address this high degree of religious ignorance.

If we turn now to reflect more directly on the culture and mission of campus ministry, what are some of the challenges they face? Besides religious illiteracy, campus ministers at universities and colleges with many residential students deal with students who have a great deal of free time, nearly all of it unsupervised by adults. Some campuses recruit students to be supervisors in the residence halls. They are often only a year or two older than first-year students. These RAs, resident advisers as they are often called, are put in the difficult situation of being expected on occasion to confront the bad behavior of their peers. They struggle with students' consumption of alcohol and use of other drugs and witness multiple forms of sexual misbehavior. Left mostly to themselves, most students are not mature enough to make good decisions on all these matters, and peers rarely try to correct each other.

Nor has it helped that since the 1960s, the work of campus ministers has been organized and professionalized as a separate unit within the university. James Burtchaell explained that the divide between the academic and the pastoral widened when administrators delegated pastoral responsibilities to a different group than the faculty: student services, RAs, and campus ministers:

> When the administrators in their turn created a class of religious functionaries—chaplains, secretaries, deans of students, et al.—to relieve [faculty], too, of responsibilities, that ecclesial piety and discipline were shown to be only loosely and incoherently bound to the central purpose of the colleges.[17]

In response to this division of the academic and the religious, some efforts by faculty and staff on a number of Catholic campuses (some at big, but more often at smaller campuses) are working to strengthen greater collaboration between campus ministry and faculty, and between faculty members themselves. Speaking at a national conference on "Callings" at the Jesuit University of Santa Clara in March of 2007, Sharon Parks, a one-time professor of education at Harvard, noted that higher education is undergoing a major shift away from a century-old German model of the research university with its emphasis

on objectivity, division into departments and disciplines, and hierarchical administration to a dramatic redefining of boundaries that now, at the dawn of the
twenty-first century, emphasize the importance of double majors and "interdisciplinary and trans-disciplinary studies." She points to "the blurring of town-
and-gown boundaries, catalyzed by 'service learning,'" which she says is now
"morphing into 'community-based learning.'"[18] She also notes that too many
faculty still look down upon service learning as soft and fear that promoting
it could weaken their standing in the eyes of their colleagues. And though she
decries the growing consumerism in American culture and on many of the
nation's campuses, she nonetheless presents a very positive—perhaps overly
positive—picture of the academy at the beginning of the twenty-first century.
She believes that we are witnessing an overdue revolution. If so, it may facilitate
great collaboration between faculty and campus ministers. I hope she is right but
believe that she may be overstating the case.

Many campus ministers are unable to see the critical importance of the intellectual development of students. While faculty tend to underestimate the importance of the moral and religious development of their students, campus ministers
tend to underestimate how a deeper intellectual formation actually supports the
goals of campus ministry. I have found that most campus ministers do an excellent job promoting service opportunities, retreats, and immersion trips. These
activities have proved quite effective in engaging students, forming community,
and developing habits of service, especially if they are followed up with sufficient
reflection and study. Few campus ministers have the budgets or the inclination
to sponsor lecture series that bridge the academic and the religious dimensions
or have found ways to involve faculty appropriately in their ministry—such as
inviting them to speak with students at dinners about their own lives as people
of faith, or in general promoting the intellectual life as a way also to foster lives
of faith.[19]

The 1985 bishops' pastoral letter states that "it is vital that campus ministry
creates a climate in which theological learning is respected," and that such a climate is best supported by campus ministers who "are perceived as being serious
about continuing their own theological education"(par. 54). It is not that campus
ministers are anti-intellectual; rather, they seem so focused on building community, programming, and relationships that support students' personal and
emotional development that intellectual formation rarely gets the attention it
deserves.

Both faculty and campus ministers tend to overlook the importance of
students' Catholic intellectual formation. They often do not root Catholic social
teaching in Catholic dogmatic teaching and, as a consequence, focus on justice
issues, sounding more like the Democratic Party than an integrated version of
Catholic social teaching. On the other hand, there are Catholics whose energy is

devoted only to ending abortion and gay marriage, and they sound more like the Republican Party. Pope Francis has tried, not without resistance from both sides of the political divide, to overcome this unfortunate division of what should be integrated. Even on Catholic campuses, the church's teachings on sexual morality and abortion are less emphasized than teachings on serving the poor and social justice. In general, then, both faculty and campus ministers, and Catholics in general, have trouble articulating in a compelling way a holistic understanding of Catholic teaching and religious formation.[20]

Finally, I think most people in higher education—faculty and campus ministry staffs both—struggle with how to understand diversity and its benefits and limits. A recent issue of the *Journal of College and Character* devoted to religious diversity states in its editorial that morality is "the neglected topic in diversity discussions on campus."[21] Articles in this issue describe why faculty avoid such discussions (they list fear of conflict, of proselytizing, and of crossing the boundaries between church and state). They note that many campus ministers, for their part, turn such discussions away from religion and instead promote tolerance, which, it would seem, they do not associate with religion. As one campus minister at Wellesley, where religion is apparently discussed, wrote, the point is to "move from Christian hegemony to a multi-faith community."

Most nonreligiously affiliated universities basically celebrate the cultural and ethnic differences they have and want to find ways to increase them. They promote mutual respect and hospitality—which are very good practices—but put to the side issues of faith and morality. Many students, as already noted, on Catholic campuses lack an adequate understanding of their own religious tradition and know even less about other religions. They are aware that there are many religions, but they often think that they all teach about the same thing, except for a few "details," such as Jesus Christ. They often believe religion is just a matter of opinion and don't see the point of studying it seriously.

At Catholic universities, faculty and campus ministers should engage directly the questions of different religions, learn what they have in common and how they differ, seek to understand the significance of the differences according to each of the religions, and, as a consequence, begin an important intellectual and religious journey that in a global world of religious pluralism we ignore at our peril. Not every faculty member or campus minister needs to become an expert in interreligious dialogue or the comparative study of religion, but they should recognize that the current pervasive ignorance about religions leads to stereotyping, misinterpretation, misunderstanding, and, tragically, violence. One of the recent developments that makes this kind of substantive ecumenical and informed interfaith conversation possible is the growing expectation that campus ministers on Catholic campuses should serve and provide support for the religious development of students who practice forms of Christianity other than

Catholicism or who practice other religions. Faculty and campus ministers at Catholic universities should be especially well equipped to foster this conversation, given the fact that Catholicism officially promotes interreligious dialogue and is able to avoid both fundamentalism and relativism.

I have pointed out several typical problems that face faculty and campus ministers at Catholic universities. I have also noted that both faculty and campus ministers find the issue of religious diversity difficult to deal with. Again, these are broad generalizations, and many exceptions can surely be found.

Some Recommendations for Greater Collaboration

Faculty and campus ministers have different primary responsibilities. I believe in this division of labor. This division, however, is not a total separation, and certainly is not an opposition. The primary purpose of faculty is the intellectual development of the student. Nothing will help faculty achieve that goal at a Catholic university more than a deep appreciation of what Catholic intellectual traditions mean for their disciplines and for the formation of the whole person. Familiarity with Catholic approaches to the intellectual and moral life prevents any facile or arbitrary separation of intellectual and moral development. Bernard Prusak reminds us of the moral development that implicitly shapes students when they prepare well for any class. Doing so requires

> temperance with respect to the many possible pleasures of undergraduate life. Discussion classes demand—and offer opportunities for the development of—justice and respect toward others in the give-and-take of ideas, humility when an idea must be withdrawn or modified, and courage to stand by an idea that is unpopular.[22]

Faculty who understand and appreciate a Catholic philosophy of education will recognize that the development of the mind presupposes the acquisition of important moral habits. They will educate the "whole person." In the long run, faculty members who are able to recognize the relevance of Catholicism for their discipline are forced to think about more things than only about their own discipline. David Chappell, the author of a recent book on the civil rights movement, wrote that Dr. Martin Luther King "had a more accurate view of political realities than his more secular liberal allies because he could draw on biblical wisdom about [sinful] human nature. Religion didn't just make civil-rights leaders stronger—it made them smarter."[23] Whatever strengthens Catholic intellectual life on campus will benefit the important work of both campus ministers and the faculty.[24]

Here are some simple recommendations that will increase on Catholic campuses greater collaboration between faculty and campus ministry:

For Faculty

(1) Take the time to learn about the campus ministry programs.
(2) Learn about the Catholic intellectual tradition.
(3) Explore the relationship between academic learning and moral development.
(4) Whether Catholic or not, show up occasionally at campus liturgical celebrations.
(5) Volunteer to participate as a mentor or an observer at one campus ministry retreat a year.
(6) Raise key questions about the purpose of a college education and of life in your classes at appropriate moments.
(7) Study the documents of Vatican II.[25]
(8) Explore fruitful forms of interdisciplinary research, seminars, and teaching.
(9) Become familiar with Catholic social teaching.[26]
(10) Encourage students to take the study of religion seriously.

For Campus Ministers

(1) At the beginning of the academic year, ask professors to allow you to speak briefly in their class about programs that you offer and what you do.
(2) In the campus ministry office set up a small library of books and DVDs, with movies such as *The Diary of a Country Priest, Babbette's Feast, Of Gods and Men, A Man for All Seasons, Grand Torino, A Hidden Life,* and many others.
(3) Encourage Bible study (with commentaries), not just sharing personal opinions about texts.
(4) Invite faculty to give talks about what matters to them and what they care about most.[27]
(5) Start a monthly lecture series and ask local faculty to respond to the speakers.
(6) Close the gap between conservative and liberal versions of Catholic teaching.
(7) Lead a study on Vatican II[28] and invite some faculty to discuss these documents with you.

(8) Start a series on the study of different religions and Catholicism's relationship with them.[29]

(9) Find ways to increase male participation in campus ministry events.[30]

(10) Develop the habit of reading books on the Catholic intellectual tradition.

Ultimately, Christianity is not only about ideas, nor even mainly about behaviors, but rather about an encounter with a person, Jesus Christ, experienced also in and through one another, especially the poor, who are too often conspicuous by their absence on many Catholic campuses. Such an encounter, expressed by how believers live, opens up rich and deep possibilities for living the intellectual life. Liturgy and service, coupled with study and disciplined reflection, form the whole person.

In summary, then, there is a need to open up the academic disciplines, to hold conversations between faculty and campus ministers, and to increase religious literacy and literacy about religions.

Conclusion

People are fond of quoting a saying attributed to St. Francis: "Preach the Gospel at all times; use words if necessary." The saying underscores the need to walk the talk; deeds, indeed, are important. At the same time, I am also fond of 1 Peter 3:15: "Always be ready to make your defense to anyone who demands from you an accounting for the hope that is in you; yet do it with gentleness and reverence."[31] The call to witness and defend the faith transcends just going to college and getting a good job. Catholics need to inform and deepen their faith. And to do that, they need both deeds and words. Nicholas Lash, a British Catholic theologian, once remarked that "care with language" is the "first casualty of original sin." Good theologians watch their language in the presence of God.[32] So do good campus ministers and faculty members. A Catholic university is one of the best institutions to foster good deeds and craft carefully words that enable Christians to give the accounting they are called to give of their faith in this life.

15

Catholic Studies Programs and Catholic Identity

Introduction

The previous chapter examined the relationship between academics and campus ministers and offered some suggestions for how to strengthen it. This chapter focuses on the initiatives that some faculty at some Catholic universities have taken to make the Catholicity of their universities more visible and to offer more opportunities for the spiritual formation of the students.

As mentioned earlier in this book, there are good reasons not to generalize about Catholic higher education in the United States. First, it is not a centrally governed set of educational institutions, but a "free enterprise" system founded mainly by different religious orders, some of which, even those founded by the same order, compete even with each other for faculty, including members of their own order, as well as students and donors. Second, not being centrally organized, the two hundred or so Catholic colleges and universities are very different in size, the types of student they enroll, location, and culture. Third, some exist in big cities, others in small towns, and a few in rural settings. Fourth, some of these institutions have no graduate programs, while a few aspire to be research universities. Different types of people administer and staff these institutions. Fifth, some small colleges have student bodies that are almost exclusively Catholic, while some student bodies are less than 20% Catholic. Some are mostly residential with traditional undergraduates ages eighteen to twenty-two, and others are commuter schools with adults who attend classes mainly in the evenings and on weekends. Sixth, a few have small teacher/student ratios; others generate revenue through extensive online learning programs. And finally, a few have doctoral programs in Catholic theology, but the vast majority do not.

As different as these institutions are, there are still some common identifiable trends that affect how Catholic people think about them. First, for a long time, the presence of religious orders reassured families that their institutions were indeed Catholic. But the numbers of religious have dropped dramatically since the mid-1960s. Today, very few religious and priests serve as full-time faculty members, and of them most are approaching retirement. Second, most of these institutions are now led by lay presidents. Third, before 1960, there were many

The Future of Catholic Higher Education. James L. Heft, S.M., Oxford University Press. © Oxford University Press 2021.
DOI: 10.1093/oso/9780197568880.003.0016

women's Catholic colleges founded by religious orders of sisters, but in the following decades most of them merged with larger men's colleges, which typically were led by men. Fourth, at most Catholic universities today, the theological views and religious backgrounds of faculty and students differ more than ever before on issues such as abortion, homosexual marriage, women's rights, and the relationship that a Catholic university should have with the church. Finally, in the 1920s and 1950s there were animated debates about the academic quality of Catholic colleges and universities—a debate brought to a fever pitch by John Tracy Ellis's famous 1955 article that lamented their widespread mediocrity. Today, however, most debates are not about their academic quality, but about their Catholicity.

In the last forty years, several new small Catholic colleges have been founded, mainly by laypersons who want a clearer focus on Catholicism in both curricular and student life. These colleges include Thomas Aquinas, founded in 1971 in California; Christendom, founded in 1977 in Virginia; and Thomas More College, founded in 1978 in New Hampshire. Ave Maria College was founded in Michigan in 1998 but was renamed Ave Maria University when it was relocated to Florida in 2003. The founders of these institutions believed that the existing Catholic colleges and universities had capitulated to the worst trends of the 1960s, to the cultures of relativism and secularism, in a misguided effort to win approval from their secular peers. What needed to be done, they claimed, was to begin all over again and establish new colleges that were truly Catholic. They have no need for Catholic studies programs (CSPs) since their whole institution is Catholic. Typical of their criticism of major Catholic universities is Christendom's board member Fr. George Rutler who, on the fiftieth anniversary of the Land O'Lakes statement, wrote:

> The heads of Catholic colleges and universities who gathered at Land O'Lakes were fraught with a deep-seated inferiority complex, rooted in an unspoken assumption that Catholicism is an impediment to the new material sciences, and eager to attain a peer relationship with academic leaders of the secular schools whose own classical foundations were crumbling and whose presidents and deans were barricading their offices against the onslaught of Vandals in the guise of undergraduates.[1]

It is not only the leaders of some of these recently established Catholic colleges who are critical of the Land O'Lakes statement. In less sweeping terms than Rutler's, John Garvey, president of the Catholic University of America, established in 1889, stated in a 2017 interview that Catholic universities now need a closer relationship with the hierarchy that would replace the essentially "hands off" stance reflected in the Land O'Lakes statement, which, in his view, called for "an academic freedom from any sort of influence, lay or clerical," a phrase quoted from the statement that he interpreted as wanting no relationship at all with the church. Garvey believed that what Land O'Lakes called for is not "the view of *Lumen Gentium*, it's not the view of *Ex corde ecclesiae*, it's not the view of John Paul II, or Benedict, or Francis."[2] That's a pretty sweeping condemnation.

But then there are those administrators and faculty members who believe it is not necessary to start all over again and found new institutions. They have set out to strengthen the Catholicity of their existing institutions by creating CSPs. The purpose of this chapter is to examine these programs and evaluate their effectiveness. What did the founders of these programs see happening that led them to create CSPs? What do some of the existing programs look like? What are their strengths and weaknesses, and their future?

Catholic Studies Programs: Origins

Three years after the publication in 1990 of *Ex corde ecclesiae*, the late Donald Briel, founder of the first and still largest CSP, explained why he felt the need to create it. In a retrospective essay included in a *Festschrift* published in his honor in 2017, he recalls that when as a first-year student he walked onto the Notre Dame campus in 1965, he experienced an integrated Catholic culture, where priests and brothers of the Congregation of the Holy Cross wore religious habits everywhere on the campus. They were not just in administrative offices and the faculty in classrooms, but they also lived with students in residence halls. The university then required eight courses in philosophy and eight in theology, while additional courses in literature and history explained the Catholic foundations of Western culture. Catholicism pervaded the entire university.[3]

By 1969, however, Notre Dame's tapestry of Catholicism, according to Briel, had unraveled. The Holy Cross priests and brothers had adopted secular clothing and the students, all men, were no longer required to wear coat and tie for dinner. Many on the faculty began to oppose the large number of required theology and philosophy courses; faculty began to promote social and political activism. Vietnam protests were organized on many campuses, student sit-ins in administrators' offices demanded change, and the civil rights movement captured the imaginations of many students and faculty. Perhaps the most serious hollowing out of the Catholic character of the university was, again according to Briel, the loss of the ecclesial context of theology. In place of Catholic theology, the practice of *fides querens intellectum*, academic theology took its place and became just another discipline like all the others. By the late 1960s, the cultural forces of secularism and pluralism had begun to shape the attitudes of faculty at Catholic universities; many faculty no longer bothered themselves with the religious formation of students, offloading that onto campus ministry.[4]

For Briel, another clear indication of the unraveling was the 1967 Land O'Lakes statement. In calling for "true autonomy and academic freedom in the face of authority of any kind, lay or clerical, external to the academic community itself" (critics of the statement refer to this sentence often), it severed the university's important relationship with the church. Nevertheless, the authors claimed that, naively according to Briel, Catholicism would be "perceptively present and effectively operative."[5]

In retrospect, the authors of that 1967 statement could hardly have anticipated the upheaval in American culture that followed the optimism of the elections of Pope John XXIII as pope, the promise of great renewal in the church through Vatican II, and the first Catholic, John F. Kennedy, in the White House, and that the coherent Catholic subculture of the 1950s would dissolve so quickly. Who would have expected right on the heels of Vatican II that so many religious would leave their orders, that increasingly aggressive forms of secularism would further privatize the role of religious faith, and that the vulgarization of public life and media would alienate many of the young from the church?

Despite these powerful cultural changes pulsating through American society already by 1967, the authors of the Land O' Lakes statement believed that Catholic universities were being called by the times to be the "critical reflective intelligence" not only for society but also for the church. They were confident that in the coming years the church would enjoy "the benefit of continual counsel from Catholic universities." Following Notre Dame's long-time president Theodore Hesburgh's oft-repeated description of the university as the place where the church does its thinking, they believed that the time had come for the church to consult with and begin to learn from its universities.

It gradually became clear, however, that to provide such guidance, the university needed committed Catholic intellectuals in many disciplines, not just in theology. For a variety of reasons described in other chapters in this book, such intellectuals were hard to find, at least in the numbers needed to solidify in multiple disciplines the intellectual mission of universities. Since Catholic intellectuals were many fewer than Catholics with PhDs, those who retained a sense of Catholicism sought ways to create special programs for students desirous of a more integrated Catholic experience. Briel, a great admirer of John Henry Newman and Christopher Dawson, set about creating an academic program at the University of St. Thomas that integrated knowledge and affirmed the complementarity of faith and reason. While not ignoring academic rigor, he emphasized the Catholic intellectual tradition rather than academic freedom and institutional autonomy. Rather than abandoning responsibility for the moral life of the students, he established cocurricular programs for their religious formation.

According to Briel, CSPs needed to go beyond mere career preparation and begin reversing the fragmentation of knowledge. He embraced the church's role in the intellectual life of the academy. He refused to adopt "critical thinking" at the expense of creative and commonsensical thinking. How successful was Briel's reformation of Catholic higher education, and have others follow his lead?

Evaluations of Catholic Studies Programs

Thomas Landy, a sociologist at the College of the Holy Cross, wrote one of the first articles about the appearance and growth of CSPs. In the early 1990s, he founded *Collegium*, an eight-day summer institute launched to help junior faculty and doctoral students learn about the Catholic intellectual life and encourage them to join the faculties of Catholic colleges and universities. In his 1998 article, he described these new CSPs, which by then numbered seven, beginning with the most extensive and well-funded one at the University of St. Thomas in St. Paul, Minnesota.[6] In general, Landy thought that these programs helped these colleges and universities to "address their religious identity and pass along Catholic tradition to students."[7] If since Vatican II most Catholic colleges and universities had become interested mainly in opening themselves up to the rest of the world and move beyond what some critics described as "ghetto Catholicism," he explained that the faculty who created these new programs believed that the Catholic identity of their institutions could no longer be taken for granted. They proceeded to design, integrate, and make available courses that offered students a more robust exposure to the Catholic tradition.

But not everyone at these universities was happy with the curricular initiatives of their colleagues. Some feared that they were "restorationist" projects, that their leaders wanted to retreat to the pre–Vatican II "Catholic ghetto," and that their programs had become protected curricular islands that exempted the rest of the faculty from also teaching the Catholic intellectual tradition. Some faculty felt that the establishment of such programs made them feel as though they could not be trusted to support the mission of the university. In short, on many campuses, these programs met opposition from faculty not involved in them.

The next national conversation about Catholic higher education in general, and implicitly about CSPs, took place in the pages of *Commonweal* in April of the following year.[8] At that time, the American bishops were themselves about to meet and approve their second proposal (the one in which the Vatican required the *mandatum* for theologians) for implementing Pope John Paul II's 1990 apostolic exhortation on Catholic higher education, *Ex corde ecclesiae*.[9] Many leaders of Catholic higher education feared that Rome would force the American hierarchy to crack down on what they perceived as the hard-fought post–Vatican II achievements. The editors' introduction to the six *Commonweal* articles reflected that widespread anxiety: "Next November when the bishops of the United States gather for their annual meeting they are very likely to approve a set of canonical requirements that would irredeemably alter the character and mission of U.S. Catholic higher education." The future of these institutions, the editorial continued, was "gravely threatened."[10] If the new juridical requirements (especially the *mandatum* that Catholic theologians were expected to acquire from their local bishop) were imposed on Catholic universities, the editorial warned, they will lose their "autonomy, academic freedom, and pluralism."

In the face of such threats, what were leaders of Catholic higher education to do? Peter Steinfels recommended three things: first, a "return to the basics" as outlined quite positively in the first half of *Ex corde*; second, an acceptance of the great diversity among Catholic colleges and universities, such as "a strictly doctrinally defined Franciscan University of Steubenville and a cosmopolitan Georgetown and a more religiously homogeneous but academically open Notre Dame, as well as liberal arts colleges serving working-class women or minorities"; and third, a request for leadership from the bishops: "let bishops be bishops, not errand boys," by which he meant that bishops needed to take into consideration the actual realities of Catholic higher education in the United States rather than "reach a paper solution or get a good report card from Rome."[11] With one notable exception, all the other authors participating in this *Commonweal* conversation did not recommend establishing CSPs, though several commented on them.

Many of the fears raised by these authors were echoed by lawyer Paul Saunders, who in the mid-1980s served as counsel to Charles Curran in *Curran v. The Catholic University of America*. Saunders believed that

> implementation of the proposed norms (which included the *mandatum* for theologians and the expectation that at least 50% of the faculty will be Catholic) will, in short, raise a hornet's nest of legal issues that will not be resolved easily or quickly and that may result not only in the loss of federal or state aid, but in liability by the university to those who will be adversely affected by such implementation.[12]

Such predictions have since proven to be alarmist. Other authors in that same issue of *Commonweal* saw the situation differently. Fr. Andrew Greeley, a sociologist, novelist, and consistent proponent of Catholic education, accused Catholic colleges and universities of fleeing from their Catholicism. He claimed that mandates would make no difference. What was needed, he wrote, were Catholic research and CSPs. He had had enough of the "silly season, a time of shallow, angry, ideological romanticism," of "clergy dressing in sweat suits and nuns in Bermuda shorts."[13]

John Cavadini, then chair of the theology department at Notre Dame, called for scaling down the rhetoric and not describing the controversy as an "impasse" between bishops and universities. He encouraged academics to admit that there were real problems and to abstain from "calls for academic freedom [which is never absolute anywhere] without corresponding calls for Catholic identity." However, he did not want Catholic universities to become simply "an arm of the Church" or be turned into "glorified pulpits" any more than he wanted theology departments to become "unremittingly critical of the *magisterium*."[14] He recommended that the bishops take a five-year moratorium before deciding how to implement *Ex corde* so that the Catholic colleges and universities could think more deeply about how, in serious and creative ways, they might embody the bold call for a robust Catholic identity sounded in the first part of the pope's apostolic constitution. He acknowledged that solid CSPs could be an appropriate response to the need for a clearer Catholic identity, but he did not recommend establishing more of them.

Similar points made by authors in this special issue of *Commonweal* have been echoed in other articles that discuss CSPs. Worries about creating a "Catholic ghetto" within the university, of cutting off the academic freedom needed to explore and critique the Catholic tradition, of turning universities into seminaries, of forcing the breadth and richness of the Catholic tradition into narrow formulations that pass for orthodoxy, and of general faculty opposition were voiced when discussing the pros and cons—mostly cons—of CSPs. Landy had noted already in his 1998 article that faculty at some institutions feared that if many CSPs got off the ground, they would be locked into prolonged and fruitless debates about what would pass as "authentic" Catholicism. Other faculty feared that creating a specific set of Catholic courses would make direct oversight by bishops more likely, giving them a clearer target that would threaten academic freedom. Some administrators, according to Landy, feared that CSPs would marginalize Catholic content and reduce them to simply one more option in the curriculum, such as women's studies or environmental studies.

In 1999, Francis W. Nichols, professor of theology at Saint Louis University, offered a generally positive view of CSPs' contributions. He described the historical evolution of theology from mainly a catechetical and apologetic emphasis in the 1950s into academic theological departments, and then in more recent years into religious studies departments. But like other critics, he then asked whether faculty in such religious studies departments would see Catholic studies as a criticism of their own lack of an exclusive concentration on Catholicism. According to Nichols, the biggest challenge was defining what constituted Catholic studies, a task that required faculty to ask what is meant not only by "Catholic" but also by "studies." Given the increasing religious illiteracy, he wondered how courses that were primarily interdisciplinary could also be pedagogically remedial. He worried that interdisciplinary courses would have their own difficulties, not least of which were the increasing number of theologians who no longer devoted themselves to the study and teaching of the Catholic intellectual tradition itself. Though Nichols viewed CSPs as generally a positive development, he wrote that it was a "diverse work in progress" that nonetheless seemed "destined for a secure place" in the future.[15]

The 2011 volume *The Catholic Studies Reader* offers the best proof that Nichols was basically right about the complex academic nature of CSPs.[16] The seventeen essays in this volume, edited by James T. Fisher and Margaret M. McGuinness, offer a thoughtful overview of the various ways in which CSPs, which they describe as an "emerging discipline," are constructed in both Catholic and non-Catholic universities throughout the country. They admit that the assumptions that undergird CSPs today would be virtually incomprehensible to Catholics who, with the great confidence that characterized the "Catholic Revival" of the 1930s and 1940s, had established national professional societies for Catholics proud about the distinctive Catholic character of their research and disciplines.[17] The assumption then was that most if not all the faculty needed to be Catholic. Members of the religious orders in substantial numbers confidently led their institutions' distinctive mission, though without much faculty participation in their governance. Today, scholars of all faiths (and even none) are welcome in most Catholic universities, where only a handful of religious remain. CSPs are often interdisciplinary and include more than theology and philosophy, thereby exposing students to study Catholicism through multiple lenses. Many faculty, Fisher and McGuiness report, are simply not sure what to make of CSPs.[18] They conclude that there seems to be no "clear consensus" about what makes for a CSP:

> Does placing existing courses under the heading "Catholic Studies" create an interdisciplinary area of study? Catholic universities, of course, require all students to complete a minimum number of religion/theology courses in order to graduate, but what other fields are important? Are there particular disciplines to which all Catholic Studies students should be exposed? Is literature more important than art; is art more important than sociology?[19]

By 2011 CSPs had assumed at least three different configurations: (1) a cluster of cross-listed courses that treat Catholicism (e.g., LaSalle University), (2) a required introductory course followed by multiple relevant courses (e.g., Fordham and Georgetown models), and (3) an infusion of the Catholic intellectual tradition in the general education program and in faculty research programs in as many academic disciplines as possible (e.g., Dayton model).

Some Current Programs

The number of CSPs has increased since Tom Landy's 1998 article. As of 2018, some of these programs list more than fifty courses, some connected in clusters as minors or even majors, and in at least two instances as graduate degree programs. Few universities can boast about its CSP as does St. Thomas University in St. Paul, where Don Briel started his program of curricular and cocurricular reform. It started out in 1993 as an interdisciplinary degree program and then in 1996 was established as a center. Each year about one hundred freshmen indicate that they intend to major or minor in Catholic studies. They currently have 233 students in the undergraduate program (154 majors and 69 minors) and 56 students in their graduate program. Besides a residential program of religious formation and courses in Rome, St. Thomas also has on campus two houses for men and one for women in which students majoring in the program can live together. One of the major purposes of these residential arrangements was the religious formation of the students. Recently, St. Thomas established a master of arts in Catholic studies, available in online and blended formats. A fifteen-million-dollar endowment makes these opportunities possible.

Other programs, while not nearly as extensive, are growing at places like Loyola Chicago, Santa Clara, Seton Hall, and John Carroll, to mention only a few. Some remain quite small. At the time of this writing, DePaul University, currently the largest Catholic university in the country (over fifteen thousand undergraduates), lists on its website sixty-three courses as part of its CSP and thirty-nine faculty as teachers. However, they currently have only fifteen majors and seven minors. Detroit Mercy, in existence since 1999, had its first graduates in its certificate program (eighteen credit hours in several disciplines) in 2006, and currently has twenty-five undergraduates enrolled in their program. More students than these, of course, take courses in Catholic studies. At Loyola Chicago fifty students enroll in their Catholic studies program, partially supported by their newly founded Hank Center for the Catholic Intellectual Heritage. Catholic studies has become an important undergraduate community; it hosts an annual interdisciplinary/mixed media forum and semiannual retreats. St. Louis University has seventy-five students enrolled for minors in Catholic studies and plans to establish a major program in the near future. For the minor, two specifically Catholic courses are required; with approval, these students may choose courses in philosophy, theology, and history.

Some Catholic universities, like the University of Dayton where I served for nearly thirty years, have tried to create a culture in which the Catholic intellectual tradition is respected and understood by all the faculty. At least one of the faculty in all the disciplines and professional programs is expected to do research in that tradition. Instead of establishing a CSP, the faculty leadership at

University of Dayton decided to continue to have dimensions of Catholic intellectual traditions become an integral part not only of the required general education program but also in all of the degree programs—with, of course, mixed results.[20] The Dayton model requires substantial support for ongoing faculty development programs.

Another way to emphasize the importance of a Catholic university's commitment to its Catholic intellectual tradition is what they invest in certain academic programs. Twenty-five years ago, the leadership at Dayton decided that if Catholic theology was to be recognized as academically distinguished within the university, it would be best to build a PhD program. That doctoral program now enrolls nearly forty students, and an additional thirty master's degree students. Dayton's doctoral program gives special emphasis to the dialogue between theology and the social sciences. On the undergraduate level, about thirty students major in religion, with nearly twice that number minoring in religion. They offer several clusters of courses that explore Catholicism through several disciplines. The University of Dayton is not the only Catholic university fostering multidisciplinary courses that explore Catholicism without calling them Catholic studies. It is therefore important to look carefully at not just the names of programs and courses, but also at what universities actually offer in their courses, both as core requirements and as electives.

Some secular universities also offer CSPs, such as the University of Illinois at Chicago, where almost half the students are Catholic. It lists nineteen courses but only two faculty members. The cross-listing of courses makes it difficult to determine just how many students take CSP courses. The University of California at Santa Barbara, like a number of other secular universities, established a chair of Catholic studies and offers courses on both the undergraduate and graduate levels.[21] At Stanford, where 25% of the undergraduates are Catholic (not unusual at many of the Ivy League universities), efforts to establish a chair in Catholic studies have not succeeded, though the money needed for it was available. At Yale, a vital Catholic campus ministry program draws two thousand students weekly for Sunday Eucharist (total student population of Yale is thirteen thousand); it also provides space for students to study. At the University of Southern California, a private university established by but no longer affiliated with the Methodists, I teach courses in Catholic history, theology, and interreligious dialogue. Catholic alumni of the university recently built an exquisite campus ministry complex with offices, meeting rooms, a lounge area, and a church administered as a parish by the archdiocese.

Given this brief and partial 2018 survey, it should be obvious that since the 1970s, efforts to strengthen Catholic identity at Catholic universities through CSPs have intensified. While they are at very different levels of maturity, they address a need that, in the judgment of some faculty and administrators, has not been sufficiently met by the ordinary offerings of the curriculum: a focus on Catholic tradition in multiple disciplines. Moreover, in view of the growing Catholic populations of undergraduate students on secular campuses and a greater openness to the study of religion (Harvard excepted), leaders on secular campuses allow religious studies departments, and even Catholic studies courses, as well as endowed chairs in Catholic theology (or sometimes called Catholic thought) to be established.[22]

Some Generalizations

For over three decades I have been working on issues related to Catholic universities and their distinctive mission, first at the University of Dayton, but then also in my own research and writing, especially as provost of the university (1989–1996) and then as its chancellor (1996–2006). A fuller understanding of the university as an institution and what it takes to change the culture of such a complex entity as well as formulate and implement long-term priorities for the entire institution—that opportunity was, for me personally, the greatest benefit of those very challenging and interesting years in administration. I also had the privilege of serving on the board of the Association of Catholic Colleges and Universities for nearly a decade and chaired that board during the time that the Catholic bishops in the United States finally implemented *Ex corde* in 1999. Throughout all these years, I was privileged to visit and speak at numerous Catholic campuses around the country. It is this background that I bring to the evaluation of these CSPs.

Has the establishment of CSPs been successful in deepening the Catholic mission and identity of Catholic colleges and universities? The first thing to be said is that CSPs constitute a genuine if sometimes uneven effort on the part of faculty and administrators to make more explicit the Catholic mission and identity of the university. This effort is often a tacit admission that without such initiatives, the mission of their institutions risks becoming invisible, a sad consequence of years of inattentiveness on the part of the leadership and faculty of these universities.[23] Speaking more positively, it is also a clear statement that transmitting the Catholic identity of the institution should no longer be placed upon the shoulders of only a theology department. ✗

Establishing CSPs also implies that the responsibility for Catholic identity cannot be left only to campus ministry programs, as important as their role is. Campus ministry staffs work at religious and moral formation but typically do not do well in addressing the intellectual formation of Catholics, as explained in the previous chapter. The intellectual character of CSPs helps students understand that Catholicism has a public role despite the peculiar understanding of the separation of church and state in the United States.

✗ Does everyone teaching have to be Catholic? If not, how can they transmit Cath. identity?

On the other hand, problems remain. If faculty who lead these programs are perceived by their peers as academically weak—pious, well-intentioned people who lack intellectual gravitas and rigor—the programs will only be tolerated by the rest of the faculty, if not openly opposed. As Fisher and McGuinness recognize, "some tension" exists between faculty who want CSPs to be solely academic disciplines and those who favor them primarily as vehicles also for moral development and forming future leaders for the church. That very tension, they write

> can serve to sensitize those in non-Catholic and secular universities to the role this discipline plays in implementing the mission of Catholic colleges, while at the same time, pushing those Catholic institutions who view Catholic Studies as a way to appease donors, bishops, and graduates worried about Catholic identity to recognize its validity as an academic discipline that can increase our understanding of theology, culture, faith, traditions and lived practices of Catholicism.[24]

If at Catholic universities the Catholic studies courses lack intellectual rigor, ignore legitimate criticism of the tradition, or avoid tough questions, many faculty will perceive them simply as ways to indoctrinate students.[25] And if these programs are driven by faculty who do not respect what other faculty in the university have committed themselves to in terms of their research and teaching, the program will never be what it should be—a leaven within the entire curriculum.

Catholic studies is an "emerging discipline." By its very nature it might be better described as a "field of study" rather than a "discipline." Its content is not easily specified. Understanding its complexity prevents simplistic generalizations about the many forms it takes. Faculty who ask for "CliffsNotes" on the Catholic intellectual tradition or ask what "exactly" it includes will deform into a series of bullet points a living and multifaceted intellectual tradition. Swiss theologian Hans Urs von Balthasar described truth as "symphonic," that is, a blending of notes, creating rich harmonies. To understand more adequately the symphonic character of the Catholic tradition, he recommended that theologians pay close attention first to aesthetic experiences (embodiments of beauty and the arts) and then to their dramatic forms (embodiments in the lives of persons, especially the saints, and history), and only finally, for theologians, to engage in theological reflection, an always inadequate effort to speak about God and the things of God (integrated Catholic theology).[26] In other words, the Catholic tradition is never just intellectual, definitional, or easily summarized.

Before concluding, I want to revisit the debates that have continued over the effects of the Land O'Lakes statement on Catholic higher education. On the fiftieth anniversary, in 2017, the president of Notre Dame, John Jenkins, CSC, referred to some of the document's critics, including Bishop David O'Connell, former president of the Catholic University of America, and Patrick Reilly, the president and founder of the Cardinal Newman Society. The former said that document caused "confusion" in the church, while the latter, sounding somewhat like Fr. George Rutler quoted at the beginning of this chapter, decried its "devastating impact on Catholic higher education."

Jenkins admitted that the drafters of the document had overlooked some of the very real challenges they would have to face if they were to have implemented its vision successfully. They underestimated, Jenkins admitted, the difficulty of finding enough theologians and scholars in other disciplines who were rooted in the Catholic intellectual tradition: such scholars "would need to have both the ability and interest not only to conduct research at the highest level in their chosen areas, but also to be intellectual leaders of colleagues across the disciplines, and to foster interdisciplinary, integrative conversation." Those of us who have engaged in interdisciplinary research and teaching know the challenges they pose. Jenkins also admitted that a critical weakness in the document was its failure to make any suggestions about what the relationship between the church and the Catholic university should be, an omission that allowed its critics to assume that the authors of the document didn't want any such relationship. Even though *Ex corde ecclesiae* affirmed, as did the authors of the Land O'Lakes statement, the importance of academic freedom and institutional autonomy (a point often missed by its critics), it called for Catholic universities to stay in communion with the universal church. How best to do that remains, I would add, also a "work in progress."[27]

I believe that Jenkins offers a fair assessment of the current situation, and that critics like Rutler and Reilly see none of the document's good points, nor would they mention, much less compliment, people like Jenkins who affirm the document's value but also offer a thoughtful criticism of its shortcomings.

Conclusion

Catholic studies, led by capable faculty and supported by thoughtful administrators, should help in focusing more clearly the Catholic mission and identity of very diverse Catholic colleges and universities. Some campuses enjoy resources that others lack. Some have a core of faculty who can lead this effort credibly, while others do not. In retrospect, Landy's 1998 article holds up well. I repeat what one author affirmed a decade ago: Catholic studies is here to stay. May these programs grow in depth and intellectual vitality. On the other hand, the existence of CSPs is, as mentioned earlier, a tacit admission on the part of some administrators and faculty that their university no longer communicates a sufficiently integrated vision of Catholicism. In that light, CSPs are important or, perhaps better, "necessary but not sufficient." Most Catholic universities need more than CSPs. All of the faculty need to learn how to contribute, in ways appropriate within their disciplines, to the distinctive intellectual and moral mission of a Catholic university. Otherwise, CSPs appear as religious curricular islands separated from the secular mainland of the university.

Even in granting the problem of lack of Catholic distinctiveness, one gets the feeling that restorationists are going about it all wrong. To attract more faculty to take Cath. seriously, catholics have to shed their form of insecurity. Focus on Cath. Intl. tradition is the answer.

Conclusion

The Future of Catholic Higher Education
in the United States

To historians, all history is revisionist history, and for conservatives it is a term of derision for any history that places the experiences of groups other than wealthy white men at the center of the story. Given the increasing variety of perspectives from which history is written today—anticolonialist, feminist, queer, and social history, among others—the complexity of understanding well what has happened and how it should be understood is daunting. Many revisionists are up front about how their own standpoint shapes their view of the past and, while not claiming objectivity, still want their stories taken seriously. Henry Glassie, whom I quoted in chapter 11, explains that subjectivity, not to be equated with subjectivism, distorts if hidden but can be controlled if identified and exposed.[1] The need to identify one's subjectivity is true for scholars not only in the liberal arts but also in the sciences.

If our understanding of the past is always limited and our ability to interpret even our own time is biased, isn't trying to predict the future a fool's errand? To avoid falling into despair over how little can be predicted with any confidence, I will offer, by way of conclusion, only a few thoughts on what I hope to be fairly defensible generalizations about the future of Catholic higher education in the United States. Drawing upon what I have written in this book, I will focus on three areas: vision and leadership, faculty, and the Catholic Church. I will add a few comments about finances—although I did not devote a chapter to that topic (I do not think I am competent enough to do so), I know that at many colleges and universities making the budget and marshaling resources remain a great challenge, especially for universities and colleges that are tuition driven.

I want to stress first the importance of vision and leadership for the future of Catholic higher education.[2] In the first three chapters of this book, I stressed the importance of Jesus, Mary his mother, and St. John Henry Newman as "north stars," individuals who should influence the shape of the mission of a Catholic university. Most readers would expect to see Newman as a guide, but what about Jesus and Mary? For Christians, Jesus is the axis of history, the unique person at the center of their religious belief and practice. In a special way for Catholics, Mary also occupies a key but ancillary position that, as I have explained, shows

The Future of Catholic Higher Education. James L. Heft, S.M., Oxford University Press. © Oxford University Press 2021.
DOI: 10.1093/oso/9780197568880.003.0017

that Jesus is truly human (he didn't drop from heaven fully grown) and therefore also needed to be raised like any other child then, educated in his religion and in the ways of wisdom.

The person of Jesus reminds leaders of Catholic educational institutions that ultimately individual people are what education is about. Universities tend to focus on ideas, abstractions, hypotheses, theories, and verifiable knowledge. How do people verify who they are? To the extent that the humanities and the arts are important—and they should be very important at Catholic colleges and universities—the stories of individual people, their triumphs and tragedies, teach us the meaning of life. At the center of Christianity is a person, three persons, not a philosophy or a set of moral rules. Students are not primarily customers nor faculty solely experts. They are persons working together in a learning community that seeks not just knowledge but also wisdom. Administrators are not bureaucrats. They are servants, or people who minister to, as in ad-ministers. Jesus gathered a community around him to help him. It is no different for those in a Christian educational community. We are together and dedicated to seeking wisdom and doing good to others. Before education is a nonprofit business, it is a beneficial community, one that aims to be good as well as do good.

What about the role of Mary, the Mother of Jesus? As St. Pope John wisely noted sixty years ago, the place, significance, and agency of women constitutes one of the great movements of our own times. Thinking of Mary educating Jesus in the ways of wisdom and then staying with him throughout his life, encouraging him to help a young couple escape embarrassment at their wedding celebration, present at the foot of the cross where all the apostles but one had abandoned him, says something about awareness, fidelity, courage, and love, which ought to be characteristic virtues of the Christian academy. Feminist authors have astutely exposed the tendency of academic culture, largely male until recently, to compartmentalize thinking and multiply abstractions. Jesus and Mary offer a more personalized and inclusive vision for Catholic education, one in which we can speak of communities of learning and the search for wisdom.

Finally, unlike Jesus and Mary, John Henry Newman actually writes about university education, and does so with a clear emphasis on the liberal arts, moral formation of students, and the freedom that theologians need for their work. He also explains how theology plays a role in shaping the mission of the entire university and how disciplines should be understood to relate to each other. Today's Catholic colleges and universities are certainly different than Newman's 1850 Oxford University and its colleges. Nevertheless, in key respects, Newman's vision of education, I have argued, should be embraced by Catholic colleges and universities today.

What kinds of leaders, then, should Catholic colleges and universities seek? Authors of books on leadership often list qualities for a successful university president that only someone approaching divinity would possess. Frank Rhodes, who served as a distinguished president of Cornell University for many years, tells the humorous story of a member of Yale's board of trustees who in the middle of the nineteenth century gave the following description of the president they needed:

> He had to be a good leader, a magnificent speaker, a great writer, a good public relations man, a man of iron health and stamina, married to a paragon of virtue. His wife, in fact, had to be a mixture of Queen Victoria, Florence Nightingale and the best dressed woman of the year. We saw our choice as having to be a man of the world, but an individual with great spiritual qualities; an experienced administrator, but able to delegate; a Yale man, and a great scholar; a social philosopher, who though he had the solutions to the world's problems, had still not lost the common touch. After lengthy deliberation, we concluded that there was only one such person. But then a dark thought crossed our minds. We had to ask—**is God a Yale man?**[3]

As I have shown in chapter 10 on teaching and research, great teachers are not all alike. Nor are all great presidents. What qualities, then, should presidents of Catholic colleges and universities have? First, they need to grasp the distinctive vision that Catholic colleges and universities should possess. That vision includes the centrality of the person, the importance of community, and the search for wisdom. The major officers of a Catholic university need to express that vision clearly and attractively to many audiences—faculty, students, donors, and bishops. The president takes seriously both the intellectual and moral formation of students. At Catholic universities, presidents should make it clear that students are there to learn not only how to make a living but also, more importantly, how to make a life worth living. Finally, the president needs to coordinate the different groups within the university community—faculty students and staff—and never tire of articulating the vision that makes Catholic colleges and universities a valuable and distinctive contribution to the pluralism of higher education in the United States.

Second, it is impossible to have a good university without faculty who are competent in their disciplines, humble in their search for knowledge, and dedicated to the university's mission. I described in chapter 9 some ways to hire faculty who support the mission, emphasizing that they need to grasp that mission as a theologically and philosophically rooted intellectual tradition. They also need to care about the moral formation of students and be willing to collaborate in appropriate ways with staff who work directly with the students, such as campus ministers and student services staff. It does not mean that a Catholic university hires as faculty only Catholics, nor does it mean that people of other Christian denominations, other religions, or no religion will be unable to contribute to the Catholic mission. Indeed, some may be very attracted to that mission. Diversity in a faculty can strengthen the mission, as long as that diversity is within the mission, not parallel to or against it. Catholicism is a big tent—so big that even within the mission, difference of opinion should be welcome, vigorous debates possible, and disagreements respected. Finally, if the leadership of the university does not shape the criteria for promotion and tenure to support a vision of teaching and research that welcomes the exploration of religious and ethical perspectives, fosters the integration of knowledge, and encourages a distinctive core curriculum, it will have failed in one of its most important responsibilities.

Throughout this book, I have stressed the importance of the distinctive character of the Catholic intellectual tradition. In several chapters, I have offered descriptions of some of the characteristics of that tradition. Some people have asked me why I don't just speak of Catholicism—why instead I talk about the Catholic intellectual tradition. The main reason I have used this phrase is that the greatest danger today, especially in the academy, is to think of religion as only personal and private, or worse yet, superstitious and anti-intellectual. I have also emphasized it as a tradition, but not as traditional, as in "we've always done it that way." It is helpful to distinguish between tradition and traditionalism: tradition is the living faith of the dead, while traditionalism is the dead faith of the living, as I believe G. K. Chesterton once wrote. A tradition is dynamic and multifaceted, gives life, draws on centuries of wisdom, generates debate, and enriches the present. To be contemporary is to be relevant, but to treasure a living tradition is to be on the path to wisdom.

Therefore, faculty need to embody and teach the Catholic intellectual tradition, which is not just personal but also social, is not just private but also public, and is not just one idea but many ideas that often are in a dynamic tension. It is not just contemporary but also carries within it the wisdom of centuries of exploration that has been handed down even for thousands of years. If the Catholic intellectual tradition is to be found anywhere in this world, it should be found alive and well among faculty at Catholic colleges and universities.

Third, there are the ever-present and pressing issues of finance. Over the years, as provost, chancellor, and now president of a research institute, I have been guided by people who are excellent in financial matters. One consequence of this has been successive excellent audit reports. A second consequence is that since I was able to delegate these matters to people far more competent than me, I really don't know much about them, especially if I try to get into details. However, there are some general observations I think that even I can make.

Surveys that I cited earlier in this book indicate that sometimes boards have hired presidents more skilled in finance than steeped in vision, especially when the bottom line is hemorrhaging. A financially astute president can figure out how to stop the budgetary bleeding, but without a distinctive vision of education, the school will not draw the students or the donors it needs to sustain itself and grow. Good management, of course, is important: no margin, no mission. But without a vision, the people perish (Prov. 29:18), good faculty don't apply, and donors are uninspired. Without a distinctive vision compellingly presented, a Catholic university as Catholic will cease to exist, even if it somehow continues to enroll students and meet the payroll. The person who monitors the finances doesn't have to be the president, but the president needs to be able to articulate the mission compellingly. Every budget is a mission statement.

It should be recalled that when the accreditation agencies for universities and colleges began to gain influence in the 1930s, they were concerned about not only academic quality but also the financial health of an institution. The major Protestant universities initially received support from the churches that founded them. However, they soon realized that to meet their needs and support their aspirations, they needed to break away from their church support and raise money on their own. In short, by the late nineteenth and early twentieth century, these major private universities developed fundraising capabilities.

The story at Catholic universities was different. As we have noted in this book, religious orders founded and staffed the vast majority of Catholic colleges and universities. They never asked for money from the bishops or local churches. These priests, brothers, and sisters led these institutions, filled most of the faculty positions, and, other than what was needed for their own room and board, never took salaries. As a consequence, the cost of tuition remained very low. It also meant that they didn't see the need to build an endowment—they became the "living endowment" of their institutions.[4] This unique arrangement won them accreditation and worked well at most of these institutions as long as there were many religious and priests. But that supply rapidly disappeared after Vatican II ended in 1965. It was only then that most Catholic universities began to think seriously about fundraising. They were about a century behind the major private universities. Today, most Catholic colleges and universities have yet to build adequate endowments.

For the future of Catholic colleges and universities, then, success in fundraising will likely determine whether they remain in existence. Money follows vision. Therefore, again, it is crucial that leadership present that vision in ways that connect with potential donors. This should be obvious but nonetheless needs to be stressed, for at a number of institutions that are in financial difficulty, short-sighted administrators think that spending money to raise money is to spend money they don't have. However, if they are able to articulate the vision and establish a good fundraising staff, this infrastructure will more than pay for itself.

I have one other suggestion for those universities and colleges founded by Catholic religious orders. Most of these orders are now personnel poor and property rich. I suggest that they sell some of their property, turn the proceeds into endowments, and give them to the universities they founded to strengthen their Catholic mission and support low-income students who otherwise would be unable to attend. Some religious orders have already begun to do this.

Fourth, and finally, though this book is about Catholic higher education in the United States, I have also emphasized in several chapters the importance of the Catholic university's proper and enduring relationship to the Catholic Church, not just locally but also globally. C. S. Lewis once wrote that for every modern book that he read, he also read one written during another period of history. Otherwise, he feared that he would become captive to the errors of the local village. Similarly, being attentive not just to the Catholic Church in the United States but also to the universal church will make it less likely that Catholic universities will succumb to academic fads or lapse into political parochialism. If for a period of time in the late 1960s Catholic universities may have thought it best to keep the hierarchy at arm's length, I have argued that that relationship be maintained, but all the while protecting their institutional autonomy and academic freedom as affirmed in Ex corde ecclesiae.

I have argued elsewhere that since World War II, Christianity, as well as other religions, may be entering a second axial age.[5] Having survived the critique of the Enlightenment, the church has no longer retained the shape of Christendom, when the church wanted to control not only its own affairs but also public and political affairs. The Enlightenment created educational institutions and civic governments free of church control and argued for the freedom of religion and the rights of conscience. When the Catholic Church at Vatican II officially recognized the autonomy of secular institutions and encouraged ecumenical and interreligious dialogue, it changed profoundly a set of assumptions that had shaped the understanding of its role in society that it had held since the late fourth century. In 1990, the Catholic Church document Ex corde ecclesiae affirmed the academic freedom and autonomy of Catholic colleges and universities. These are extraordinary game-changers that we might be tempted to take for granted. By supporting academic freedom, the church has also recognized tenure, which protects the rights of the faculty through due process. The bishops have acknowledged that they do not have, and should not have, the power to hire and fire faculty at nonpontifical Catholic colleges and universities. Since Vatican II, the Vatican has mistreated some theologians, but there is more recourse to due process than ever before.

These protections are to be treasured, not taken for granted, and certainly not abused. More than any other institution in the Catholic Church, Catholic colleges and universities have created practices of governance that entrust the mission of the university to lay boards of trustees and protect lay faculty, men and women, from arbitrary dismissal. It takes time to adjust to such sweeping changes. Historians think that the first axial age lasted for several centuries. I have argued that the challenge, or better, the great opportunity that exists now at our Catholic colleges and universities is the freedom to create a distinctive mission led by laymen and -women, among whom we will find most of the Catholic intellectuals of the future.

I return finally to the question I posed at the beginning of this book: will Catholic universities take the secularization path that major Protestant universities took at the turn of the last century? If Catholic universities and colleges hire solid leadership, recruit boards of trustees that understand Catholic education at a university level, and strengthen the Catholic intellectual tradition through careful faculty hiring and formation, I believe that they will not lose their Catholic identity and will thrive and offer to the world a truly distinctive education.

Notes

Introduction

1. For a reliable and public domain English translation of *De Docta Ignorantia*, see Arthur Haskins, *On Learned Ignorance*, 2nd ed., 2nd printing (Minneapolis: Arthur J. Banning Press, 1985), 55402.
2. See James Heft, Reuven Firestone, and Omid Safi, eds., *Learned Ignorance: Intellectual Humility Among Jews, Christians and Muslims* (New York: Oxford University Press, 2011), especially the introduction and chapter 2, "Learned Ignorance and Faithful Interpretation of the Qur'an in Nicholas of Cusa (1401–1464)," by Pim Valkenberg.
3. Nicholas Lash, *Seeing in the Dark* (London: Darton, Longman and Todd, 2005), p. 15.
4. Philip Gleason, *Contending with Modernity: Catholic Higher Education in the Twentieth Century* (New York: Oxford University Press, 1995), p. 290. For a thoughtful critique of Ellis's article, see Brian Conniff, "John Tracy Ellis and the Figure of the Catholic Intellectual," *Catholic Education: A Journal of Inquiry and Practice* 10, no. 1 (September 2006), pp. 76–88. Conniff evaluates some of Ellis's assertions and puts them in a historical context that involves Flannery O'Connor and Thomas Merton.
5. Paul Van K. Thomson, "Should Catholic College Be Abolished?," *Columbia College Today*, Fall 1966, pp. 36–41.
6. Ibid., p. 41.
7. John Cogley, "The Future of an Illusion: Catholic Universities Face the Fate of the Papal States," *Commonweal*, June 2, 1967, p. 310.
8. Ibid., p. 313.
9. Peter Schrag, "Our First Great Catholic University?," *Harper's Magazine*, May 1, 1967, pp. 41–49, at 49.
10. Cogley, "The Future of an Illusion," p. 314.
11. Ibid.
12. For the text of the Land O'Lakes statement, see Alice Gallin, ed., *American Catholic Higher Education: Essential Documents, 1967–1990* (Notre Dame, Indiana: Notre Dame Press, 1992), pp. 7–12.
13. Don Briel, Kenneth Goodpaster, and Michael Naughton, "Our Reason for Being: Restoring the Pillars of Catholic Education," *America*, February 1, 2016, p. 14.
14. David O'Brien, "The End of Catholic Education?," in letters to the editor, *America*, February 22, 2016, p. 6.
15. Much of this diagnosis may be found in the introduction to Una Cadegan and James L. Heft, eds., *In the Lógos of Love: Promise and Predicament in Catholic Intellectual Life* (New York: Oxford University Press, 2016), p. 3.
16. Una Cadegan, "The Cliff and the Tower," in *In the Lógos of Love*, p. 11.
17. Ibid., p. 12.

Chapter 1

1. George Dennis O'Brien is an exception. His *The Idea of a Catholic University* (Chicago: University of Chicago Press, 2002) presents Jesus as a sacrament, a reality that engages the believer both intellectually and existentially. His treatment of Jesus remains, however, on a somewhat abstract level. See my review in *Commonweal,* July 12, 2002, pp. 24–25.

2. Harvey Cox, a Baptist theologian who for many years taught at the Harvard School of Divinity (he retired in 2009 at the age of eighty), published *When Jesus Came to Harvard: Making Moral Choices Today* (New York: Houghton Mifflin Company, 2004), in which he asked what the Jesus of Galilee had to do with Harvard University. In the 1980s Harvard asked him to teach a course in a newly created Moral Reasoning division of the undergraduate curriculum. Cox examined past course catalogs to see when the last course with Jesus in the title was taught and discovered that one was taught by Professor George Santayana, who by 1912 had left Harvard. The Jesus that Harvard wanted Cox to teach, however, had nothing to do with claims of divinity or theological beliefs about him; they really wanted a course on morality. In chapter 12 on liberal education, it becomes even clearer that in recent years, faculty at Harvard voted against any study of religion since they think it promotes superstition.

3. Tertullian, *Prescription of Heretics,* chapter 7. For a discussion of Tertullian's thought and influence, see Hans von Campenhausen, *The Fathers of the Latin Church* (Stanford: Stanford University Press, 1964), and about the debate concerning the proper relationship between Athens and Jerusalem, see pp. 17–18. For a fuller development of the relationship between philosophy and faith, see Jack A. Bonsor, *Athens and Jerusalem: The Role of Philosophy in Theology* (Rahwah, NY: Paulist Press, 1993).

4. See Paul Gooch, "Paul, the Mind of Christ, and Philosophy," in *Jesus and Philosophy*, ed. Paul K. Moser (New York: Cambridge University Press, 2009), pp. 84–105.

5. James Heft, ed., *A Catholic Modernity? Charles Taylor's Marianist Award Lecture* (New York: Oxford University Press, 1999), pp. 118–119.

6. I have a friend, a humanist, who has published several award-winning books. He recently wrote a fascinating—to me at least—exploratory essay on miracles. I asked him where he thought he could publish it. He replied, "I have absolutely no idea."

7. Sandra Mize, "On the Back Roads: Searching for American Catholic Intellectual Traditions," in *American Catholic Traditions: Resources for Renewal*, ed. S. Y. Mize and William Portier (Maryknoll, NY: Orbis Books, 1997), p. 5.

8. See James Heft and Jan Stets, eds., *Empty Churches: Non-Affiliation in America* (New York: Oxford University Press, 2021). This interdisciplinary study brought into extended conversation scholars from the disciplines of psychology, social psychology, sociology, political science, history, philosophy, and theology and two mothers who have young adult children, all of whom explore the reasons for this important development. We also asked them to evaluate the phenomenon—something many social scientists typically avoid—and explain whether they think it is good, bad, or a mix of good and bad, and why.

9. See Alvin Plantiga, *God and Other Minds: A Study of the Rational Justification of Belief in God* (Cornell, NY: Cornell University Press, 1967), and a second edition with a new preface by Plantinga published in 1990; and *Warranted Christian Belief* (New York: Oxford University Press, 2000). Also see John Haldane, *Faithful Reason: Essays Catholic and Philosophical* (London and New York: Routledge, Taylor & Francis Group, 2004) and *Seeking Meaning and Making Sense* (Exeter, UK: Imprint Academic, 2008). See also David Tracy, *The Analogical Imagination: Christian Theology and the Culture of Pluralism* (New York: Crossroad, 1981), in which he explains the public nature of theology, the way that classics (not just in theology) attain a normative status in a nonauthoritarian way.

10. On the WWJD movement, see Tom Beaudoin, "A Peculiar Contortion," *America* (September 18, 1999), pp. 16–19. The Reverend Janie Tinklenberg, a youth pastor at a Reformed church in Holland, Michigan, began the current WWJD movement.

11. George Denis O'Brien's book (see note 1 of this chapter) draws a perhaps overly sharp difference between a secular and a Christian university. As explained in chapter 13 on the role of Catholic theology, religious studies, while not the same as theology, is now an established discipline on many secular campuses. Some bridges can be built between theology and religious studies. See also Mark Roche's review of O'Brien's book in *Journal of Higher Education* 75, no. 2 (2004), pp. 234–237. Before joining the faculty at Notre Dame, Roche taught at the Ohio State University.

12. Andrew Greeley, *The Catholic Myth* (New York: Simon and Schuster, 1990).

13. Robert Bellah, "Religion and the Shape of National Culture," *America* 181 (July 1999), p. 3.

14. Ibid., p. 11.

15. Robert Wuthnow, *Loose Connections: Joining Together in America's Fragmented Communities* (Cambridge, MA: Harvard University Press, 2002).

16. I particularly like the description Robert Imbelli gives of a deep "sacramental consciousness" at the heart of the various historical forms Catholicism has taken over the centuries (see "Vatican II: Twenty Years Later," *Commonweal* 109, no. 17 [October 8, 1982], pp. 522–526). Despite the diversity of those cultural forms, Catholicism retains, according to Imbelli, certain "foundational sensitivities," among which he numbers five: (1) the corporeal, as the body sacramentalizes the spirit; (2) the communal, for the community gives birth to a sacramental consciousness; (3) the universal, inasmuch as Catholicism addresses the private and the public, the natural and the cultural, the personal and the institutional; (4) the cosmic, as all of creation is involved in the redemptive work of God in Christ; and (5) the transformational, because the human is not just covered over by Christ making it acceptable to God the Father, but rather is truly transformed and made holy.

17. From W. H. Gardner and N. H. Mackenzie, eds., *The Poems of Gerard Manley Hopkins*, 4th ed. (New York: Oxford University Press, 1970), p. 90.

18. From Ralph W. Franklin, ed., *The Poems of Emily Dickinson: Reading Edition* (Cambridge, MA: Belknap Press of Harvard University Press, 1998).

19. Brian Daley, "Christ and the Catholic University," *America*, September 11, 1993, p. 9.

20. Louis Dupré, "The Joys and Responsibilities of Being a Catholic Teacher," in *Faith and the Intellectual Life*, ed. James L. Heft (Notre Dame, IN: Notre Dame Press, 1996), p. 70.

Chapter 2

1. I am speaking of long-time history professor at the University of Dayton, Irving Beauregard, whose student, Philip Gleason, became a professor at the University of Notre Dame and a distinguished historian of Catholics in the United States and author of the magisterial study of Catholic higher education, *Contending with Modernity* (New York: Oxford University Press, 1995).

2. I will be drawing here freely from Johnson's book, *Truly Our Sister: A Theology of Mary in the Communion of Saints* (Boston, Massachusetts: Continuum, 2005), and more recently from her article "Galilee: A Critical Matrix for Marian Studies," *Theological Studies* 70 (2009), pp. 327–346; I also have found very helpful the reflections, sent to me by email, by the late Fr. Francois Rossier, S.M., then the director of the International Marian Research Institute.

3. Johnson cites (in *Truly Our Sister*, p. 96) Raymond E. Brown, "The Meaning of Modern New Testament Studies for an Ecumenical Understanding of Mary," in his *Biblical Reflections on Crises Facing the Church* (New York: Paulist Press, 1975), p. 105.

4. John L. McKenzie, *Dictionary of the Bible* (New York: MacMillan Press, 1965), p. 575. For a description of *midrash* as a literary type, see Ray Brown, *The Jerome Biblical Commentary*, 3rd ed. (Englewood Cliffs, New Jersey: Prentice Hall, 1990), p. 1082, where he states that "midrashic interpretation . . . uses such reflections to make the text relevant to the questions, need, and interests of its audience."

5. New Testament scholar John Meyers points out that even though scripture doesn't explain the educational process, "the day-to-day interactions of mothers with children in the household were of foundational significance in passing most aspects of Israelite culture from one generation to another" (cited by Elizabeth Johnson, *Truly Our Sister*, p. 202).

6. Beverly Roberts Gaventa, *Mary: Glimpses of the Mother of Jesus* (Columbia, South Carolina: University of South Carolina Press, 1995), p. 68.

7. Stressing Mary's role of educating the child and young Jesus should not diminish the importance of Joseph's role, brought out more clearly in the first two chapters of Matthew's Gospel. Elizabeth Johnson tells the story she heard from a woman in Harlem who wanted the church to preach less about Mary and more about Joseph, "because he raised that boy like his own kid, which he wasn't" (*Truly Our Sister*, p. 193).

8. Johnson, *Truly Our Sister*, p. 117.

9. In the early church, one way Christians professed orthodox teaching was by what they believed about Mary: namely, that she really was Jesus's mother (Jesus was

truly human), and that she was also, according to the Council of Ephesus (431), the *Theotokos*, the Mother of God (that Jesus was truly divine).

10. Johnson, *Truly Our Sister,* p. 205.

11. Roland E. Murphy, *The Tree of Life: An Exploration of Biblical Wisdom Literature,* 3rd ed. (Kentwood, Michigan: Eerdmans, 2002), p. 4.

12. Ibid., p. 1. The only exceptions, Murphy adds, are very late additions (Sir. 44–50 and Wis. 11–19).

13. Ibid., p. 133.

14. Again, I am indebted to Fr. Francois Rossier, SM, for these reflections. See note 2.

15. Francois Rossier, SM, email dated July 27, 2009.

16. Roland Murphy, *The Tree of Life,* p. 146. As for a helpful description of Lady Wisdom, Murphy cites Burton Mack: "She is a teacher, one who shows the way, a preacher and a disciplinarian. She seeks out human beings, meets them on the streets and invites them in for a meal. The bewildering sexual aspects include sister, lover, wife and mother. She is the tree of life, the water of life, the garment and crown of victory. She offers to human beings life, rest, knowledge and salvation" (n. 22, p. 149).

17. See Bertrand Buby, *Scripture in the Marian Writings of Father William Joseph Chaminade* (Dayton, OH: North American Center for Marianist Studies, 2000), Monograph Series, Document #44, p. 2, citing the work of Fr. Jean Baptiste Armbruster, SM.

18. Boethius, *The Consolation of Philosophy* (Dirigreads.com Publishing, 2018), pp. 7–8.

19. Ibid., p. 10.

20. Ibid., p. 22.

21. Ibid., p. 23.

22. Ibid., p. 27.

23. Pamela Sheingorn, "'The Wise Mother': The Image of St. Anne Teaching the Virgin Mary," in *Gendering the Master Narrative: Women and Power in the Middle Ages,* ed. Mary C. Erler and Maryanne Kowaleski (Ithica, New York: Cornell University Press, 2003), p. 107. *Pseudo Matthew,* another apocryphal gospel, states: "No one could be found who was better instructed than she [Mary] in wisdom and in the law of God, who was more skilled in singing the songs of David [Psalms]," also p. 107.

24. Ayers Bagley, http://iconics.cehd.umn.edu/St_Anne/St_AnneText.htm.

25. For a much-needed study of the role of Catholic colleges and women in America, see Tracy Schier and Cynthia Russett, eds., *Catholic Women's Colleges in America* (Charles Village, Baltimore: Johns Hopkins University Press, 2002).

26. John XXIII, *Pacem in terris,* par. 41.

27. Walter Ong, *Fighting for Life: Contest, Sexuality, and Consciousness* (Ithica, New York: Cornell University Press, 1981), p. 121.

28. Ibid., pp. 119–134.

29. Ibid., pp. 135–136. In ecclesiastical universities, especially seminaries such as the *Gregorianum* in Rome, oral examinations are still the preferred way to test students.

30. Ibid., p. 139.

31. I thank Prof. Fred Jenkins, associate dean of the University of Dayton Libraries, for this reflection.

32. John W. O'Malley, S.J., *What Happened at Vatican II* (Cambridge, Massachusetts: The Belknap Press of Harvard University Press, 2008).

33. John O'Malley, *Four Cultures of the West* (Cambridge, Massachusetts: Harvard University Press, 2004).

34. In my opinion, the loss of the Latin language should be lamented. Without knowing Latin, many important ancient and medieval texts that shed light on the history of women, and certainly on Mary, are now in danger of being unread only because they are untranslated. A similar argument can be made for the retention of the great tradition of Gregorian chant lest it be lost to the church as well.

35. See Jean M. Twenge, *iGen: Why Today's Super-Connected Kids Are Growing Up Less Rebellious, More Tolerant, Less Happy, and Completely Unprepared for Adulthood* (Ojai, California: Atria Books, 2017). Though the title suffers a bit from exaggeration, Twenge's study is carefully done. See especially chapters 3, "In Person No More: I'm with You but Only Virtually," and 4, "Insecure: The New Mental Health Crisis."

36. Richard Kearney, "Losing Our Touch," *The New York Times*, Opinion Page (August 30, 2014), p. SR4.

37. April Dammann, *Corita Kent: Art and Soul: The Biography* (Santa Monica, California: Angel City Press, 2015).

38. *Aufzeichnungen aus den Jahren* 1875/79. *Gesammelte Werke*, Musarion-Ausgabe (Munich, 1922 ff.), vol. 9, p. 480, cited by Josef Pieper, *In Tune with the World: A Theory of Festivity* (New York: Harcourt, Brace & World, 1965), p. 10.

39. Bertrand Buby, *Mary: The Faithful Disciple* (Mahwah, New Jersey: Paulist Press, 1985).

40. Elizabeth A. Johnson, C.S.J., *Truly Our Sister* (New York: Continuum Books, 2006).

41. In a text entitled "La Magna Charta," Lubich comments on Mary's visit to Elizabeth: "Our Lady didn't go to Elizabeth in order to sing the Magnificat, but in order to help her. So with us, we should not go to our neighbors in order to reveal to them the Christian treasure that we carry in our hearts, but in order to carry with them their sufferings and burdens and share their joys and responsibilities. Then if we do this in a complete (perfect) way, it will not be long until we can open our hearts to our brother in order to share with him our richness and to love together the One who pushes us to see each other and treat each other as brothers" (translated by Amelia J. Uelmen, "Mary, Model of Dialogue in the Thought, Work and Writings of Chiara Lubich," unpublished paper, p. 17).

42. Michael L. Fitzgerald, "Mary as a Sign for the World According to Islam," in *Mary in Time and in Eternity*, ed. William McLoughlin and Jill Pinnock (Herefordshire, England: Gracewing, 2007), p. 298. British theologian Tina Beattie writes about her experience as a volunteer in helping Lourdes pilgrims take baths in its healing waters. She was very impressed with another volunteer and asked what parish she was from. The woman replied that she didn't have a parish and was a Muslim. Years before she visited Lourdes with her ill son, she mentioned that Muslims honor Mary and that she had no problem taking part in the ritual of the baths (Beattie, "An Immense Material Presence," *The Tablet*, September 13, 2008), p. 9.

43. Amantha Perera, "How the Mother of Madhu Survived a Civil War," *Time*, August 31, 2009, p. 4. It is not that unusual in India for Hindus, Muslims, and Christians to celebrate some of their feasts with each other.

44. See Maureen Orth, "The World's Most Powerful Woman," *National Geographic*, December 2015, pp. 30–59.

45. Mary Gordon, "Getting Here from There: A Writer's Reflections on a Religious Past," in *Spiritual Quests: The Art and Craft of Religious Writing*, ed. William Zinsser (Boston: Houghton Mifflin, 1988), p. 27.

46. Barbara Taylor Brown, "Our Bodies, Our Faith," *Christian Century,* January 27, 2009, p. 24. She cites with approval a hymn by Brian Wren, one stanza of which reads: "Good is the flesh that the Word has become, good is the birthing, the milk in the breast, good is the feeling, caressing and rest, good is the body for knowing the world, Good is the flesh that the Word has become."

47. Rowan Williams, *Christ on Trial: How the Gospel Unsettles Our Judgment* (Kentwood, Michigan: Eerdmans, 2000), p. 63. Williams is actually commenting on the idea originally broached by Donald Nicholl, layman, theologian, and father of a family.

48. Jennifer Popiel, email to the author April 5, 2017.

49. Prof. Una Cadegan brought this point to my attention.

50. See Sandra Mize, *Joining the Revolution in Theology: The College Theology Society, 1954–2004* (Lanham, Maryland: Rowan and Littlefield, 2007).

Chapter 3

1. Ian Ker, *John Henry Newman: A Biography* (Oxford and New York: Oxford University Press, 1988), p. 4.

2. Frank Turner, "Newman's University and Ours," in *The Idea of a University/John Henry Newman,* ed. F. M. Turner (New Haven, CT: Yale University Press, 1996), p. 285.

3. Cited by Edward Jeremy Miller, "The Complicated Cardinal," *Philadelphia Inquirer*, September 14, 2010, p. A13. Miller's suggestions have helped improve this chapter greatly.

4. Nicholas Lash, "Introduction" to Newman's *An Essay in Aid of a Grammar of Assent* (Notre Dame, Indiana: Notre Dame Press, 1979), p. 12.

5. John T. Ford, "John Henry Newman as a Contextual Theologian," *Newman Studies Journal* 2, no. 2 (2005), p. 68.

6. St. John Paul II, "Letter to Archbishop Vincent Nichols. *L'Osservatore Romano* (English ed.), p. 2.

7. http://www.vatican.va/holy_father/benedict_xvi/homilies/2010/documents/hf_ben-xvi_hom_20100919-beatuf-newman_en.html.

8. P. J. Fitzpatrick, "Newman's Grammar and the Church Today," in *John Henry Newman: Reason, Rhetoric and Romanticism,* ed. D. Nicholls and F. Kerr (Bristol, UK: Bristol Press), p. 121. In Fitzpatrick's view, Newman depreciated reason to make

faith more acceptable to modern people and, as a consequence, ends up relying on papal authority too much.

9. Jaroslav Pelikan, *The Idea of a University: A Reexamination* (New Haven, CT: Yale University Press, 1992), p. 9. Newman scholar M. Katherine Tillman criticizes Pelikan for ignoring theology's important role in the *Idea*, mistakenly turning over to philosophy the integration of knowledge (Tillman, "Philosophy of Education," in *The Oxford Handbook of John Henry Newman*, ed. F. Aquino and B. King [Great Clarendon Street, Oxford: Oxford University Press, 2018]), p. 424.

10. Richard Schiefen, "Newman, Basilians and Catholic Higher Education," in *The Basilian Way of Life and Higher Education*, ed. J. Thompson (Saskatoon, Saskatchewan: St. Thomas More Press), p. 44.

11. Theodore M. Hesburgh, "Looking Back at Newman," *America*, March 3, 1962, p. 720. In that same article Hesburgh claimed that "it is easier to write about what a Catholic university should be than to create and administer one in reality—to bring the total idea into being. Newman, in fact, never did create the university he wrote about, nor did he have to administer it." M. Katherine Tillman (see note 9) corrects Hesburgh, writing in *America* magazine () that as the founding rector of the Catholic University of Ireland, Newman "hired its faculty, defined its curriculum, built its church and officially administered it from 1854 to 1858."

12. George Dennis O'Brien, *All the Essential Half-Truths about Higher Education* (Chicago, Illinois: University of Chicago Press, 1998), p. 8.

13. Ian Ker, editor's introduction, in *J. H. Newman, The Idea of a University: Defined and Illustrated* (Oxford, UK: Clarendon Press, 1976), p. xxix.

14. D. N. Livingstone, "The Idea of a University: Interventions from Ireland," *Christian Scholar's Review* 30, no. 2 (2000), p. 188.

15. Marvin O'Connell, "Newman and the Irish Bishops," *Newman Studies Journal* 1, no. 1 (2004), p. 61.

16. C. F. Harrold, "Introduction," in J. H. Newman, *The Idea of a University, Defined and Illustrated* (New York: Longmans, Green & Co., 1947), p. xv.

17. In 1873, Newman wrote of the Irish bishops that "Dr. Cullen meant these men to advise and control me, and to be at once his own informants of what I was doing," in Edward Jeremy Miller, "Revisiting Campuses with Newman," typed manuscript, p. 19, citing *Autobiographical Writings*, p. 296.

18. John Henry Newman, *Letters and Diaries*, vol. 24 (Oxford, 1973), p. 46. How bishops were to leave the university alone and at the same time "control" it is one of the ambiguities that Newman sustains when referring to the relationship between a Catholic university and the hierarchy. At about the same time, Newman wrote to his friend Robert Ornsby that "Cullen wishes well to the University, but while he is as ignorant as anyone how to do it good, he has not the heart to have perfect confidence in anyone. . . . Here is the *origo mali*—an Archbishop without trust in any one. I wonder he does not cook his own dinners."

19. Ian Ker, *John Henry Newman: A Biography* (New York: Oxford University Press, 1990), pp. 372–375.

20. Ian Ker, editor's introduction, *The Idea of a University: Defined and Illustrated* (Clarendon, 1976), pp. xvi–xvii.

21. Ibid., p. xxxvii.

22. Julie Reuben, *The Making of the Modern University* (Chicago, Illinois: University of Chicago Press, 1996).

23. David Hollinger, "Money and Academic Freedom a Half-Century after McCarthyism," in *Unfettered Expression: Freedom in American Intellectual Life,* ed. P. J. Hollingsworth (Ann Arbor, Michigan: University of Michigan Press, 2000), p. 173.

24. Edward Jeremy Miller, "John Henry Newman's Idea of *Alma Mater*," *Newman Studies Journal* 8, no. 2 (2011), p. 25.

25. Martin Svaglic, *John Henry Newman: The Idea of a University* (Notre Dame, Indiana: University of Notre Dame Press, 1986, 3rd printing), pp. 125–126.

26. Ibid., p. 126.

27. Ibid., preface, p. xlv.

28. Ibid., p. 378.

29. Ibid., pp. 134–139.

30. Clark Kerr, *The Uses of the University* (Cambridge, Massachusetts: Harvard University Press, 2001), p. 95.

31. John Mearsheimer, "Teaching Morality at the Margins," *Philosophy and Literature* 22 (1998), pp. 279–298. Bernard Prusak cites this statement by Mearsheimer in his article "Catholic Higher Education as Transformation," *Journal of Catholic Higher Education* 37 (2018), p. 187.

32. John Henry Newman, *The Rise and Progress of Universities,* ed. M. Katherine Tillman (Leominster and Notre Dame, IN: Gracewing and University of Notre Dame Press, 2001), pp. 228–229.

33. Brian Wicker, "Newman and the Idea of an Education for Gentlemen," *Cross Currents* 30, no. 2 (Summer 1980), p. 168. See also James L. Heft, "The 'Gentleman' and the Christian," *The Cresset* 66, no. 12 (June 2003), pp. 5–13.

34. Prusak, "Catholic Higher Education as Transformation," p. 185.

35. Mark R. Schwehn, "From Faith and Learning to Love and Understanding: A Possible Future Agenda for Church-Related Higher Education," *The Cresset,* Lent (2018), p. 4.

36. Svaglic, "John Henry Newman: The Idea of a University," p. 39.

37. Ibid., pp. 19–20.

Chapter 4

1. Hugh Heclo and Wilfred M. McClay, eds., *Religion Returns to the Public Square: Faith and Policy in America* (Washington DC: Woodrow Wilson Center Press and Charles Village, Baltimore: Johns Hopkins University Press, 2003), from an essay by Heclo that introduces the volume but revised as an article in the *Wilson Quarterly,* Winter 2003, p. 68.

2. The issue, dated April 8, 1966, was released so that it would appear during the celebrations of Easter and Passover. The article stated: "If nothing else, the Christian atheists are waking the churches to the brutal reality that the basic premise of faith— the existence of a personal God, who created the world and sustains it with his love— is now subject to profound attack." The author of the article apparently had not read Voltaire or Nietzsche.

3. Jose Casanova, *Public Religions in the Modern World* (Chicago, Illinois: University of Chicago Press, 1994).

4. Ibid., p. 211.

5. See the conclusion of Louis Dupré's important study, *The Enlightenment and the Intellectual Foundations of Modern Culture* (New Haven, Connecticut: Yale University Press, 2004), pp. 338–339.

6. Charles Taylor, *A Secular Age* (Cambridge, Mass.: Harvard University Press, 2007).

7. I have found two summaries of Taylor's book particularly helpful. Peter Steinfels, "Modernity and Belief," *Commonweal*, May 9, 2008, pp. 14–21, and James K. A. Smith, *How (Not) to Be Secular: Reading Charles Taylor* (Grand Rapids, MI: Eerdmans, 2014). See my review of Smith's book in *Journal of Metaphysics* 68, no. 2 (December 2014), pp. 447–448.

8. Peter Berger, Grace Davie, and Effie Fokas, *Religious America, Secular Europe?* (Burlington, VT: Ashgate, 2008), p. 12

9. Charles Taylor, "Secularization," unpublished manuscript, p. 4.

10. See my review of Marsden's three books, *The Secularization of the Academy: Religion in America*, ed. George M. Marsden and Bradley J. Longfield (New York: Oxford University Press, 1992); *The Soul of the American University: From Protestant Establishment to Established Nonbelief* (New York: Oxford, 1994); and *The Outrageous Idea of Christian Scholarship* (New York: Oxford University Press, 1997), in *Journal of Religion and Law* 16, no. 2 (2001), pp. 461–470. James Burtchaell, *The Dying of the Light: The Disengagement of Colleges and Universities from Their Christian Churches* (Grand Rapids, Michigan: Eerdmans, 1998); and Philip Gleason, *Contending with Modernity* (New York: Oxford University Press, 1994).

11. Marsden, *The Soul of the American University*, p. vii.

12. Burtchaell, *The Dying of the Light*, p. 311.

13. See my review of Burtchaell's book in *Catholic Education: A Journal of Inquiry and Practice* 2, no. 4 (June 1999), pp. 494–511.

14. Gleason, *Contending*, p. 320.

15. Philip Gleason, "American Catholic Higher Education Since WWII," unpublished paper, p. 12.

16. David O'Brien, *From the Heart of the American Church: Catholic Higher Education and American Culture* (Maryknoll, NY: Orbis Books, 1994).

17. The first among them, *American Catholic Higher Education: Essential Documents 1967–1990* (Notre Dame, Indiana: Notre Dame Press, 1992). Since then she also published *Independence and a New Partnership in Catholic Higher Education* (Notre

Dame, Indiana: Notre Dame Press, 1996) and *Negotiating Identity* (Notre Dame, Indiana: Notre Dame Press, 2000).

18. Alice Gallin, "American Catholic Higher Education: An Experience of Inculturation," in *Trying Times: Essays on Catholic Higher Education in the 20th Century*, ed. William M. Shea and Daniel Van Slyke (Atlanta, Georgia: Scholars Press, 1999), pp. 99–119.

19. Personally, I am grateful to Luther, whose writings I studied in graduate school only to discover that I was until then a closet Pelagian, that is, someone who relied for salvation too much on his own good works and not on God's graciousness.

20. John Roberts and James Turner, *The Sacred and the Secular University* (Princeton, New Jersey: Princeton University Press, 2000), p. 121. See also Turner's recent collection of essays, *Language, Religion and Knowledge* (Notre Dame, Indiana: Notre Dame Press, 2003), where he spells out some of the contributions of Catholic intellectual traditions.

21. Denys Turner, *Faith Seeking* (London: SCM Press, 2002), p. 136.

22. David Riesman and Christopher Jencks, *The Academic Revolution* (New York: Doubleday Press, 1968).

23. An example of mistaking a part for the whole is shown in the essays contained in Steven Brint, ed., *The Future of the City of Intellect* (Redwood City, California: Stanford University Press, 2002). One of the most illuminating exceptions in the volume is Richard Chait's essay, "The 'Academic Revolution' Revisited." Chait provides statistics that clearly demonstrate the wide range of institutions that make up higher education in the United States today and how unevenly the "academic revolution" has taken root in them.

24. William L. Portier, "Marsden and American Catholic Higher Education," *Delta Epsilon Sigma Journal* 42, no. 3 (Fall 1997), p. 113.

25. *Ex corde ecclesiae*, par. 18, a quotation taken from St. John Paul II's address at UNESCO, June 2, 1980, n. 22, *AAS* 72 (1980), p. 750.

26. John Coleman, summarizing Casanova's argument, "The Second Coming of Religion," *Commonweal*, September 23, 1994, p. 22.

27. See "Most Lay Presidents of Catholic Colleges Lack Formal Religious Training," *Chronicle of Higher Education*, June 16, 2003, https://www.chronicle.com/most-lay-presidents-of-catholic-colleges-lack-formal-religious-training-survey-finds/.

Chapter 5

1. This chapter is an edited and updated version of an article that Leo O'Donovan and I wrote, "A University That Evangelizes? *Ex corde ecclesiae* Six Years Afterwards," *Horizons* 23 (1996), pp. 103–112.

2. See James Heft, Reuven Firestone, and Omid Safi, eds., *Learned Ignorance: Intellectual Humility among Jews, Christians and Muslims* (New York: Oxford University Press, 2011).

Chapter 6

1. *Gaudium et spes, Pastoral Constitution on the Church in the Modern World*, Preface, Vatican Council II: Constitutions, Decrees, Declarations, ed., Austin Flanery, O.P. (New York: Costello Publishing Company, 1996), p. 163.
2. See "Humble Infallibility," my chapter in *Learned Ignorance: Intellectual Humility among Jews, Christians and Muslims*, ed. James L. Heft, Reuven Firestone, and Omid Safi (New York: Oxford University Press, 2011), pp. 89–106. The fivefold historical conditioning of even infallible statements is explained in the 1973 Vatican document *Mysterium ecclesiae*, issued by the Congregation for the Doctrine of the Faith.
3. See J. Robert Dionne, *The Papacy and the Church* (New York: Philosophical Library, 1987), p. 24.
4. See Nicholas Lash, "Letters," *The Tablet*, April 28, 2012, p. 17.
5. Jon Nilson, "The Impending Death of Catholic Higher Education: The Doomsday Clock for Catholic Higher Education Is Ticking Toward Midnight," *America*, May 28, 2001, pp. 10–13.
6. Monika Hellwig, "The Survival of Catholic Higher Education," *America*, July 16, 2001, pp. 23–24.

Chapter 7

1. James L. Heft, *John XXII (1316–1334) and Papal Teaching Authority* (Lewiston, New York: Edwin Mellen Press, 1986), pp. 97–99.
2. "It goes without saying that this book is in no way an exercise of the magisterium but is solely an expression of my personal search 'for the face of the Lord' (cf. Ps. 27:8). Everyone is free, then, to contradict me. I would only ask my readers for that initial good will without which there can be no understanding." Benedict XVI, *Jesus of Nazareth* (New York: Doubleday, 2007), pp. xxiii–iv.
3. See John W. O'Malley, "A Lesson for Today? Bishops and Theologians at the Council of Trent," *America* 205 (October 31, 2011), pp. 11–13. O'Malley explains: "The bishops at Trent were typical of the Catholic episcopacy at the time. They had little formal training in theology, even though they otherwise might be well educated according to the standards of the day. If they had university degrees, those decrees tended to be in canon law. The theologians at Trent, however, came exclusively from universities or comparable institutions, and some were men of great distinction. They were not hand-chosen to promote a particular perspective but represented a random sampling of theological 'schools.' The bishops did well to hear them out before proceeding to their own deliberations." See also his book, *Trent: What Happened at the Council* (Cambridge, Massachusetts: The Belknap Press of Harvard University Press, 2013), pp. 84–85, 92, 108, 131, 145, 154, and 189.
4. Joseph Komonchak, "Modernity and the Construction of Roman Catholicism," *Cristianismo nella storia* 18 (1997), p. 374. See also Thomas Albert Howard, *The Pope*

and the Professor: Pius IX, Ignaz von Döllinger, and the Quandary of the Modern Age (New York: Oxford University Press, 2017).

5. Joseph Komonchak, loc. cit., "Modernity and the Construction of Roman Catholicism," *Cristianismo nella Storia* 18 (1997).

6. Sheridan Gilley, *Newman and His Age* (Westminster, Maryland: Christian Classics, 1990), p. 348. Henry Edward Cardinal Manning, archbishop of Westminster and head of the English Roman Catholic Church from 1865 to 1892, also deeply distrusted Newman (p. 341).

7. John O'Malley, *What Happened at Vatican II* (Cambridge, Massachusetts: The Belknap Press of Harvard University Press, 2010), pp. 55–56.

8. Shortly before being elected pope, Joseph Cardinal Ratzinger wrote: "The pope is not an absolute monarch, whose will is law, but completely the opposite: he must always seek to renounce his will and call the Church to obedience, but he himself must be the first to obey." Quoted in Andres Torres Queiruga, "*Magisterium* and Theology: Principles and Facts," *Concilium: Theology and Magisterium* (2012, Vol. 2), ed. Felix Wilfred and Susan A. Ross, p. 55.

9. Quoted in Avery Cardinal Dulles, "The Freedom of Theology," *First Things*, May 2008, p. 21. The distinction between the *inspiration* and the *assistance* of the Holy Spirit is important. Inspiration creates revelation; assistance interprets it. Theologians, bishops, and even popes are not inspired but only assisted in interpreting revelation, over which they have no authority to change or deny.

10. Ian Ker, *John Henry Newman: A Biography* (London: Oxford University Press, 1988), p. 701.

11. Ibid., p. 703. Newman continues: "Truth is the guiding principle of theology and theological inquiries; devotion and edification, of worship, our emotional nature; of rule, command and coercion. Further, in man as he is, reasoning tends to rationalism; devotion to superstition and enthusiasm; and power to ambition and tyranny."

12. Ibid., p. 704. Friedrich von Hügel (1852–1925), writing in 1918 during the anti-Modernist period in the church, described himself as seeking to do "all that I can to make the old Church as inhabitable intellectually as I can—not because the intellect is the most important thing in religion—it is not; but because the old Church already possesses in full the knowledge and the aids to spirituality, whilst, for various reasons which would fill a volume, it is much less strong as regards the needs, rights and duties of the mental life."

13. It was originally published in 1859 as an article in *The Rambler* and, with some additions, again in 1871 as an appendix to the third edition of *The Arians of the Fourth Century*. See John Henry Newman, *On Consulting the Faithful in Matters of Doctrine*, ed. John Coulson (New York: Sheed and Ward, 1961).

14. Cardinal Basil Hume, "Development of Marriage Teaching," *Origins* 10 (October 16, 1980), p. 276.

15. Again, von Hügel, who acknowledged a great intellectual and spiritual indebtedness to Newman, distinguished three important, interacting dimensions in the life of the church: the institutional, the intellectual, and the mystical. See his *The Mystical Element of Religion as Studied in Saint Catherine of Genoa and Her Friends*,

Vol. 1: *Introduction and Biographies*, 2nd ed. (James Clark and Co., 1961), pp. 50–82, esp. at p. 61.

16. Avery Dulles, "*Successio apostolorum: Successio prophetarum--Successio doctorum,*" in *Concilium: Who Has the Say in the Church?* (1981, Vol. 8), ed. Hans Kung and Jürgen Moltmann, p. 64.

17. Cited by Larry N. Lorenzoni in *America*, October 4, 2010, p. 44.

18. Ibid.

19. Yves Congar, "Towards a Catholic Synthesis," in *Who Has the Say in the Church*, p. 69. "Infallibility—a terribly weighted term which we need to use very warily—is a function of truth. We must not make infallibility the foundation stone of our structures and make truth a function of it."

20. Ibid., p. 75.

21. See my " 'Sensus fidelium' and the Marian Dogmas," in *Mater Fidei et Fidelium: Collected Essays to Honor Theodore Koehler on His 80th Birthday* (Dayton, Ohio: Marian Library Studies, Vol. 17–23, University of Dayton, 1991), pp. 767–786.

22. See Alasdair MacIntyre, *Three Rival Forms of Moral Inquiry: Encyclopaedia, Genealogy, and Tradition* (Notre Dame, Indiana: University of Notre Dame Press, 1990).

23. Jaroslav Pelikan, *The Vindication of Tradition* (New Haven, CT: Yale University Press, 1984), p. 80.

24. See my "Tradition: A Catholic Understanding," in *The Idea of Tradition in the Late Modern World: An Ecumenical and Interreligious Conversation,* ed. Thomas Albert Howard (Eugene, OR: Cascade Books, 2020), pp. 33–55.

25. John Henry Newman, *Apologia pro Vita Sua,* ed. Martin J. Svaglic (Walton Street, Oxford: Clarendon Press, 1967), p. 224. Also, for "night battle," see *Fifteen Sermons Preached Before the University of Oxford* (Notre Dame, Indiana: University of Notre Dame Press, 1997), p. 201.

26. *Letters and Diaries of John Henry Newman,* vol. 21 (Nelson, 1970), pp. 48–49, cited in Joseph Komonchak, "The Catholic University in the Church," in *Catholic Universities in Church and Society: A Dialogue on Ex corde ecclesiae,* ed. John P. Langan (Washington, DC: Georgetown University Press, 1993), p. 46. Some authors have found fault with Newman for being hypersensitive, just as Erasmus, writing to his friend Thomas More, faulted theologians of his day as "a remarkably supercilious and touchy lot" (Nicholas Lash, *Seeing in the Dark: University Sermons* [Darton, Longman and Todd, 2005], p. 19). Newman was indeed sensitive, but not supercilious. It would have shocked Newman to learn that he would be canonized. That he was canonized should be an encouragement for all theologians.

27. John Henry Newman, *Letters and Diaries, vol.* 20 (Nelson, 1970), p. 447, cited in Komonchak, "The Catholic University in the Church."

28. John Henry Newman, *The Idea of a University* (Notre Dame, Indiana: Notre Dame Press, 1982), introduction and notes by Martin Svaglic, p. xxxvii.

29. *Ex corde ecclesiae,* 1990, par. 12. In another chapter, I spell out what I believe to be the appropriate understanding of academic freedom for a Catholic university.

30. Quoted in Ian Ker, "Wisdom of the Future," *The Tablet*, September 18, 2010, p. 14.

31. Raymond A. Schroth, "How We Got Here," *Conversations on Jesuit Higher Education*, no. 41 (Spring 2012), p. 4.

32. If, however, the teaching of bishops reflects only one school of theological thought, conflicts arise, as was the case with Newman and the growing neo-scholastic orthodoxy of the nineteenth century.

33. Komonchak, "The Catholic University in the Church," p. 45.

34. See my "Catholic Universities as Open Circles," *Origins* 35 (March 23, 2006), pp. 660–663.

35. Komonchak, "The Catholic University in the Church," p. 50.

36. Elizabeth Johnson, *Quest for the Living God: Mapping Frontiers in the Theology of God* (Continuum, 2008).

37. The text, as well as all the major statements regarding Johnson's book and her exchanges with the bishops' doctrinal committee, can be found in Richard R. Gaillardetz, ed., *When the Magisterium Intervenes: The Magisterium and Theologians in Today's Church* (Liturgical Press, 2012).

38. NCCB, Doctrinal Responsibilities, par. 8.

39. See his *Consuming Religion: Christian Faith and Practice in a Consumer Culture* (Continuum, 2005) and "When Mediating Structures Change: The *Magisterium*, the Media, and the Culture Wars," in Gaillardetz, ed., *When the Magisterium Intervenes* (Collegeville Minnesota, Liturgical Press, 2012), pp. 140–153.

40. Terrence W. Tilley, "Culture Warriors," *The Tablet*, November 22, 2012, pp. 9 and 11, describes astutely how identity politics polarizes the church in the United States.

41. "*Quaestio Disputata*: The Magisterium in an Age of Digital Reproduction," in Gaillardetz, ed., *When the Magisterium Intervenes*, pp. 140–153.

42. In a recent article in *U.S. Catholic*, Heather Grennan Gary quotes from a letter that Cardinal Donald Wuerl, archbishop of Washington, DC, sent to his seminarians, warning them that "there are theological writers who present teachings contradictory to that of the church's magisterium." He tells them that if they have doubts about whether something a theologian writes contradicts the teaching of the church, they need only consult the *Catechism of the Catholic Church*. "What Women Theologians Have Done for the Church," *U.S. Catholic* 78 (January 2013), pp. 12–17. See www.uscatholic.org/print/26587.

43. In an article suggesting ways to improve the processes used by the CDF, Gerald O'Collins notes that "frequently the texts coming from the ITC and, especially, the PBC [Pontifical Biblical Commission] have handled their sources more skillfully, argued their case more compellingly, and, in short, produced more convincing documents than those coming from the CDF itself. Would the CDF enhance its standing by authorizing and publishing as its own the texts of the PBC and the ITC?" See "Art of the Possible," *The Tablet*, July 14, 2012, p. 7.

44. Dulles, "The Freedom of Theology," pp. 22–23.

45. O'Collins, "Art of the Possible," pp. 6–7.

Chapter 8

1. George Marsden, *The Soul of the American University: From Protestant Establishment to Established Nonbelief* (New York: Oxford University Press, 1994), pp. 5 and 6.

2. John Paul II, *Ex corde ecclesiae: Apostolic Constitution of the Supreme Pontiff John Paul II on Catholic Universities*, Vatican website: http://w2.vatican.va/content/john-paul-ii/en/apost_constitutions/documents/hf_jp-ii_apc_15081990_ex-corde-ecclesiae.html.

3. *Some Characteristics of Jesuit Colleges and Universities: A Self-Evaluation Instrument*, Association of Jesuit Colleges and Universities website: http://static1.squarespace.com/static/55d1dd88e4b0dee65a6594f0/t/56043648e4b0eddafbc448b4/1443116616873/Characteristics+FINAL+Dec+20122.pdf.

4. Ibid., p. 19.

5. Ibid., p. 1.

6. Paula Moore, "Catholic Higher Education Embraces Efforts to Assess Identity," *Update: The Newsletter of the Association of Catholic Colleges and Universities*, Summer 2014, pp. 14, 16. See also James L. Heft, "Leadership in Catholic Higher Education," in *American Catholic Higher Education in the 21st Century: Critical Challenges*, ed. Robert R. Newton (Boston: Linden Lane Press, 2015), pp. 92–93.

7. Taken together, these developments were described by Christopher Jencks and David Riesman in their book, *The Academic Revolution* (Garden City, NY: Doubleday, 1968).

8. AAUP, "1915 Declaration of Principles on Academic Freedom and Academic Tenure," p. 295, AAUP website: https://www.aaup.org/NR/rdonlyres/A6520A9D-0A9A-47B3-B550-C006B5B224E7/0/1915Declaration.pdf.

9. Ibid., p. 293.

10. AAUP, "1940 Statement of Academic Freedom and Tenure," p. 14, AAUP website: https://www.aaup.org/file/1940%20Statement.pdf.

11. AAUP, "Recommended Institutional Regulations on Academic Freedom and Tenure," AAUP website: https://www.aaup.org/report/recommended-institutional-regulations-academic-freedom-and-tenure.

12. AAUP, "The 'Limitations' Clause in the 1940 Statement of Principles," *Academe* 74, no. 5 (September–October 1988), pp. 52–59.

13. See Michael W. McConnell, "Academic Freedom in Religious Colleges and Universities," *Law and Contemporary Problems* 53, no. 3 (1990), pp. 203–324, passim.

14. Avery Dulles, "The Teaching Mission of the Church and Academic Freedom," *America*, April 21, 1990, p. 399. I deal with additional questions about the relationship between theologians and bishops in a separate chapter.

15. AAUP, "1940 Statement," p. 14.

16. AAUP, "1915 Declaration," p. 295.

17. Mark Roche, *Realizing the Distinctive University: Vision and Values, Strategy and Culture* (Notre Dame, Indiana: Notre Dame Press, 2017), p. 55. These figures are

based on statistics from various government funding agencies available on agency websites.

18. Eyal Press and Jennifer Washburn, "The Kept University," *The Atlantic*, March 2000, pp. 39–42, 44–52, 54.

19. Alasdair MacIntyre, *Three Rival Versions of Moral Inquiry: Encyclopaedia, Genealogy, and Tradition* (Notre Dame, Indiana: University of Notre Dame Press, 1990).

20. Jaroslav Pelikan, *The Idea of a University—A Re-examination* (New Haven, CT, and London: Yale University Press, 1992), p. 47.

21. See also Caroline J. Simon, "Can Two Walk Together Unless They Be Agreed," *The Cresset* 82, no. 1 (Michaelmas 2018), pp. 13–22. She also distinguishes three models of a Christian liberal arts college: a very fragmented secular university with nearly no institution-wide agreement on purpose; a university that requires all faculty to agree to a statement of faith or the authority of the Roman Catholic *magisterium*; and those universities that are somewhere in "the messy middle," inhabited " by colleges and universities that aspire to be communities of truth-seekers who acknowledge human limits and dependence upon God's grace made possible through the person and work of our Lord Jesus Christ, yet do not codify this shared purpose in creedal statement or behavior codes." There are obvious similarities between Simon's messy middle and my "open circle," but my understanding of academic freedom and its relationship to the *magisterium* of the Catholic Church is more nuanced.

22. AAUP, "Recommended Institutional Regulations on Academic Freedom and Tenure."

23. Thomas Nagel, *The View from Nowhere* (New York: Oxford University Press, 1986).

24. Alasdair McIntyre, "The End of Education," *Commonweal*, October 16, 2006, pp. 10–12, 14.

25. AAUP, "1915 Declaration," p. 293.

26. Charles Taylor, *A Catholic Modernity?*, ed. James L. Heft (New York: Oxford University Press, 1999), p. 16.

27. David Burrell, *Faith and Freedom: An Interfaith Perspective* (London: Blackwell, 2004).

28. John Noonan, "Religious Law Schools and the First Amendment," *Journal of College and University Law* 20, no. 1 (1993), p. 45.

29. John Paul II, *Ex corde ecclesiae*, par. 32.

30. Mark W. Roche, "Principles and Strategies for Reforming the Core Curriculum at a Catholic College or University," *Journal of Catholic Higher Education* 34, no. 1 (Winter 2015), pp. 59–75.

31. John Paul II, *Ex corde ecclesiae*, par. 12.

32. In particular, we should remember not only those who suffer *for* the church but also those who suffer *from* the church. I highly recommend Catherine Wolff's edited volume, *Not Less Than Everything: Catholic Writers and Heroes of Conscience, from Joan of Arc to Oscar Romero* (San Francisco: Harper One, 2013).

Chapter 9

1. Mark W. Roche, *Why Choose the Liberal Arts?* (Notre Dame, Indiana: Notre Dame Press, 2010), p. 2. According to the American Academy of Arts and Sciences, between 2012 and 2014 the numbers of degrees in the humanities dropped by 9%. Among all bachelor's degrees, only 6% are in the humanities, the lowest percentage since records began to be kept in 1948. https://www.amacad.org/humanities-idicators/higher-education/bachelors-degrees-humanities#31600.

2. See, for example, Gavin D'Costa, *Theology in the Public Square: Church, Academy and Nation* (Blackwell, 2005); Brad S. Gregory, *The Unintended Reformation: How a Religious Revolution Secularized Society* (Cambridge, Massachusetts: Harvard, 2012), especially chapter 6, "Secularizing Knowledge"; Parker Palmer, *The Courage to Teach* (San Francisco, California: Jossey-Bass, 1998); Jaroslav Pelikan, *The Idea of the University: A Reexamination* (New Haven, Connecticut: Yale, 1992); Christian Smith, *The Secular Revolution* (Berkeley, California: University of California Press, 2003); Peter Steinfels, *A People Adrift* (New York: Simon and Schuster, 2003)); Warren A. Nord, *Religion and American Education* (Chapel Hill, North Carolina: University of North Carolina Press, 1995); and William Deresiewicz, *Excellent Sheep: The Miseducation of the American Elite and the Way to a Meaningful Life* (New York: Simon and Schuster, 2014).

3. Quoted by Joseph Appleyard, in "Student Formation in Catholic Colleges and Universities," in *American Catholic Higher Education in the 21st Century: Critical Challenges* (Linden Lane Press at Boston College, 2015), p. 59.

4. For the exchange between John Garvey and Mark W. Roche, "Hiring for Mission," *Commonweal*, January 26, 2017, pp. 10–16, Also weighing in on this discussion were David O'Brien, "Mission before Identity: A Response to John Garvey and Mark Roche," *Commonweal*, March 24, 2017, pp. 8–9 and Joshua Hochschild, "The Catholic Vision: Hiring for Mission Is about More Than 'Counting Catholics,'" *Commonweal*, May 19, 2017, pp. 8–10. Following *Ex corde*, Garvey endorses hiring a majority of Catholics to form an intellectual community "governed by a Catholic worldview." Roche argues that what makes a university Catholic is more complex than hiring a majority of Catholics, especially when the university aspires to be a great university. For his part, O'Brien stresses, as he has for years, that mission, though related to identity, should be the starting point, lest Catholic universities become sectarian. Hochschild lists questions that he believes candidates for faculty positions should be able to answer—questions that, in my opinion, even few Catholic theologians could answer.

5. Michael J. Buckley, *The Catholic University as Promise and Project: Reflections in a Jesuit Idiom* (Washington, DC: Georgetown University Press, 1998), p. 15. I agree with Buckley, but in an age such as our own, dominated as it is by the "immanent frame," to draw on Charles Taylor's magisterial study *A Secular Age* (Harvard, 2007), pushing through that frame (the secular-academic) into the transcendent dimension (religious) will prove difficult for many faculty.

6. Fr. Dennis Holtschneider, president of the Association of Catholic Colleges and Universities (ACCU), in an unpublished paper given at a conference at St. Mary's University in San Antonio, Texas, September 20, 2019.

7. The winter issue of the *Journal of Catholic Higher Education*, 32, no. 1, (2013) published by the ACCU, addressed in greater detail how degree programs in both the liberals arts and business can reflect the distinctive mission of a Catholic university.

8. While the Catholic intellectual tradition has much to offer the modern academy, I also want to stress that all serious research—whether on the French Revolution, immunology, the reform of the tax code, or nanotechnology—contributes to the Catholic mission of a university, for they all help to understand reality and what serves the common good.

9. See, for example, James Heft, "A Study of Catholicism: An Interdisciplinary Faculty Seminar," *Horizons* 29 (2002), pp. 94–113. See also James Heft, "Ethics and Religion in Professional Education: An Interdisciplinary Seminar," *Current Issues in Catholic Higher Education* 18 (Spring 1998), pp. 21–50.

10. George M. Marsden, "What Can Catholic Universities Learn from Protestant Examples," in *The Challenge and Promise of a Catholic University*, ed. Theodore M. Hesburgh (Notre Dame Indiana: Notre Dame Press, 1994), p. 197, cited by Appleyard, "Student Formation in Catholic Colleges and Universities," p. 58.

11. Andrew Delbanco, *College: What It Was, Is, and Should Be* (Princeton, New Jersey: Princeton University Press, 2012), p. 65.

12. http://www.udayton.edu/artssciences/about/images/Habits_of_Inquiry.pdf.

13. A detailed description of the University of Dayton CAP can be found at http://www.udayton.edu/provost/cap/cap_101.php—go to the Approved Academic Senate Documents.

Chapter 10

1. *The Chronicle of Higher Education*, August 7, 1991, p. A1.

2. *The Chronicle*, July 31, 1991, p. A20.

3. Charles J. Sykes, *Profscam: Professors and the Demise of Higher Education* (Washington, DC: Regnery Publishing, 1988).

4. William Deresiewicz, *Excellent Sheep: The Miseducation of the American Elite and the Way to a Meaningful Life* (New York: Simon and Schuster, 2014).

5. Henry Rosovsky, *The University: An Owner's Manual* (New York: W. W. Norton & Company, 1990), p. 165.

6. Ibid., p. 85.

7. Ibid.

8. Alexander W. Astin and Mitchell J. Chang, "Colleges That Emphasize Research and Teaching: Can You Have Your Cake and Eat It Too?," *Change: The Magazine of Higher Learning* 27, no. 5 (1995), pp. 45–50.

9. Alfred North Whitehead, *The Aims of Education* (New York: Free Press, 1929), pp. 97–98.

10. Leon Botstein, "Structuring Specialization as a Form of General Education," *Liberal Education* 77, no. 2 (March/April 1991), pp. 10–19

11. Rosovsky, *The University*, p. 92.

12. Ibid.

13. See Roger Lancelyn Green and Walter Hooper, *C. S. Lewis: A Biography* (New York: Harcourt Brace Jovanovich, 1974), pp. 40–41.

14. Whitehead, *The Aims of Education*, p. 93.

15. See Kalman Yaron, "Martin Buber (1878–1965)," *Prospects: Quarterly Review of Comparative Education* 23, no. 1/2 (1993), pp. 135–146.

16. A. Bartlett Giamatti, "To Make Oneself Eternal," in *A Free and Ordered Space: The Real World of the University* (New York: W. W. Norton, 1990), pp. 193–194.

17. Rosovsky, *The University*, p. 90.

18. Ernest Boyer, *College: The Undergraduate Experience in America* (New York: Harper and Row, 1987), p. 131.

19. For example, Ernest Lynton and Sandra Elman, *New Priorities for the University* (San Francisco: Jossey-Bass, 1987); Richard I. Miller, *Evaluating Faculty for Promotion and Tenure* (San Francisco: Jossey-Bass, 1987); and Donald A. Schön, *Educating the Reflective Practitioner* (San Francisco: Jossey-Bass, 1987). Even though all three books were published in 1987, the issues they address remain perennial.

20. Humphrey Carpenter, ed., *The Letters of J. R. R. Tolkien* (Boston: Houghton Mifflin, 1981), p. 370, quoted in Jaroslav Pelikan, *Scholarship and Its Survival: Question on the Idea of Graduate Education: A Carnegie Foundation Essay* (Princeton, NJ: Princeton University, 1983), p. 6.

21. Jacob Neusner and Noam Neusner, *Reaffirming Higher Education* (New York: Routledge, 2017), p. 21.

22. The two largest Catholic universities in the United States are St. John's University on Long Island and DePaul University in Chicago, both founded by the Congregation of the Mission (CM), known as Vincentians. Each is located in a major metropolitan center and currently enrolls between twenty thousand and twenty-five thousand students. Many Catholic universities enroll between five thousand and ten thousand students. A not insignificant number enroll less than five thousand students.

23. Glenna Jennings, "At Table: Everyday Space of Expression and Connection," *University of Dayton Magazine* 12, no. 3 (Spring 2020), p. 43.

24. James Turner, *The Future of Christian Learning: An Evangelical and Catholic Dialogue*, ed. Thomas Albert Howard (Grand Rapids, MI: Brazos Press, 2008), p. 91.

25. Ibid., p. 94.

26. A colleague of mine, Antonio Damasio, author of many books, including most recently, *The Strange Order of Things: Life, Feeling, and the Making of Cultures* (New York: Pantheon Books, 2018), clearly recognizes that there is more to what makes a human being human than matter alone. For a study of the mind/brain relationship see also his *When Self Comes to Mind: Constructing the Conscious Brain* (New York: Pantheon Books, 2010).

Chapter 11

1. James L. Heft, ed., *A Catholic Modernity?: Charles Taylor's Marianist Award Lecture* (New York: Oxford University Press, 1999). Taylor's lecture may also be found, along with nine other lectures by scholars who had also received the Marianist Award, in James L. Heft, ed., *Believing Scholars: Ten Catholic Intellectuals* (New York: Fordham University Press, 2005). Each year, the University of Dayton gives the Marianist Award to a Catholic scholar who has made a major contribution to the intellectual life.

2. Heft, *A Catholic Modernity?*, p. 16.

3. Ibid., p. 35.

4. Charles Taylor, *Sources of the Self: The Making of Modern* Identity (Cambridge, Massachusetts: Harvard University Press, 1989), pp. 495–521. Taylor also singles out the virtues of faithfulness, awareness of responsibility, veracity, and goodness.

5. Ibid., p. 517.

6. Ibid., p. 520.

7. Quoted by Adam Begley, "The Mensch of Montreal," *Lingua Franca*, May/June 1993, p. 39. Other critics of Taylor are similarly generous in their administration for his work. For example, Judith Shklar of Harvard, who admits that she does not "share a single one of Taylor's assumptions, reactions, or conclusions," still affirms that "there can be no doubt that Taylor's learning and conviction make this [*Sources*] a major work and that anyone who regards hermeneutics as the best way to illuminate the tangle of moral selfhood will find this a deeply rewarding book" (*Political Theory*, February 1991, review of *Sources*, pp. 105–109). In another more recent major work, *A Secular Age*, published by Harvard in 2007, Taylor returns to what many commentators believe is an even more penetrating analysis of modernity than he did in *Sources*. I briefly describe his contribution in that work in chapter 4 on secularization and Catholic universities.

8. Charles Taylor, *The Ethics of Authenticity* (Cambridge, Massachusetts: Harvard University Press, 1991), pp. 22–23.

9. Heft, *A Catholic Modernity?*, p. 29.

10. Ibid., pp. 36–37.

11. Ibid., p. 54.

12. Ibid., p.84.

13. Ibid., pp. 99 and 102.

14. Ibid., p. 105.

15. Isaiah Berlin, introduction to Charles Taylor, James Tully, Daniel M. Weinstok, eds., *Philosophy in an Age of Pluralism: The Philosophy of Charles Taylor in Question* (Cambridge, England: Cambridge University Press, 1994), p. 3.

16. Brian Daley, S.J., "The Pursuit of Excellence and the 'Ordinary Manner': Humility and the Jesuit University," in *For That I Came: Virtues and Ideals of Jesuit Education*, ed. William J. Obrien (Washington, D.C.: Georgetown University Press, 1997), p. 28. Daley elaborates: "With only modest hopes of monetary reward but ample opportunities for other compensation in academic rank, solemn ceremony, and the subtler vanities based on where one has studied and who has published one's latest

book—with the more tempting possibilities of adulation and ego-building available in a professor's daily dealings with a classroom full of eager young people who depend on his or her approval for advancement—those who want to teach as a service need some safeguard to suffuse their scholarship and educational energy with love that builds." That safeguard, he adds, is humility.

17. See James L. Heft, Reuven Firestone, and Omid Safi, eds., *Learned Ignorance: Intellectual Humility among Jews, Christians and Muslims* (New York: Oxford University Press, 2011). Sponsored by the Institute for Advanced Catholic Studies, this conference hosted participants for a week in Jerusalem to discuss their papers on learned ignorance. My contribution to the volume is a chapter entitled "Humble Infallibility" (pp. 89–106).

18. Mark Schwehn, "The Christian University: Defining the Difference," *Current Issues in Catholic Higher Education* 20, no. 2 (Spring, 2000), p. 17.

19. Henry Glassie, "Meaningful Things and Appropriate Myths: The Artifact's Place in American Studies," *Material Life in America, 1600–1860*, ed. Robert Blair St. George (Boston: Northeastern University Press, 1988), pp. 87–88. I am grateful to Una Cadegan, who introduced me to the thought of Glassie.

20. Mark R. Schwehn, *Exiles from Eden: Religion and the Academic Vocation in America* (New York, Oxford: Oxford University Press, 1993), pp. 51 ff.

21. Jeffrey Stout, *Ethics after Babel: The Languages of Morals and Their Discontents* (Boston Massachusetts: Beacon Press, 1988), p. xi.

22. See Schwehn, *Exiles*, pp. 51–52.

23. See George Marsden's *Soul of the American University* (New York: Oxford University Press, 1994) and *The Outrageous Idea of Christian Scholarship* (New York: Oxford University Press, 1997).

24. Heft, *A Catholic Modernity?*, p. 89. In fact, several segments of Taylor's "Catholic Modernity" lecture may be found in his book, *A Secular Age* (Cambridge, Massachusetts: The Belknap Press of Harvard University Press, 2007).

25. At the beginning of his Marianist lecture, Taylor explained that the nature of philosophical discourse, at least as he practices it, leads him to "try to persuade honest thinkers of any and all metaphysical or theological commitments" (p. 13). He employs, it could be said, an "indirect" method. Michael Novak, a Catholic thinker, saw Taylor's indirect approach quite differently than Marsden. "The followers of the philosopher Leo Strauss are fond of saying that John Locke was not as religious as he seemed; rather, he employed religious language in order to persuade religious hearers. It seems to me that Taylor is often doing the reverse. He writes as if he were less religious, and less traditional, than he is. While convincing us that he is authentically modern, and on the whole happy about that (although rightly worried), he never quite gives his whole heart, mind, and soul to modernity" (review of *The Ethics of Authenticity* in *First Things*, May 1993, p. 42).

26. Heft, *A Catholic Modernity?*, p. 119.

27. Ibid.

28. Ibid., p. 25.

29. Ibid., p. 24.

30. See Kenneth Garcia, *Academic Freedom and the Telos of the Catholic University* (New York: Palgrave MacMillan Press, 2012). See especially chapter 6, "The Consequences of Caesar's Gold." To qualify for federal grants, leaders of some Catholic universities had to prove that they were not "sectarian." Garcia cites court testimonies of several of these leaders who tried to persuade the government that religion in their institutions played no pervasive role.

31. See James Burtchaell, *Dying of the Light: The Disengagement of Colleges and Universities from their Christian Churches* (Grand Rapids, Michigan: Eerdmans, 1998), and my review (*Catholic Education: A Journal of Inquiry and Practice* 2, no. 4 [June 1999], pp. 495–503) and his response 3, no. 2, [December 1999], pp. 256–259). Burtchaell emphasizes the need for strong presidential leadership, ridiculing many of them for their "vacuous leadership." He fails, in my opinion, to give enough attention to the historical, cultural, and ecclesial complexities of the 1960s.

32. Alice Gallin, *Negotiating Identity* (Notre Dame, Indiana: Notre Dame Press, 2000). See also her *Independence and a New Partnership in Catholic Higher Education* (Notre Dame, Indiana: Notre Dame Press, 1996), which describes the movement to adopt lay boards of trustees. See David O'Brien, *From the Heart of the American Church: Catholic Higher Education and American Culture* (Maryknoll, NY: Orbis Books, 1994). Both of these authors offer important historical information indispensable for understanding the developments in Catholic and American higher education over the last forty years.

33. *Ex corde ecclesiae*, par. 6, introduction.

34. Heft, *A Catholic Modernity?*, p. 55.

35. Ibid., p. 56.

36. Ibid.

Chapter 12

1. John W. O'Malley, "Jesuit Schools and the Humanities," *Studies in the Spirituality of Jesuits* 47, no. 1 (Spring 2015), pp. 1–34. See also Bruce Kimball's *Orators and Philosophers: A History of the Idea of Liberal Education* (New York: Columbia University Press, 1986).

2. O'Malley, "Jesuit Schools and the Humanities," p. 10.

3. Cited in ibid., p. 12.

4. Andrew Delbanco, *What Is College For?* (Princeton, New Jersey: Princeton University Press, 2012), p. 14.

5. John Henry Newman, *The Idea of a University*, 3rd ed. (Notre Dame, Indiana: University of Notre Dame Press, 1986), introduction and notes by Martin J. Svaglic, p. 81.

6. Delbanco, *What Is College For?*, p. 15.

7. Cited by Henry Rosovsky, *The University: An Owner's Manual* (New York: W. W. Norton and Company, 1990), p. 108.

8. Terrance Sandalow, "The Moral Responsibilities of Universities," in *Moral Values and Higher Education: A Notion at Risk*, ed. By Dennis L. Thompson (Provo UT, Brigham Young University Press, 1991), pp. 149–171. See also my "Can Higher Education Foster Moral Development," *Origins* 22, no. 33 (January 28, 1993), pp. 559–565.

9. Sandalow, Ibid., p. 170.

10. Alexander C. Kafka, "Michelle Alexander's Leap of Faith" *Chronicle of Higher Education*, 63, no. 6 (2016), pp. B10–B11, cited by Douglas Jacobsen and Rhonda Jacobsen, "Can Christianity Save the Humanities?," *The Cresset*, 80 (Michaelmas 2017), p. 16.

11. Martha C. Nussbaum, *Not for Profit: Why Democracy Needs the Humanities* (Princeton, New Jersey: Princeton University Press, 2010).

12. Ibid., p. 2.

13. Ibid., pp. 25–26.

14. Ibid., pp. 83–84.

15. Ibid., p. 55.

16. O'Malley, "Jesuit Schools and the Humanities," pp. 28–31.

17. Louis Dupré, "On Being a Christian Teacher of the Humanities," *Christian Century*, April 29, 1992, pp. 452–455. This article appeared originally in a slightly altered form in James L. Heft, ed., *Faith and the Intellectual Life* (Notre Dame, Indiana: University of Notre Dame Press, 1996), a collection of addresses given by recipients of the Marianist Award for distinctive intellectual achievement and contribution to the intellectual life.

18. Paul Mariani, the University Professor of English at Boston College, provides an extensive and valuable list of literature, poetry, art, philosophy, theology, history, music, and video that embody the Catholic sacramental literary imagination. See "Charism and the Literary Imagination," *Integritas* 1, no. 2 (Spring 2013), pp. 16–19. *Integritas* is a publication of Boston College.

19. Dupré, "On Being a Christian Teacher of the Humanities," pp. 453–454.

20. For many years at the University of Dayton I taught a course on Christian ethics. I spent the first week discussing the virtue of reverence, which, according to the phenomenologist Dietrich von Hildebrand, is the foundation of the moral life. According to him, people without reverence are sociopaths for whom nothing is sacred. See von Hildebrand's *Fundamental Moral Attitudes* (New York: Longmans, Green and Co., 1950). I also played Aretha Franklin's hit song, "Respect."

21. Mark Roche, *Why Choose the Liberal Arts?* (Notre Dame, Indiana: Notre Dame Press, 2010), chapters 1 and 2.

22. Mark Roche, *The Intellectual Appeal of Catholicism and the Idea of a Catholic University* (Notre Dame, Indiana: Notre Dame Press, 2003), pp. 6–7. Defending the liberal arts in a utilitarian society presents major challenges. Even more difficult is to defend poetry, a subset of English that even many English professors would struggle to do. Dan Gioia, a widely recognized Catholic poet, made an eloquent case for the importance of poetry in an essay, "Can Poetry Matter?," which originally appeared in the

April 1991 issue of the *Atlantic Monthly*. At the end of his essay, he offers six "modest proposals" that would reinstate poetry as part of America's public culture. See "Can Poetry Matter?," in *Can Poetry Matter?: Essays on Poetry and American Culture*, 10th Anniversary ed. (Graywolf Press, 2002), pp. 1–21.

23. Hugh Heclo, *On Thinking Institutionally* (New York: Oxford University Press, 2008), p. 92.
24. Douglas Belkin, "Liberal Arts Colleges, in Fight for Survival, Focus on Job Skills," *Wall Street Journal*, Online Edition (April 25, 2017), p. 1, https://www.wsj.com/articles/liberal-arts-colleges-in-fight-for-survival-focus-on-job-skills-1493051024.
25. Nussbaum, *Not for Profit*, pp. 3–5.
26. Dennis O'Brien, "The End of Moral Education," *America*, February 1, 2016, pp. 34–36.
27. Mark Roche, *Why Choose the Liberal Arts?*, pp. 82 ff.
28. *The Teaching of the Arts and Humanities at Harvard College: Mapping the Future*, https://harvardmagazine.com/sites/default/files/mapping_the_future_of_the_humanities.pdf, pp. 15 and 42.
29. https://www.insidehighered.com/news/2017/04/26/duke-undergraduate-curricular-reform-vote-tabled-indefinitely-after-years-work.
30. A major troublesome movement in all of higher education in the United States, secular and religious, is the increasing dependence on part-time faculty, many of whom receive no benefits and must work at several campuses just to make ends meet.
31. Jane S. Shaw, "Higher Learning; Meet Lower Job Prospects," *Wall Street Journal*, Eastern Edition, 261, no. 29 (February 5, 2013), p. A13, https://www.wsj.com/articles/SB10001424127887323807004578282423881446066.
32. Charles Taylor, *A Catholic Modernity? Marianist Award Lecture* (New York: Oxford, 1999), p. 19.
33. Ibid., pp. 26–27.
34. Philosopher Josef Pieper offers a powerful defense of the liberal arts and its relationship to worship in his classic *Leisure: The Basis of Culture* (New York: Mentor Omega Book, 1963), introduction by T. S. Eliot. Pieper makes clear the relationship between leisure, cult, and culture.
35. Louis Dupré, "Catholic Education: What Is It? What Should It Be?," in *Catholic Commission on Intellectual and Cultural Affairs* (Notre Dame, Indiana: Notre Dame, 1987), p. 69.

Chapter 13

1. Karl Rahner, *Foundations of Christian Faith* (New York: Seabury Press, 1978); Avery Dulles, *The Craft of Theology* (New York: Crossroad Books, 2000); Joseph Ratzinger, *Introduction to Christianity* (New York: Herder and Herder, 1973); Elizabeth A. Johnson, *She Who Is: The Mystery of God in Feminist Theological Discourse* (New York: Crossroad Books, 1992); for an introduction to the thought

of Hans Urs von Balthasar, see David Schindler, *Hans Urs von Balthasar and the Dramatic Structure of Truth* (New York: Fordham University Press, 2004); Rosemary Haughton, *The Catholic Thing* (Springfield, Illinois: Templegate Publishers, 1979); Thomas Rausch, *Systematic Theology: A Roman Catholic Approach* (Collegeville, Minnesota: Liturgical Press, 2016); and Gustavo Gutierrez, *A Theology of Liberation* (Maryknoll, New York, 1971).

2. Charles Taylor, *A Catholic Modernity?* (New York: Oxford, 1999), p. 24.

3. Austin Farrer, "The Christian Apologist," in *Light on C. S. Lewis*, ed. Jocelyn Gibb and Owen Barfield (New York: Harcourt, Brace & World, 1967), p. 26.

4. 1 Peter 3:15–16.

5. *"Gaudium et Spes: Pastoral Constitution on the Church in the Modern World,"* in *The Basic Sixteen Documents of Vatican Council II*, ed. Austin Flannery (New York: Costello Publishing Co., 1995), p. 163.

6. See my review of Wilson D. Miscamble's *American Priest: The Ambitious Life and Conflicted Legacy of Notre Dame's Father Ted Hesburgh* (New York: Image, 2019), 464 pp., in *American Catholic Studies* 130, no. 4 (2019), pp. 85–87.

7. An edited version of that address was published in *Commonweal*, March 26, 2010, "Distinctively Catholic: Keeping the Faith in Higher Education."

8. See, for example, James Heft, "Ethics and Religion in Professional Education: An Interdisciplinary Seminar," *Current Issues in Catholic Higher Education* 18, no. 2 (Spring 1998), pp. 21–50. This article was also included in Irene King and John Wilcox, eds., *Enhancing Religious Identity: Best Practices from Catholic Campuses* (Washington, DC: Georgetown University Press, 2000), pp. 175–199). See also James Heft, "Exploring a Catholic Vision of Engineering," in *Engineering Education and Practice: Embracing a Catholic Vision*, ed. James Heft and Kevin Hallinan (Notre Dame, Indiana: University of Notre Dame Press, 2012), pp. 13–40. These descriptions of some of the faculty seminars that I led at the University of Dayton make clear, I hope, that the leaders of these seminars did not "impose" Catholic doctrine, but rather engaged faculty in open and sustained conversation about ethical and religious dimensions inherent in their disciplines.

9. David Burrell, "A Catholic University," in *The Challenge and Promise of a Catholic University*, ed. Theodore M. Hesburgh (Notre Dame, Indiana: University of Notre Dame Press, 1994), p. 43.

10. See David Tracy, *The Analogical Imagination* (New York: Harper, 1972).

11. Philip Gleason, *Contending with Modernity: Catholic Higher Education in the Twentieth Century* (New York: Oxford University Press, 1995), p. 164, citing the words of a report presented at the symposium.

12. Rowan Williams, *Christ on Trial: How the Gospel Unsettles Our Judgment* (Grand Rapids, Michigan: Eerdmans Publishing Company, 2000), p. 63. Nicholl noted that the traditional exclusion of women is a situation that Christians have begun to remedy only recently. Rowan continues, "Less obviously and equally importantly, however, we would have to say 'children' as well. Given that Jesus had strong comments to make about attending to children and recommended that his followers should imitate children, there is something very odd about a Christian discourse that ignores children."

Rowan quotes Nicholl, "How can you live in accordance with the teaching about being children if you are forever hiding yourself away from children?"

13. I am drawing freely from my chapter, "Theology's Place in a Catholic University," in *Theological Education in the Catholic Tradition: Contemporary Challenges*, ed. Patrick Carey and Earl C. Muller (New York: Crossroads Publishing Co., 1997), pp. 192–206.

14. Adam Gregerman, "Superiority without Supersessionism: Walter Kasper, the Gifts and the Calling of God Are Irrevocable, and God's Covenant with the Jews," *Theological Studies* 79, no 1 (March 2018), pp. 36–59.

15. See Francis Schüssler Fiorenza, "Theology in the University," *Bulletin of the Council of Societies for the Study of Religions*, April 1993, p. 34. To speak of one's own religious tradition as "superior" may seem arrogant. Yet this is the very position, for example, of committed Jews or Muslims. Otherwise, they would cease to be Jews or Muslims or would convert to another religious tradition that they thought made more sense than the one they found wanting. Or they just feel at home in their tradition and are not interested in comparing religions or looking for another.

16. Lawrence Cunningham, "Gladly Wolde He Lerne and Gladly Teche: The Catholic Scholar in the New Millennium," *The Cresset*, June 1992, pp. 4–16.

17. Jack Miles, editor of the two-volume *The Norton Anthology of World Religions* (New York and London: W. W. Norton & Company, 2015), in a subsequent book, *Religion as We Know It: An Origin Story* (New York and London: W. W. Norton & Company, 2020), which is a revised version of his introduction to the 2015 two-volume work, traces the history of the development of the field of religious studies and its importance: "Religious studies in the twenty-first century is open to all qualified participants. . . . Broadening the textual basis for religious studies and exploding the temporal frame around it were important nineteenth-century developments. Broadening the composition of the population that would engage in religious studies was even more important" (pp. 104–105).

18. John Cavadini, "A Theologian's View: Avoiding a Rush to Judgment," *Commonweal* 126, no. 7 (1999), p. 22, and, more recently, "Why Study God," *Commonweal*, September 30, 2013, pp. 12–18. A version of that article appears as an *excursus* in a book coauthored by John Cavadini and Christian Smith, *Building Catholic Higher Education* (Eugene, Oregon: Cascade Books, 2014). See also Cavadini's article, "College Encounter: Dialogue and Witness in Catholic Education," *America*, May 9, 2016, pp. 22–25.

19. In chapter 5, I have addressed the question of evangelization for Catholic universities in general.

20. Pope Paul VI, *Evangelii nuntiandi*, October 20, 1974 (AAS 66) p. 568.

21. Mentor Omega Book, 1962, a translation of *L'Amour des lettres et le désir de Dieu*, originally published by *Les Editions du Cerf* (Paris), based on a series of lectures given in 1955–1956 to monks in France. Also, see Mark Schwehn's excellent article, "From Faith and Learning to Love and Understanding: A Possible Future Agenda for Church-Related Higher Education," *The Cresset* 81, no. 3 (2016), pp. 4–13.

22. Christopher Ruddy, "Young Theologians: Between a Rock and a Hard Place," *Commonweal*, April 21, 2000, pp. 17–19. Hans Urs von Balthasar wrote powerfully

about how theologians should write their books on their knees (see "Theology and Sanctity," *Word and Redemption: Essays in Theology*, vol. 2 (New York: Herder and Herder, 1965). Pierre Hadot makes a similar point but applied to philosophers. He explains that before the rise of the universities in the twelfth and thirteenth centuries, much of the authority of a philosopher depended on his wisdom and the example of his way of life, rather than on his conceptual brilliance (see his *Philosophy as a Way of Life* [Oxford, UK: Blackwell, 1995]). Finally, I was privileged to be a member of the founding board of trustees for *Collegium*, an initiative to give young academics interested in the study of religion both an understanding of the possible relationships between faith and reason and a chance to deepen their spiritual lives. The director of the program, Prof. Thomas Landy, emphasized the importance of including a retreat day for prayer and the study of spiritual traditions. I suggested that we stay with the intellectual formation. Landy was right. That need for spiritual grounding is now even more important than it was twenty-five years ago when *Collegium* was founded.

23. Michael Lacey, "The Backwardness of American Catholicism," *Proceedings of the 46th Annual Convention of the Catholic Theological Society of America* 46 (1991), p. 2.

24. See my article, "It Is Time to Get Past the Snobbery against Pastoral Theology," *America*, Short Take, July 24, 2017, p. 8.

25. Cavadini and Smith, *Building Catholic Higher Education*, p. 81.

26. See chapter 7 on bishops and theologians in which I give the example of Pope John XXII (1316–1334) asking the theologians at the University of Paris not to judge his three sermons on the beatific vision, since they were only exploratory.

27. John O'Malley, "Were Medieval Universities Catholic?," in *Catholic History for Today's Church: How Our Past Illuminates Our Present* (Lanham, Maryland: Rowan and Littlefield, 2015), pp. 177–181.

28. Cited by John Padberg, *In All Things: Religious Faith and American Culture*, ed. Robert Daly (Kansas City, Kansas: Sheed and Ward, 1990), p. 4.

Chapter 14

1. A version of this chapter was originally given in 2007 as a presentation to a national meeting of campus ministers who served at both private and secular universities.

2. For an excellent description of the student formation movement in the United States, and how Catholic colleges and universities have embodied it, see Joseph Appleyard, "Student Formation in Catholic Colleges and Universities," in *American Catholic Higher Education in the 21st Century: Critical Challenges*, ed. Robert R. Newton (Chestnut Hill, Massachusetts: Linden Press, 2015), pp. 33–59.

3. See Philip Gleason, *Contending with Modernity: Catholic Higher Education in the 20th Century* (New York: Oxford University Press, 1995), especially chapter 13, pp. 297–304.

4. See David O'Brien, *From the Heart of the American Church* (Maryknoll, New York: Orbis Press, 1995).

5. The reduction in the number of campus ministry programs may be because many dioceses combined youth, young adult, campus, and sometimes vocation ministries into one organization. It also may have been the economic downturn of 2008 that forced these consolidations.

6. Brandon Sanchez, "Infographic: The Role of College Campus Ministries," https://www. americamagazine.org/faith/2018/11/30/infographic-role-college-campus-ministries.

7. I am grateful to Barbara McCrabb, the assistant director for higher education for the United States Conference of Catholic Bishops, for her suggestions on this part of the chapter. She was responsible for directing both the quantitative and qualitative studies, which are currently being followed up on.

8. Christian Smith, "Getting a Life: The Challenge of Emerging Adulthood," *Books and Culture*, November/December 2007, p. 10.

9. Jeffrey Arnett, *Emerging Adulthood: The Winding Road from the Late Teens through the Twenties* (New York: Oxford University Press, 2004), cited by Smith, ibid.

10. For a detailed description of a very Catholic subculture in Cleveland, Ohio, in the 1950s, see the first chapter of Kenneth L. Woodward's *Getting Religion: Faith, Culture, and Politics from the Age of Eisenhower to the Era of Obama* (New York: Convergent, 2016). A more recent edition of this book has appeared with an additional chapter on President Trump.

11. See historian John McGreevy, *Parish Boundaries: The Catholic Encounter with Race in the Twentieth Century Urban North* (Chicago, Illinois: University of Chicago Press, 1996).

12. William Portier, "Here Come the Evangelical Catholics," *Communio* 3-1, no. 1 (Spring 2004), pp. 35–66. Sociologist and theologian Stephen Bullivant documents the beginning of the fall-off in attendance at Sunday Eucharist in England from the late 1940s with increasing affluence, single-family homes, televisions, cars, and popular culture. See his *Mass Exodus: Catholic Disaffiliation in Britain and America Since Vatican II* (Oxford University Press, 2019). Also see James Heft, S.M. and Jan Stets, eds., *Empty Churches: Disaffiliation in America* (New York: Oxford University Press, 2021). This edited volume includes chapters by sociologists, political scientists, historians, social psychologists, theologians, philosophers, gerontologists, and several people with children in their twenties.

13. The bishops' 1985 pastoral letter mentions a variety of challenges that students face in religious belief (par. 45). For a concise description of the typical objections to Christian belief, see Robert Barron, "YouTube Heresies: On Today's Virtual Areopagus," *America*, May 25–June 1, 2009, pp. 21–23. Barron lists four: scientism, ecclesial angelism, biblical fundamentalism, and Marcionism.

14. Appleyard, "Student Formation in Catholic Colleges and Universities," p. 46.

15. Richard B. Hays, a scripture scholar at Duke University, tells how difficult it was for some of his colleagues in the Divinity School to support as one of their goals in teaching divinity students "a commitment to living a life ordered toward holiness, justice, peace and reconciliation." His colleagues did not disapprove of such goals but doubted it should be part of their job description: "As one of our theologians put it, the committee's list of goals mixed together intellectual aims with moral and religious

ones in a way that he found problematic; better to stick to purely intellectual goals and leave the moral and religious elements out of it." See Richard B. Hays, "The Palpable Word as Ground of *Koinonia*," in *Christianity and the Soul of the University*, ed. Douglas V. Henry and Michael D. Beaty (Grand Rapids, MI: Baker Academic, 2006), p. 21. After considerable discussion, the faculty eventually approved the goal.

16. Christian Smith, *Soul Searching: The Religious and Spiritual Lives of American Teenagers* (New York: Oxford, 2005); see chapter 6, "On Catholic Teens," pp. 193–217. It should be noted that most of these Catholic teenagers were not attending Catholic schools.

17. James Burtchaell, *The Dying of the Light: The Disengagement of Colleges and Universities from the Christian Churches* (Grand Rapids, Michigan: Wm. B. Eerdmans, 1998), p. 821.

18. Sharon Daloz Parks, "Callings: Fostering Vocation through Community-Based Learning," *Explore: An Examination of Catholic Identity and Ignatian Character in Jesuit Higher Education* 11, no. 1 (Fall 2007), pp. 6–7.

19. In preparation for these remarks, I read through eight issues of *Crossroads*, the official publication of the Catholic Campus Ministry Association, beginning with an issue dated December 2004 and ending with one dated summer 2007. Some issues were devoted to a single theme, for example, marketing, evangelizing, reaching out, and crisis management. Occasionally a book was reviewed or reading was recommended. I found only a few isolated statements about the importance of the relationship between the intellectual and religious dimensions of development.

20. The late Cardinal Bernardin desired to close some of the divisions between liberal and conservative Catholics by promoting what came to be called the "consistent life ethic." Closing that gap remains a difficult task since, although abortion and capital punishment are now condemned, but with different degrees of authority, it is still believed that self-defense with lethal force and a war might be considered just under strict conditions. Some Catholics have mistakenly believed that the consistent life ethic requires Catholics to oppose all abortions (despite the legitimate moral principle of double effect in rare cases), all wars, and capital punishment. Simple responses to complex issues are rarely helpful. Cardinal Bernardin did not understand it in this simplistic way.

21. See the November 2007 issue of *Journal of College and Character* 9, no. 2.

22. Bernard Prusak, "Catholic Higher Education as Transformation," *Journal of Catholic Higher Education* 37 (2018), p. 180.

23. Cited by Hays, "The Palpable Word as Ground of *Koinonia*," p. 26.

24. Mark Edwards makes a compelling and sophisticated case for faculty to take seriously religion in their teaching and research. See his *Religion on Our Campuses: A Professor's Guide to Communities, Conflicts, and Promising Conversations* (New York: Palgrave Macmillan, 2006). Though addressed to faculty at secular universities, it would also be very useful for faculty-led discussions on a Catholic campus.

25. Use John W. O'Malley, S.J., *What Happened at Vatican II?* (Cambridge, Massachusetts: The Belknap Press of Harvard University Press, 2008).

26. E.g., a short but excellent introduction by Kenneth Himes, *101 Questions and Answers on Catholic Social Teaching*, 2nd ed. (Mahwah, New Jersey: Paulist Press, 2013).

27. For years, the Office of Religious Life at the University of Southern California has asked students to invite professors to speak about "What Matters to Me and Why." These talks take place at noon once a month and are attended on average by one hundred students and faculty. The campus ministry at Yale invites faculty to come and talk about their faith; see Kerry Robinson's chapter in *Empty Churches* (cf. note 12 earlier), in which she describes many of the programs of Yale's Catholic campus ministry.

28. Also use O'Malley's, "What Happened at Vatican II?."

29. See James Heft, *Catholicism and Interreligious Dialogue* (New York: Oxford University Press, 2011).

30. See John L. Allen Jr, "Lay ecclesial ministry and the feminization of the church," https://www.ncronline.org/blogs/all-things-catholic/lay-ecclesial-ministry-and-feminization-church. Allen estimates that 80% of lay ministers are now women, and outnumber diocesan priests.

31. Translation is from Hays, "The Palpable Word as Ground of *Koinonia*," p. 33.

32. See interview with Nicholas Lash, "Performing Scripture," *Christian Century*, December 11, 2007, p. 30. The second comment about theologians being careful about their language is attributed to Gerald O'Collins, SJ.

Chapter 15

1. Fr. George W. Rutler, "The Idea of a Catholic University 50 Years after Land O'Lakes," *Crisis Magazine*, July 20, 2017, https://www.crisismagazine.com/2017/idea-university-50-years-land-olakes-statement.

2. John L. Allen Jr. and Ines San Martin, "Garvey: Francis Fosters New Look at Church Authority and Higher Education," *Crux*, July 10, 2017, https://cruxnow.com/interviews/2017/07/garvey-francis-fosters-new-look-church-authority-higher-education/.

3. Donald Briel, "A Reflection on Catholic Studies," in *Renewal of Catholic Higher Education*, ed. Matthew T. Gerlach (Bismarck, North Dakota: University of Mary Press, 2017), p. 22.

4. Ibid., p. 23.

5. Ibid., p. 25

6. Thomas Landy, "Catholic Studies at Catholic Colleges and Universities," *America* 178, no. 1 (1998), pp. 12–17. See also the insightful commentaries on the meaning and value of Catholic studies in James T. Fisher and Margaret M. McGuinness, eds., *The Catholic Studies Reader* (New York: Fordham University Press, 2011).

7. Landy, "Catholic Studies at Catholic Colleges and Universities," p. 12.

8. *Commonweal*, 126, no. 7 (1999).

9. See chapter 6 on *Ex corde* and the *mandatum*.

10. Editorial, "Keeping Colleges Catholic: What's at Stake?," *Commonweal* 126, no. 7 (1999), p. 13.

11. Peter Steinfels, "A Journalist's View: Does Rome Have the Best Answer?" *Commonweal* 126, no. 7 (1999), p. 17.

12. P. Saunders, "A Lawyers' View: Look before You Leap," *Commonweal* 126, no. 7 (1999), p. 26.

13. Andrew Greeley, "A Sociologist's View: What Catholics Do Well," *Commonweal* 126, no. 7 (1999), pp. 27–28.

14. John Cavadini, "A Theologian's View: Avoiding a Rush to Judgment," *Commonweal* 126, no. 7 (1999), pp. 21–22. Cavadini may have referred to an "impasse" because of the title that the editors of *The Chronicle of Higher Education* gave to my article, "Have Catholic Colleges Reached an Impasse?" (vol. 46, no. 12, November 12, 1999, pp. B6–7). In that article, I argued that there need be no impasse between the bishops and Catholic colleges and universities. At the time, I was also chairing the board of the Association of Catholic Colleges and Universities.

15. Francis Nichols, "Catholic Studies Are Here to Stay," *Commonweal* 126, no. 7 (1999), pp. 30–32.

16. Fisher and McGuinness, *The Catholic Studies Reader*.

17. See Philip Gleason, *Contending with Modernity: Catholic Higher Education in the Twentieth Century* (Oxford, 1995), chapter 7, "The Catholic Revival Reaches Full Flood," p. 150, where he gives as examples of the intellectual revival of Catholicism the establishment of separate Catholic professional groups, such as the American Catholic Historical Society (founded in 1919), the Catholic Biblical Association (1936), the American Catholic Sociological Society (1938), the Catholic Art Association (1938), the Catholic Economists (1941), the Catholic Theological Society of America (1946), and Catholic psychologists who gathered in 1947.

18. Fisher and McGuiness, *The Catholic Studies Reader*, p. 2.

19. Ibid., p. 3.

20. See Una Cadegan, "Catholic Studies in the Spirit of 'Do Whatever He Tells You," in *The Catholic Studies Reader*, pp. 171–192.

21. See Ann Taves, "Catholic Studies and Religious Studies: Reflections on the Concept of Tradition," in *The Catholic Studies Reader*, pp. 113–128.

22. The establishment of endowed chairs of Catholic studies at secular universities has typically run into two problems: first, the donor wants to have a role, sometimes even a final say, in who should be appointed to the chair; and second, the faculty, who expects to have the final say in who occupies any chair, doubts that Catholic studies can be anything other than a means of indoctrination and a violation of the separation of church and state.

23. The offerings of philosophy departments today are typically more complicated and generally less connected to the courses in theology departments than they were before the collapse of the Thomistic synthesis, which lasted in most Catholic universities until the early 1960s.

24. Fisher and McGuiness, *The Catholic Studies Reader*, pp. 8–9.

25. A suspicion remains on the part of some faculty that CSPs are not sufficiently intellectual. Fr. Michael Byron found that some majors in Catholic studies were "not skilled at rigorous theological thinking" and that they don't understand the difference between "academic theology and apologetics." See "What's Catholic About It?," *America*, February 8, 2016, p. 27.

26. James Heft, "Mary in the Writings of Hans Urs von Balthasar," *Marian Studies* 31 (1980), pp. 40–55, also reprinted in part in *Communio: International Catholic Review* 7 (1980), pp. 127–139. See also Hans Urs von Balthasar, *Truth Is Symphonic* (San Francisco: Ignatius Press, 1987), . For an excellent description of the multifaceted Catholic intellectual tradition (or "imagination" as they describe it), see Santa Clara's Catholic studies website under the title "Catholic Studies Colloquium."

27. John Jenkins, "The Document That Changed Catholic Education Forever," *America*, July 11, 2017, https://www.americamagazine.org/faith/2017/07/11/document-changed-catholic-education-forever.

Conclusion

1. Henry Glassie, "Meaningful Things and Appropriate Myths: The Artifact's Place in American Studies," in *Material Life in America, 1600–1860,* ed. Robert Blair St. George (Boston: Northeastern University Press, 1988), pp. 87–88.

2. See my *Catholic High Schools: Facing the New Realities* (New York: Oxford, 2011), in which I devote two chapters to the topic of leadership, one that is based on moral and the other on theological foundations. Leadership in Catholic educational institutions requires a distinctive set of assumptions absent in most books on leadership.

3. Frank Rhodes, "The Art of the Presidency," *The Presidency* 1, no. 1 (Spring 1998), p. 17. I cite this amusing but dreadfully sexist story in the chapter on leadership in my book *Catholic High Schools*, pp. 104–105.

4. See Philip Gleason, *Contending with Modernity* (New York: Oxford University Press, 1995), pp. 184 ff.

5. See James L. Heft, "Understanding and Responding to Non-Affiliation," in *Empty Churches: Non-Affiliation in America*, ed. James L. Heft and Jan Stets (New York: Oxford University Press, 2021), chapter 13.

Index